The Elusive Dream

The Elusive Dream

The Power of Race in Interracial Churches

KORIE L. EDWARDS

OXFORD
UNIVERSITY PRESS

2008

OXFORD
UNIVERSITY PRESS

Oxford University Press, Inc., publishes works that further
Oxford University's objective of excellence
in research, scholarship, and education.

Oxford   New York
Auckland   Cape Town   Dar es Salaam   Hong Kong   Karachi
Kuala Lumpur   Madrid   Melbourne   Mexico City   Nairobi
New Delhi   Shanghai   Taipei   Toronto

With offices in
Argentina   Austria   Brazil   Chile   Czech Republic   France Greece
Guatemala   Hungary   Italy   Japan   Poland   Portugal   Singapore
South Korea   Switzerland   Thailand   Turkey   Ukraine   Vietnam

Copyright © 2008 by Oxford University Press, Inc.

Published by Oxford University Press, Inc.
198 Madison Avenue, New York, New York 10016
www.oup.com

Oxford is a registered trademark of Oxford University Press

Library of Congress Cataloging-in-Publication Data
Edwards, Korie L.
The elusive dream : the power of race in interracial churches / Korie L. Edwards.
    p. cm.
Includes bibliographical references and index.
ISBN 978-0-19-531424-3
1. African Americans—Religion.   2. Whites—United States—Religion.
3. African American public worship.   4. Public worship—United States.
5. Race relations—Religious aspects—Christianity.   I. Title.
BR563.N4E39 2008
277.3'083089—dc22   2008014445

9 8 7 6 5 4 3 2 1

Printed in the United States of America
on acid-free paper

To my children—
May you experience the dream in your lifetime.

Preface

This book is a journey toward understanding how race manages to control, infuse, and reorganize human relations, such that whites remain dominant, even in places that embrace racial diversity. I am an African-American woman, and over my life, I have found myself in racially diverse environments from time to time, where I attended school, where I worked, and where I lived. So, I have navigated the oft-challenging terrain of cross-racial relations in America. However, in regard to consciously grappling with how race matters when it comes to religion, I attribute the commencement of this leg of the journey to one experience in particular.

I attended predominantly African-American churches for most of my life. But, after graduating from college, I relocated to a predominantly white suburb to live near my work. Mainly for convenience, I decided to attend a rather large, predominantly white church in the same area. I had visited this church with a friend in college. It was the only church of which I was aware in that part of the city. I enjoyed the services well enough, so I spent very little time looking elsewhere. Attending a large church dominated by whites was new for me, but not alien, given that I am often in situations where I am one of a few racial minorities, if not the only one.

During my time there, the pastors of the church periodically spoke against racial prejudice and encouraged the congregation to be inclusive of people of other races in our day-to-day lives. I recall one sermon, in particular, in which the pastor told a story about a minister who relentlessly challenged his congregation on issues of race to the point where all of his congregants left the church. Over time, his congregation was restored, with mostly racial minorities. The story was told as an example of how we must be willing to accept, even embrace, the sacrifices that come with being inclusive. Ironically, the pastors didn't follow this minister's example. And despite their references to racism and racial inclusion in sermons, I rarely saw an African American, Latino, or Asian up in the front of the congregation. Nor were any of the pastors or church elders racial minorities. After three years, I left the church. It didn't look like the church's stated desire of racial inclusion would become a reality any time soon. I have no doubt that the pastors at this church were well intentioned. But I was struck by the racial disparities at this church. I wondered how it was that this was happening in a place where pastors consistently spoke out against racism and where race purportedly didn't matter.

This personal encounter helped to spark my sociological imagination. I wanted to learn more about how race worked in America. I understood the consequences of race on a personal level. But I wanted to understand how racial inequality was reproduced even in institutions that should be resistant to such processes. Being an engineer back then, I had little exposure to the social sciences. So, I began to search out books on topics like racial inequality, racial identity, and cross-racial relations. The experiences and ideas presented in these books were informative. Yet, I wanted to know more, and ultimately I decided to go to graduate school to pursue answers to my questions. My interests centered on interracial relations within churches. The idea of religious racial diversity is fascinating because churches purport to be inclusive and egalitarian (at least when it comes to race and ethnicity), but are arguably more racially segregated and exclusive than most other social institutions. So, for my dissertation, I examined factors that contribute to the racial diversity of churches. This book is the eventual culmination of that project. It is my hope that it illuminates our understanding of how interracial churches are able to sustain a racially integrated congregation, and also how race impacts the cultures and structures of these churches to generate a system where whites receive the lion's share of these communities' rewards.

I want to thank the intellectual community in the Sociology Department of the University of Illinois at Chicago for its encouragement and support. You gave me the freedom to pursue those issues about which I am most passionate and nurtured me so that my passions did not rule the research. I especially want to thank my dissertation committee: R. Stephen Warner and Cedric Herring (co-chairs), Nilda Flores-Gonzalez and Tyrone Forman, and Michael O. Emerson from Rice University. Steve, you challenged me to be more explicit in my writing, admonishing me to "just say it." I hope I have done that here. You also consistently provided me with detailed, thoughtful, and critical direction and feedback throughout this research, from the first paper proposal in your race and religion seminar to drafts of this book, for which I am very grateful. Cedric, you have been an advocate and mentor; your knowledge, advice, and support, in no small way, helped me to successfully traverse the graduate school experience. Nilda and Tyrone, your thoughtful criticisms were essential to this project. And Michael, your insight and guidance, especially as someone who has similar intellectual interests as my own, have been invaluable. Of course, no aspiring Ph.D. can make it through the sometimes arduous moments of graduate school without her fellow aspirants. Thanks especially to Rhonda Dugan, Michelle Hughes, Denise Narcisse, Mary Jean Cravens, Kevin James, and Robin Shirer for your intellectual and emotional support, as well as all of the good times at Jack's and the 'Bou.

My colleagues at The Ohio State University fostered a supportive environment for junior faculty members. I am especially grateful to Lauren Krivo, Kay Meyer, and Vinnie Roscigno for their encouragement.

I also thank Theo Calderara at Oxford University Press for his helpful and detailed editorial feedback.

I could not have accomplished this without my family. I want to thank my parents for not telling me I was crazy for leaving the field of engineering for the uncharted territory of sociology. I imagine you were a bit skeptical of this career change, but you supported me anyway. Thank you to my mother, Sharon Ricketts, for reviewing the draft of the final manuscript, only telling me it was "excellent" and giving me an "A+." You continue to be my greatest fan. Most important, I want to thank my husband, Mark. You have been my rock. I could always depend on you to support and encourage me throughout this process. I am truly grateful for your love.

Finally, I thank the people of Crosstown Community Church for entrusting your sacred world to me so that others might understand and learn from your voices and experiences. I am honored and humbled by this trust.

Contents

The Elusive Dream

Introduction

The Reverend Dr. Martin Luther King, Jr., in his famous "I Have a Dream" speech, entreated Americans to pursue justice and equality and to bridge the racial gulf that divides us. Dr. King also believed that religious organizations were culpable in the perpetuation of racial division.[1] Since the 1960s, religious leaders have responded to this indictment by spawning a movement of racial reconciliation. The movement began with African-American Christians, like Thomas Skinner and John Perkins, who had intense personal experiences with racism and racial segregation. These men believed that the gospel is about reconciling people to God and to one another, that racial reconciliation is "God's one-item agenda," and that the Christian message is essential for improving race relations and people's socioeconomic condition in the United States.[2] More recently, Promise Keepers, a multitudinous evangelical men's organization, has made racial reconciliation one of its core goals. A slew of books have been written on how Christians and religious organizations within a variety of traditions can achieve racial integration.[3] And some of the largest denominations in the United States, including the Southern Baptist Convention, Evangelical Lutheran Church in America, and Presbyterian Church (U.S.A.), are promoting racial and cultural diversity in their organizations.

However, religious racial integration is a dubious enterprise. Historically, Christians and Christian organizations were complicit in establishing slavery. White evangelical Christians tend to be opposed to social and political changes that would increase socioeconomic opportunities for African Americans.[4] And whites generally have resisted attempts at racial integration in schools, workplaces, and neighborhoods.[5] So, what would make contemporary religious institutions likely to achieve racial integration?

One possible answer is that religion in the United States is voluntary. Unlike for other institutions, the forces that constrain people's decisions to be a part of a religious organization are relatively limited. Where people live or attend school or work have direct implications for their lives. There are neighborhoods with greater home appreciation or lower crime rates than others. Some schools have state-of-the-art facilities and well-equipped teachers while others struggle to have enough books for students. And certain work environments, particularly those in the private sector, pay more than others. So, people are motivated to choose neighborhoods, schools, or jobs that will lead to the greatest social and financial rewards. These choices are often limited or expanded depending on people's level of education or how much money they have. This is not the case for churches. People do not have to be so concerned about how attending an interracial church will, say, impede their children's educational attainment or depreciate their financial status. Nor do they have to have a certain level of education or amount of money to attend a church. People are free to attend any church they want for whatever reasons suit them. For those who want to be part of a racially diverse community, interracial churches provide the least costly opportunity to achieve this ambition.

A second possible explanation is that leaders and laypeople can draw upon sacred texts to anchor their beliefs and convictions about the "rightness" of racial integration. Followers may feel obligated to pursue, or at least support, racial integration out of religious commitment. However, people's interpretations of sacred texts are often informed by their interests and perspectives on the world. As these interests and perspectives change, the interpretation of such texts may also change. Southern religious leaders and slaveholders, for example, drew upon certain biblical passages to justify their beliefs about slavery. Even many abolitionists who staunchly opposed slavery on the scriptural grounds of blacks' humanity did not welcome ex-slaves living among them, relying on other passages to support racial distinctions. Many even pushed for African Americans' return to Africa.[6] Of course, religious leaders no longer subscribe to a biblical interpretation that supports slavery, deportation, or segregation. As the South became less dependent upon slavery for its economy, its ministers' interpretations of biblical passages changed. As racial integration became more culturally acceptable after the successes of the Civil Rights movement, Northern ministers, who tended to be averse to conflict, began to change their stance on segregation.[7] Similarly, an ideology of racial integration based upon sacred texts could fall into disrepute if the perspectives and interests of the interpreting persons and organizations change. Nevertheless, sacred texts can be used by religious leaders and organizations to generate, if not compel, commitment among religious adherents to a movement such as racial integration, even if only temporarily so.

These reasons for the efficacy of religiously based racial integration are each valid, to some extent. However, churches are confronted with two structural conditions that impede their efforts to bring people of different races together. While the voluntary nature of American religion frees people to attend racially integrated churches, it can also restrict churches' capacity to become racially diverse. Churches are most successful within the American context (where "success" is measured by the number of attendees) when they appeal to one group. This way they can concentrate their resources on the needs and desires of a specific demographic of people. Furthermore, people prefer to spend time with people who are like them. And they are drawn to congregations made up of people to whom they are similar.[8] Though race is not the only factor in such decisions, there is little doubt that it is one of the most important.

The second factor at play is that race is central to the structure of American life and the everyday lives of Americans. Whites and African Americans,[9] in particular, live, work, and socialize in separate places. For example, 80% of African Americans, on average, would have to move in order for their cities' neighborhoods to be racially balanced.[10] Whites dominate more stable, quality jobs with better pay and benefits and greater opportunities for advancement, while blacks are more likely to hold jobs with limited authority and prestige and lower pay.[11] The kinds of social clubs, fraternities, and religious organizations people join are also dictated by their race, exemplified by such organizations as Jack and Jill of America (a national cultural and civic organization for black youth), Alpha Phi Alpha (one of five historically black fraternities), and the African Methodist Episcopal church (one of seven black-controlled denominations). Consequently, African Americans and whites rarely interact in any meaningful way in most spheres of life. To the extent that people attend churches in their neighborhoods or learn about churches through their social networks, such as through colleagues at work, whites and African Americans are not likely to come across or even be aware of churches that are not dominated by their own racial group.

This book provides an in-depth look at how interracial churches negotiate such barriers. I contend that, in order to understand the cultural, structural, and social dynamics of interracial churches, race, particularly whiteness, needs to be situated at the heart of the explanation. Given that whiteness is the cornerstone of the racial system in the United States, it plays a fundamental role in how interracial churches function. Interracial churches will not represent a balance between whites' and racial minorities' organizational influence or religio-cultural preferences. Rather, the interrelations, religious and cultural practices, and organizational structures of interracial churches will be more representative of the preferences and desires of whites than of the racial minorities in these organizations. And the racial identities, racial attitudes, and religious perspectives of people who attend interracial churches will not challenge, but may even reinforce, whiteness in these organizations. In short, I propose that interracial churches work, that is remain racially integrated, to the extent that they are *first* comfortable places for whites to attend. This is not to suggest, of course, that the congregational life of interracial churches only represents the interests and preferences of whites. Indeed, these churches need to also appeal to the racial minorities in their religious communities. Nevertheless, whiteness plays a critical role in how interracial churches are organized, ultimately producing churches that reflect a congregational life more commonly seen in white churches than in others. Furthermore, while I can imagine interracial churches where whiteness does not dictate congregational life, these are rare exceptions. Interracial churches that understand the broader implications of race for congregation members and for the churches' culture and that intentionally structure their congregations to counter whiteness are more apt to develop and sustain egalitarian interracial religious organizations.[12]

Drawing upon personal stories, congregational experiences, and national congregational-level data, I offer a theoretical explanation for how these religious organizations in the United States sustain a racially integrated congregation. Because race in the United States is primarily about hierarchical relationships between whites and racial minorities, I do not examine interracial churches where two racial minority groups, say, African Americans and Latinos, predominate.[13] I do, however, focus on a particular variety of interracial church, those where African Americans and whites are the two primary groups within the church. This is for two reasons. The first is that I suspect that black/white interracial churches are the most challenging type to develop and sustain relative to other types of interracial churches. By no means do I intend to diminish the subordination that other racial minorities have experienced in this country. However, black/white relations in America have proven to be the most strenuous to mend. Comparing whites' relations with all racial minorities, whites are least likely to marry, live near, or attend churches with blacks.[14] The second reason that I focus on black/white interracial churches is that African Americans, unlike other racial minorities, have developed an autonomous religious institution composed of seven African-American-controlled denominations, commonly referred to as the "black church," which is wholly separate from the white-dominated religious structure.[15] Arguably, the availability of African-American churches that are within a black-controlled religious structure affords African Americans greater opportunity than other racial minorities to attend churches that are largely free of the influence of the dominant culture and where their religious and cultural preferences are practiced.[16] This also means that both African-American and white attendees of black/white interracial churches are in demand by other churches. Other churches would prefer that they expend their limited time, energy, and material resources on their organizations. In fact, African Americans may be in greater demand by other churches than whites, not only because of the historic centrality of the black church to the African-American community, but because among African Americans, it is the middle class that is most likely to attend interracial churches.[17] The human and financial resources of the middle class may make these blacks all the more important to the vitality of the black church and in greater demand by congregations within this tradition. Additionally, the presence of a black church places African Americans and whites on an equal level within racially diverse religious organizations. Each group can draw upon an independent religious culture and tradition to contribute to potentially new ones. So, throughout this volume, unless I specify otherwise, the term "interracial church" refers to congregations where African Americans and whites are the two primary groups in the church.

I must admit that, originally, I expected to discover that interracial religious organizations would provide successful strategies for overcoming racial division and inequality. These organizations seemed to have the key that has eluded us in so many other areas of American life, in our neighborhoods, workplaces, and schools. When I began this project, I visited interracial churches of various racial compositions to gain initial insight into what made these organizations capable of encouraging people of different races to voluntarily worship together. I always received a warm welcome and witnessed a racially diverse group of people who appeared to truly desire to share life together. However, as I continued to visit interracial churches across the country, I noticed a pattern. Nearly all of the churches, regardless of their specific racial compositions, reminded me of the predominantly white churches I had visited. Generally, the churches were racially diverse at all levels. Whites and racial minorities were in the pews and in leadership. There were sometimes cultural practices and markers that represented racial minorities in these congregations, such as a gospel music selection, a display of flags from various countries around the world, or services translated into Spanish. Yet the diversity did not seem to affect the core culture and practices of the religious organizations. That is, the style of preaching, music, length of services, structure of services, dress codes, political and community activities, missionary interests, and theological emphases tended to be more consistent with those of the predominantly white churches I had observed. These churches exhibited many of the practices and beliefs common to white churches within their same religious affiliation, only with a few additional "ethnic" practices or markers. It was like adding rainbow sprinkles to a dish of ice cream. In the end, you still have a dish of ice cream, only with a little extra color and sweetness.

Whiteness: The Cornerstone of Race

Race is a social system that hierarchically organizes people in a society based upon physical characteristics. While race and ethnicity overlap (e.g., African Americans are a race and an ethnic group), they are distinct and have different consequences. Races are the basis of social systems that distribute rewards, such as good jobs, desirable neighborhoods, and political power, along racial lines. People placed in the dominant stratum establish the racial classifications and have greater access to and possession of society's valuable resources and more power to reserve them for their group.[18] They are recognized as worthy of their status even if they have not done anything to achieve it. Ethnicity is largely about claims of shared culture, history, or common descent. In the West, it is not (usually) based upon perceived physical differences nor linked to systems of power relations. Ethnic differences are important, but they have not produced nearly the same level of discord and disparities as race.[19] While some European immigrants experienced prejudice, their ethnicity did not prevent them from participating in everyday American life. Guglielmo argues that Italians, for instance, were white upon arriving in this country.[20] Because of their whiteness, they were not systematically banned from eating in restaurants or sitting in particular sections of buses, nor were they ever restricted from naturalizing as United States citizens, as were immigrants from non-European countries through 1952.[21] And within a generation, they were assimilating into the dominant white society. Racial lines, then, are far more salient in this country than ethnic ones.

Within the body of work on race and ethnicity, there is a specific focus on whiteness. This research emphasizes the meaning and function of white racial identity and its centrality to systems where whites are culturally and structurally dominant.[22]

Whiteness is a social construction.[23] It is not based on biological, genetic, or other "natural" facts, but is rather an identity that possesses a set of meanings. Whiteness is assigned to people who *do not* posses those arbitrarily chosen physical attributes that disqualify them from claiming a white racial identity.[24] In other words, what it means to be white is to be *not* some other race. In the United States, the boundaries of whiteness are flexible and contingent upon the definitions of other racial groups, most often African Americans.[25] For example, some states' laws claimed that a person with one African-American grandparent was African American. Other states claimed that any person with "one drop" of African ancestry was African American. Still other states used more ambiguous language for defining who was African American, like "appreciable mixture" or "ascertainable" amounts of African ancestry.[26] These kinds of classifications continued to be upheld as recently as the mid-1980s. In 1986, the Louisiana courts declared a woman with one black great-great-great-great-grandparent as African American, even though she appeared white and had lived as a white woman her entire life.[27] Despite the arbitrary character of racial group attributes, the racial identities they define yield very different and real social, economic, and psychological consequences for people. Whites are more likely than racial minorities to secure financing for home mortgages, live in better neighborhoods, attend high-quality schools, obtain stable employment, and avoid prison.[28]

Whiteness consists of three constitutive, interdependent dimensions that work together to create and sustain white hegemony. *White structural advantage* signifies a location of dominance within a racial hierarchy. In the United States, this means political, economic, and numerical dominance.[29] Whites disproportionately control or influence political parties, the legal system, government agencies, industry, and business. This structural advantage affords whites privileges, where white privilege can be thought of as "unearned benefits" that whites receive by virtue of being able to claim a white racial identity in day-to-day life and at institutional levels.[30] Racial minorities are either fully denied the privileges that seamlessly come to whites or must strive to achieve them. Some of the everyday privileges include being able to organize life so that one is always in a crowd with other whites; to easily purchase literature, movies, or greeting cards featuring whites; and to ignore the experiences, writings, or ideas of racial minorities, if one so chooses.[31] The institutionalization of white privilege means that whites are afforded benefits that are far less accessible to racial minorities as a result of policies, laws, and customary behaviors in a society. Examples of institutional-level white privilege include possessing the power to legally define who is and who is not part of your racial group; having the capacity to pass housing policies that favor your racial group; and developing educational curriculums that emphasize your racial group's historical and social experiences.[32]

White structural advantage facilitates *white normativity*, including the normativity of white ethnicity.[33] White normativity reinforces the normalization of whites' cultural practices, ideologies, and location within the racial hierarchy such that how whites do things; their understandings about life, society, and the world; and their dominant social location over other racial groups are accepted as "just how things are." Conversely, practices and understandings that diverge from this norm are seen as deviant. And when racial minorities fill powerful positions in society, these occurrences are deemed to be special. Whites also do not need to justify their way of doing or being, nor are they accustomed to doing so. Instead, the burden of explanation rests upon those who stray from what is deemed normative. Of course, white normativity does not mean there is no variation in whites' beliefs and cultural practices.[34] A certain practice or understanding may be perceived as normative among one group of whites, yet the same practice may be perceived as abnormal among other whites. However, despite variations among white populations, there still exist overarching practices and beliefs that are embraced by whites across sociodemographic lines: "[Whites] are encouraged to ... remain true to an identity that provides them with resources, power and opportunity."[35] Whites from different backgrounds hold ideologies and attitudes that invariably disadvantage racial minorities and sustain their dominant position in the racial hierarchy.[36] They are socialized to "invest" in their whiteness by embracing these attitudes and ideologies and acting in ways that are consistent with these beliefs.[37] This hegemonic whiteness, hedged by a "commonsense" ideology of how life ought to be, normalizes the practices and understandings of whites and affirms their interests.[38]

Finally, *white transparency* is "the tendency of whites not to think ... about norms, behaviors, experiences, or perspectives that are white-specific."[39] It is a lack of racial consciousness.[40] Whites are unaware that their race has consequences for their lives. They perceive themselves as cultureless and racial minority groups as possessing distinctive cultural practices.[41] Consequently, it is difficult for whites to explain what it means to be white.[42] White transparency is in many respects the most challenging dimension of whiteness in the sense that it is very difficult to address a problem if the problem is not acknowledged. White transparency and white normativity interact in that the normalization of white practices and understandings reaffirms the elusiveness of white racial identity. Since whites' practices, understandings, and social location are perceived as normative, it is difficult for them to see how race affects their lives and to cultivate a racial consciousness.

For these reasons, whiteness is a powerful, yet elusive force in the construction of race and racial hierarchies. As such, it shapes the structure of and interrelations within any organization, including interracial churches.

Race, Segregation, and Religion in the United States

Racial segregation characterizes American Christianity and exists at multiple levels of religious organization.[43] If racial segregation is not between churches and denominations, then it is within them.[44]

White Christians began evangelistic efforts toward African slaves during the eighteenth century.[45] By the mid-nineteenth century, several denominations, particularly the Baptists and Methodists, boasted a relatively large percentage of African-American adherents. However, conversion to the Christian brotherhood did not eliminate the subordinate status of blacks, free and slave alike. In the South, prior to the Reconstruction era, African Americans were relegated to the galleries during worship services. In cases where congregations did not accept this minimal inclusion of African Americans, slave owners permitted slaves to congregate together under their supervision and the leadership of a white pastor. Free blacks were afforded some leeway in forming all-black congregations, but whites became increasingly concerned with these gatherings as the Civil War approached, for these churches provided African Americans with the space to speak against slavery. Therefore, it was difficult for free blacks to openly worship together in the South. While the North was generally more receptive to racial integration, it was still rare for African Americans to have equal access to congregational resources and leadership. Separate pews were often set aside for African-American attendees. Sunday school classes were segregated by race. And African Americans were required to receive communion after whites.[46] African-American congregations in white denominations were also excluded from full participation in denominational activities. Saint Phillips, an African-American Episcopal church, for example, was denied the right to vote during the national conventions. African-American preachers in many denominations were confined to seats in the back rows of meetings and excluded from voting on denominational issues.

In response to this exclusion from full religious participation, some African Americans began to organize their own formal and informal religious communities.[47] Since slaves were forbidden to organize, they developed plantation churches, or what Frazier referred to as an "invisible institution of the church."[48] The pastors of these invisible plantation churches were usually male slaves with at least some Bible knowledge. Free African Americans also formed their own formal Christian institutions. Richard Allen, a preacher in the white-dominated Methodist denomination, and other free blacks founded the African Methodist Episcopal church in 1787 after being physically removed from a section of a church not sanctioned for blacks during a crowded worship service.[49] After the Civil War, these formal and informal African-American religious organizations were the basis of the black church. It is reported that, by 1890, nearly 90% of African-American Protestants belonged to black-controlled denominations.[50]

The black church has historically been socioeconomically diverse and a place where African Americans, regardless of their formal skills or education, have the opportunity for mobility.[51] Even though African Americans were afforded little respect outside their community, they enjoyed this simple human dignity within the walls of the church. The black church correspondingly became a place of refuge where African Americans had the "freedom to relax" and to emotionally and culturally express themselves.[52] The church has also been the center of community life for African Americans.[53] The vast majority of African Americans, regardless of their religious affiliation, have an ownership and attachment to the African-American church.[54] The black church has been a "social outlet for artistic expression . . . ; a forum for discussion . . . ; [and] a social environment for [developing] potential leaders . . . and meaningful symbols to engender hope, enthusiasm and a resilient group spirit."[55]

As exemplified by the historical experience of Richard Allen and his African-American Christian brothers and sisters, African Americans' interests have not been accommodated in interracial religious settings. The ideologies behind religious racial segregation, in both the North and South, were threaded with themes of white supremacy.[56] As the Episcopalian national convention of 1846 exclaimed:

> [Blacks] are socially degraded, and are not regarded as proper associates for the class of persons who attend our Convention. We object not to the color of the skin, but we question [if] their intercourse with members of a church convention [is] useful . . . even to themselves.[57]

A southern Baptist newspaper said in 1874, "the aversion of the people of the South to mixed schools . . . is an instinct, divinely implanted, for the wise and beneficent purpose of keeping separate races which are, by nature, widely different in color, social qualities, and moral tendencies."[58] The primary difference between how northern white Christians and southern white Christians regarded African Americans is that those in the North believed that improvement of African Americans' condition was possible if northern white Christians performed their Christian duty and provided African Americans with opportunities to improve their lot.[59]

Converting African Americans to Christianity would, of course, be included in this endeavor.[60] Southern Christians figured that African Americans were innately different and could not attain the qualities that made the white race superior any time in the near or distant future.[61] They drew upon biblical passages to support their racist ideologies.[62]

Even during this era, however, there were white religious leaders and denominations that supported racial integration at an ideological level, if not in practice. Catholic Archbishop John Ireland, for example, in his 1890 address to a congregation in Washington, DC, claimed, "We are all equal as brothers should be and we will . . . treat alike black and white. I know no color line. I will acknowledge none."[63] Denominations, including the United Lutheran Church in America, the Congregational Christian churches, and the Presbyterian Church (U.S.A.), created national policies indicating commitments to racial integration, remnants of which are still evident today in some of these denominations.[64] As the movement for racial integration gained momentum in the twentieth century, religious bodies denounced the racist ideologies upon which their previous support of segregation was based. No longer did they see racial segregation as compatible with Christian teachings.[65] In 1919, the Commission on Interracial Cooperation was formed. Its primary aim was to improve the social conditions of African Americans. Religious denominations began to elect African Americans to positions of leadership in their assemblies. Religious conventions boycotted hotels and cities that did not make provisions for racially integrated accommodations. Further, denominations developed committees with the explicit purpose of addressing issues of race relations generally. For example, the American Missionary Association of the Congregational Christian church formed a Department of Race Relations that reported on the conditions of race relations in the United States to its constituents and provided support for interracial churches. Another example is the Race Relations Department of the Federal Council of Churches, an interdenominational organization. This department aimed to educate religious leaders about interracial relations and to address issues of racial segregation and discrimination.[66]

Despite increased interracial interactions and interests in improving American race relations at the denominational and national committee levels, the movement was considerably less successful at penetrating congregations. Still, there is evidence that some congregations, primarily in the North, were able to integrate across racial lines.[67] During the 1930s and 1940s, churches that were both interdenominational and interracial formed across the country in large cities such as Philadelphia and New York. These churches performed services only part of the year and allowed attendees to have dual memberships in both the interracial, interdenominational church and their racially homogeneous, denominational home churches. The services were conducted at various churches of different denominational affiliations, and both whites and African Americans preached. Interracial churches of the "traditional" sort also developed across the country. These churches were usually located in urban neighborhoods that were experiencing a racial transition from white to African American. They were headed by white and African-American pastors, often in a co-pastoring situation.[68] First Baptist Church of Hyde Park in Chicago, Illinois, was the first church from the American Baptist Convention to be integrated. It sustained a tradition of racial diversity that began in 1942 and lasted for well over twenty years.[69] Southern Christians were generally still very pro-segregation,[70] and therefore churches in the South were far less inclined to be integrated than were northern churches. Nevertheless, a study of southern churches in 1947 and 1948 revealed that white and African-American churches did at least participate in joint special programs.[71]

As the end of the twentieth century drew near, religious racial integration had become more pertinent to denominations and other religious bodies. Denominations continued to adopt policies of racial inclusion.[72] Religious organizations and forums committed to addressing issues of race relations again materialized. Yet still, interracial churches remain the exception at the beginning of the twenty-first century. The typical church in America continues to be composed of just one racial group.[73] That is, not a single person of a different race is in attendance. And interracial churches, where no racial group comprises more than 90% of a congregation, make up only 10% of churches in the United States.[74] Therefore, while race relations have become increasingly relevant to religious bodies, the practice of racial integration has not followed at the same pace.

There have been religious movements across the past two centuries that have attempted to bridge the racial divide in the United States, either through directly promoting racial integration or through supporting African Americans' struggle for civil rights. However, fervor for these movements waxed and waned during the nineteenth and early twentieth centuries. And, while the twentieth century witnessed a steady interest in race relations among religious organizations, interracial worship remains a difficult goal to attain. Furthermore, religious racial segregation has led to the creation of spaces where African Americans can thrive. The subordination and exclusion of blacks from white-controlled religious institutions was fodder for the formation of autonomous religious institutions made up of and controlled by African Americans. As religious racial segregation has advantages for both whites and African Americans, both groups have a vested interest in maintaining at least this form of segregation. Interracial churches are therefore confronted with powerful forces that work against voluntary racial integration.

Approaching Religious Racial Integration

I used a multimethod approach for this study. The National Congregations Study (NCS),[75] a nationally representative, congregational-level data set, has a wealth of data on congregational structure, religious practices, theologies, and interrelations, among many other areas of interest. The NCS analysis provides a broad view of the congregational life of interracial churches and how it compares to that of African-American and white churches. To understand the process of whiteness in interracial churches, I also conducted a case study of a specific church, which I call Crosstown Community Church (all names of persons, places, and organizations in this book are pseudonyms).[76] The case study is the central component of this volume. Case studies do not allow for generalizable findings, but they do provide researchers with "the opportunity to study the social mysteries" of the world.[77] They are invaluable for understanding the intricate details of group culture and social interaction and how people construct their social worlds in a given context. The case study allows me to deconstruct the contents of organizational life at Crosstown Community Church and to expose how other churches might negotiate racial barriers (see appendix A for more on the research methods).

Crosstown Community Church was a conservative Protestant church located in a large, midwestern metropolis. The church drew most of its attendees from two local neighborhoods, Mapleton and Anderson. Mapleton was a majority white, but racially diverse upper middle-class neighborhood. Anderson was a predominantly African-American, working-class neighborhood. The church had an approximate attendance of 200 people.

The congregation was also largely middle class. Both African Americans and whites held professional jobs—as managers, engineers, or doctors. Crosstown sustained a racially diverse congregation, with African Americans comprising at least 20% of attendees, for close to twenty years. By the time of this study, the church's racial composition reflected that of the local community. The majority of attendees were African American, with African Americans comprising about 65% of the church, whites 30%, and Latinos and Asians 5%. Crosstown's head pastor was also African American. As a relatively stable interracial church with a majority African-American congregation and an African-American pastor, Crosstown provided a sound case for understanding if and how whiteness influences the congregational life of interracial churches (see appendix A for more on Crosstown, Mapleton, and Anderson).

This book, then, aims to shed light on how race matters, particularly how whiteness matters, in interracial churches in the United States where whites make up a substantial proportion of the attendees. I focus on the experiences of African Americans and whites with negotiating the various dimensions of whiteness in this religious context. The central questions guiding this research have to do with how interracial churches sustain racially diverse congregations, given the extent of racial segregation, religious exclusion, and white dominance in this country. How is race, particularly as it relates to the ownership of social space and power, managed within interracial churches? Who are the people who attend interracial churches and why do they attend? The stories that unfold in the following pages will address these questions. The intent is not only to inform us about the processes that dictate relations between African Americans and whites in American churches, but to potentially expand our understanding of how race works to reproduce white hegemony, even under the most amenable circumstances.

I

Decently and in Order

Congregational Worship

It was a fall communion Sunday at Crosstown Community Church. Church lay leaders, a racially and gender-mixed group, had just passed out crackers for communion and were standing on either side of the altar at the front of the sanctuary, facing the congregation. Pastor Raymond Barnes, Crosstown's African-American senior pastor, stood with them. Behind the altar was the main stage in the sanctuary where the pulpit was located. Leslie, an African-American woman whom I guessed to be in her mid-thirties, stood alone on the main stage singing a solo from *The Rebirth of Kirk Franklin*, a contemporary, soulful gospel album. A Chinese woman accompanied her on a piano. However, with Leslie's wispy soprano voice and only the piano for instrumental accompaniment, the song lost most of its intended gospel flair.

Then, just as Leslie was finishing her solo, shouts rang out from the front of the church: "THANK YOU LAWD, THANK YOU LAWD, THANK YOU LAWD." It was Lydia, an African-American woman in her late thirties. She swayed her hands high above her head in sync with her shouts of praise, shouting louder and louder as she continued. It was as if something in the song hit Lydia emotionally, and she had been momentarily taken away from the service. At first, a few other African-American attendees murmured "amen" or "mmm hmm" in seeming encouragement of Lydia, but their affirmations ceased rather quickly as the rest of the congregation failed to express similar approval. Except for Lydia, the church became quiet and eerily still. People's heads were slightly bowed with their eyes closed. Even Pastor Barnes and other church leaders standing at the front of the church were quiet and still. Many of their heads were bowed, eyes closed, while others stared straight ahead, their gaze avoiding the spectacle that was before them.

Michael, a middle-aged white man who was the chair of the elder board (the highest-ranking lay leader in the church), was standing next to the altar preparing to bless the communion bread. He had a roaming microphone in one hand and an open Bible in the other. He appeared to want to begin to bless the communion, but just stood there looking around with a befuddled expression on his face. He seemed unsure of what to do next, as did Pastor Barnes and the other church leaders who were standing there with them. However, after about twenty seconds of shouts of "THANK YOU LAWD," Michael finally braved it. He hesitantly lifted the microphone to his mouth and began to read from the Bible. As soon as he began to speak, Lydia stood up, walked down the center aisle toward the back of the church, and proceeded to exit the sanctuary, all the while continuing to shout "THANK YOU LAWD" over and over with her hands swaying high above her head. Speaking particularly softly, Michael pressed on with communion as if nothing unusual was happening. It was difficult to hear him because he was talking quietly but also because, although Lydia had moved to the lobby, her muffled shouts of praise could still be heard inside the sanctuary.

After what seemed an eternity, the shouts stopped. Lydia quietly returned to her seat. The service had proceeded, and by the time she sat down, the communion juice was being distributed to congregants. She, as did everyone else, acted as if nothing out of the ordinary had just occurred. Yet, the palpable stillness and quiet in the sanctuary during the event revealed another story. Lydia's behavior was anything but ordinary for this congregation.

Because American churches are so autonomous, congregational worship varies considerably. During worship, "congregations engage in their most dramatic rituals, their most intentional presentation[s] of their sense of identity."[1] While worship services are not the only activities that occur within churches, they are the most central in the sense that people are proclaiming who they are, not only to themselves, but also to others. They tell us what the people who participate in these rituals and practices are about. They tell us who belongs and who does not. They tell us what is allowed, what is praiseworthy, and what is unacceptable. For these reasons, understanding worship is important for understanding congregational life. However, determining which worship practices and styles are normative and representative of "who we are" in an interracial church is complicated because most Americans are accustomed to a racially homogeneous religion. People of different racial backgrounds have developed different ideas about what constitutes normative worship. And they often come to an interracial religious space with these firm sets of understandings about what worship should be like. Events such as the one described above provide a window into the congregational worship of interracial churches, exposing the peculiar challenges and tensions these kinds of churches face as they try to forge an interracial worship experience.

Worship: How Do Interracial Churches Compare to Other Congregations?

The basic structure of worship in American churches looks rather similar regardless of racial composition. In nearly every American Christian church (96%),[2] worship services include two segments, congregational singing and a sermon or homily. However, once we move beyond this foundational worship structure, styles begin to diverge. That is, the particular practices (such as whether or not a choir sings or the length of the services) or what they look like can differ across churches. Given that American Christianity is largely racially segregated,[3] worship style and racial composition often go hand in hand.

I examined six indicators of congregational worship in the NCS: verbal affirmations (such as the call of "amen"); hand raising; spontaneous worship practices (such as dancing, jumping, or shouting); length of worship service; choir participation; and whether or not the congregation reserves a time of greeting during the worship service (see appendix B for operationalizations). An analysis of these worship practices demonstrates a pattern of what interracial congregational worship looks like and how racial composition affects worship in America.

Beginning with descriptive comparisons between interracial churches' and white and African-American churches' worship styles and practices, 63% of interracial churches participate in verbal affirmation during worship services, compared to 93% of African-American churches and 48% of white churches. Hand raising occurs in a little more than half of interracial churches, while about 90% of African-American churches and 34% of white churches participate in this practice. And 32% of interracial churches participate in spontaneous worship practices, such as jumping or dancing, where 61% and 4% of African-American and white churches, respectively, engage in some form of spontaneous worship. As for length of service, worship services of interracial churches last ninety minutes on average, which is about twenty minutes longer than the average worship service of white churches and almost forty minutes shorter than the average worship service of African-American churches. Interracial churches' likelihood of having a choir participate in the worship service as well as their likelihood of reserving time for attendees to greet one another during the worship service does not differ (statistically speaking) from that of white churches. But African-American churches are more likely than interracial churches to have choirs participate in their worship services, and they are less likely than interracial churches to have a time for greeting as a part of the worship service (see table C-1, appendix C).

Initially, interracial churches' participation in verbal affirmation, hand raising, and spontaneous worship and their average worship service length appears to fall somewhere between that of white and African-American churches. However, once other important congregational characteristics, such as age composition, religious tradition (e.g., Catholic, conservative Protestant, etc.), or whether or not the congregation adheres to charismatic religion are taken into consideration, this balance disappears (see table C-2, appendix C). What this means is that the descriptive differences in worship style and practice between interracial churches and white churches are not due to differences in racial composition, but other congregational charac- teristics, particularly the percentages of young adults that attend these churches and whether the churches are conservative Protestant.

Interracial churches' level of participation in spontaneous worship and their average worship service length continue to fall between that of African-American and white churches. This is no longer the case for verbal affirmation and hand raising. While African-American churches are 8.6 times and 4.7 times more likely than interracial churches to participate in hand raising and verbal affirmation, respectively, interracial churches' participation in these practices is no different than that of white churches. Interracial churches' likelihood of having a choir sing or a time for greeting during worship services remains the same as that for white churches. But African-American churches are seven times more likely than interracial churches to have a choir sing during worship services. And they are far less likely than interracial churches to have a time for greeting during worship services. Taken together, these results tell us that interracial churches are not inclined to adopt the worship styles and practices that are commonly observed in African-American churches. They adopt those that are more common to white churches.

Congregational Worship at Crosstown

In many ways, the congregational worship at Crosstown reflects what we see for interracial churches more generally in America. In addition to including a time of greeting during the worship service, Crosstown's worship services lasted between an hour and thirty minutes and an hour and forty minutes. Crosstown had a choir that participated in the worship services about once a month. But, typically, a trio of singers would be responsible for leading congregational singing during the worship services. A piano (or keyboard) and drums were used for instrumental accompaniment. And periodically, an acoustic guitar, trumpet, bongos, or organ would be added to the musical ensemble. Different styles of music were integrated into the worship services, including hymns, contemporary praise choruses (which have a sound reminiscent of contemporary folk or light rock music), and contemporary gospel. However, music from the contemporary praise genre was most common. Hymns and gospel music each comprised about one-quarter of Crosstown's musical repertoire.

Crosstown's worship style was not particularly effusive. This was evident in both the congregational singing and the sermons. For congregational singing, I paid particular attention to how often and how many congregants participated in the singing, clapped during up-tempo music selections, or raised their hands during congregational singing. Approximately three-quarters of the congregants would consistently participate in the congregational singing. I also observed congregants clapping during about half of the worship selections where clapping would be appropriate. However, only between one-third and one-half of the congregation would clap at these times. It was not uncommon for very few people, that is, about 10% of the congregation, to clap during up-tempo music selections. At about half of the worship services, congregants would raise their hands during congregational singing. Again, a select few, about five people, would participate in this practice. When people did raise their hands, it was not high above their heads. Rather, they raised their hands to about shoulder level with the palms of their hands facing up. Congregants who were not singing, clapping, or raising their hands during congregational singing tended to stand still, appearing to read the words of the songs that were projected onto a screen above the center of the main stage.

Despite Pastor Barnes' roots in the Church of God in Christ (COGIC, a black Pentecostal denomination), his sermon delivery style was not reflective of the rhythmic, climactic, and sometimes spontaneous style common among African-American preachers.[4] He remained behind the pulpit during most of the sermon and relied heavily upon his sermon notes, regularly referencing them throughout his sermons. His tone could be firm at times, but his speech was generally even. Furthermore, his sermon delivery was not structured to facilitate a "call and response" between him and the congregation. During the sermons, an "amen" or "mmm hmm" could be heard from the congregation, but only from a select few. They included the pastor's wife and an elderly African-American woman. Others (both African-American and white attendees) might every so often verbally respond to the sermons as well. Still, the "amens" and "mmm hmms" were very intermittent when they did occur. And it was not uncommon to hear no verbal responses from the congregation during an entire sermon.

Michael Emerson and Christian Smith find that "accountable freewill individualism," "relationalism," and "antistructuralism" are core values of white evangelicals.[5] Accountable freewill individualism is the belief that people are free to make choices and are accountable to their family, church, friends, and God for their decisions. Relationalism is placing particular importance on interpersonal relationships. Antistructuralism is the "inability to perceive or unwillingness to accept social structural influences." Crosstown's sermons emphasized these values. They focused on individual spiritual growth through obedience to God, increasing individual spiritual commitment to God or the church, and individual-level sacrifice in various areas of life, such as time, money, or job choice. Improving your relationship with God or with people, especially family, was regularly discussed. Community or social issues were very rarely mentioned during sermons. The sermons, which lasted about forty minutes, were divided into three predictable segments. Pastor Barnes, who delivered nearly all of the sermons, began by reading a Bible passage out of the New Testament, on which the sermon would be based. He then explained the meaning of the

Bible passage, often relying upon other Bible passages or magazines and books written by evangelical leaders or pastors (examples of these include *Wild at Heart;*[6] *Fresh Wind, Fresh Fire;*[7] and *Christianity Today*[8]) for further clarification. He concluded his sermons by providing guidelines on how people could apply the Bible teachings to their lives.

Crosstown seemed to possess a more culturally balanced congregational worship than other interracial churches in the NCS. This likely reflected the disproportionate representation of African-American attendees in the church: They comprised two-thirds of the congregation. Nonetheless, in many ways, Crosstown's congregational worship structure—the worship style, time committed to the worship service, sermonic culture, and, to a lesser extent, music—was consistent with findings on interracial churches in the NCS. But how does it happen that Crosstown and other interracial churches emulate the congregational worship more commonly seen in white churches? Crosstown members' thoughts about the church's congregational worship and Crosstown's response to Lydia's "shouting" shed light on this phenomenon.

Shouting for the Lord: Expressive Worship at Crosstown

At Crosstown, African-American congregants and white congregants had quite different perspectives on worship. I asked congregants to tell me what they enjoyed about the worship services at Crosstown and, conversely, what frustrated them about the worship services.[9] They could have discussed any feature of the worship services. The worship and music styles were central to their responses.

Whites consistently said that they enjoyed the music. Actually, none of the whites I interviewed expressed frustration with the music. They particularly enjoyed the variety of music styles at Crosstown, the hymns and contemporary praise songs especially. They also appreciated the "upbeat" worship style and the use of multiple instruments. One woman told me:

> I like the mix [of the music]. I think it's wonderful. If I did all hymns I think I would be dissatisfied. If I did all praise songs I think I would be dissatisfied too. I really like the mix, so keep the mix!

Another white attendee said:

> I enjoy the mixture of the styles of music from traditional hymns to the praise songs to the choir singing, the soloists. I enjoy the instruments used, the fact that it's more than just a piano or just an organ. In fact, they bring in the trumpet sometimes, the guitar sometimes, they've got drums, and it's just very upbeat and it gets me in the mood to praise him. It's very similar to something I had in college, just the musical style that we used to [have].

Whites' appreciation for the worship style can be partially explained by their familiarity with it. The worship was consistent with what some had experienced when they were in a younger, more vibrant religious environment, and Crosstown provided them with the opportunity to extend this worship experience.

African Americans, on the other hand, were not so content. About a quarter of the African Americans with whom I spoke reported that they enjoyed the worship style and music during the worship services. However, when asked if there were things at Crosstown that frustrated them, the most common feature mentioned was the worship style and music, with about 60% of African Americans expressing dissatisfaction. The most common frustration was that worship was not enthusiastic enough. One attendee explained, "I think the church is a little stiff when it comes to [praise]." Another said, "I would like a little more livelier music." One woman, who also told me that she would like the worship service to be livelier, explained what she meant by "lively":

> I like to get into the song, to really do the praise and worship. It's not just singing the song, singing the words.... I feel like if I were a member of the praise team or choir standing up there I would just be looking and saying what the heck are we doin'?! Like, they are working so hard and we are just standing/sitting here staring at them. You know, GET UP!!! You know, it's like, GET UP!!! They are workin' so hard. There have been days where I feel like, you know, [the praise leader] is just workin' and everybody, you know, you've done your work and you understand what your role is and we're just sittin' here saying, okay, nice show. So anyway, that's what I mean by lively.

Clearly, her frustrations were not just with the liveliness of the worship, but also with the limited participation during congregational singing.

Congregants, she felt, treated the singing and music as entertainment, rather than as a participatory experience. These attendees' feelings were consistent with what other African Americans expressed about the worship services at Crosstown. This suggests that African-American and white attendees were working with two different sets of cultural norms and expectations for what worship ought to look like, in this case, what constituted upbeat worship. For whites, worship at Crosstown was upbeat, but for African Americans, that was far from true. Further, where whites particularly enjoyed the worship, most African Americans were not satisfied.

When it came to a particularly expressive form of worship, like what Lydia did, this difference in people's perceptions sharpened. Lydia's shouting became a central concern at Crosstown. Rumblings about Lydia filtered through the congregation, and several people brought it up during the interviews. Expressive forms of worship, such as dancing, swaying, waving your hands high above your head, or shouting were, indeed, quite rare at Crosstown. Based upon people's responses to Lydia's actions in the worship service, this behavior made some people uncomfortable. However, in interviews and casual conversations, attendees, particularly African Americans, expressed support for shouting. One African-American woman told me:

> Sometimes I wish the order of service was a little more upbeat. I would like to see people a little bit more expressive. I'll say "amen" and I'll raise my hand to something that I think the Lord deserves the praise for and he deserves praise for everything but I'll do that. Lydia, she got up and expressed . . . I mean, she wasn't real loud with it or anything. . . . She wasn't real outlandish with it but she shouted out and a lot of people disagreed with that and then I have to go back to the scriptures where it tells us to make a joyful noise unto the Lord. This is what I would like to see a little more at Crosstown—people making a joyful noise to him. . . . I think that if you want to express yourself as far as the Lord, giving praise and honor to him, I think it should be welcomed. I think it should be a part of the service.

I was also privy to two informal conversations where attendees talked about Lydia's shouting, both of which were among a racially mixed group of people. An African American brought up the topic during both conversations, asking fellow church attendees what they thought about Lydia's behavior. Some people felt that whatever is done during the worship service should be done such that it isn't disruptive, only benefiting the individual. Lydia's behavior was inappropriate because it took away from some congregants' worship experience and did not include the whole congregation. On the opposite side were those who felt that the church should provide a space where people can freely worship God. Similar to the woman above, people should be free to worship God through shouting because the Bible says to make a joyful noise unto the Lord. Additionally, they explained that people have very difficult weeks and challenging problems they are facing in their lives and need a place to release and freely express themselves. African Americans tended to take the second position, while others were more inclined to take the first.

Above, I mentioned that the church—or at least the church leadership—ignored Lydia's shouting during the communion service. It seemed, for a time, that even though this form of worship was uncomfortable for people as exemplified by the palpable quiet and stillness of the church, that *this time*, at least, there wouldn't be any verbal reprimand. A few years earlier, there had been. During another worship service, Lydia got up and stood in an outside aisle of the sanctuary and began to shout praises to God, waving her hands above her head, and there was a swift response by the church leadership. The following week during the worship service, Lydia was asked by Pastor Barnes to come up to the pulpit with him. With her standing behind him, Pastor Barnes expressed disapproval of her actions from the previous week. One member of the church with whom I spoke about the incident called the pastor's response an all-out "rebuke." Pastor Barnes then asked Lydia to come to the pulpit and explain her worship expression, seeming to imply that she should apologize for what she had done. She approached the pulpit and explained why she worshipped as she did but did not apologize. Afterward, she returned to her seat and the worship service went on as usual. This was the last time Lydia had shouted during a worship service—until now.

After the more recent incident, there was no immediate response to Lydia's shouts of praise. I do not know why the leadership did not respond this time as it did a few years ago. It is possible that the church leadership had changed its mind on the issue. Or, they may have thought that this kind of worship expression was tolerable once every few years. But Lydia again began to shout praises during another worship service four months later. A guest speaker, an African-American man who was a long-time friend of Pastor Barnes and a leader in the evangelical racial reconciliation movement, was giving the sermon. Again, it appeared that something particularly relevant or important just hit Lydia, and she began to shout "HALLELUJAH, HALLELUJAH, HALLELUJAH" over and over. Lydia was seated in the front of the church. The guest speaker looked at her when she began to shout. He had a puzzled look on his face for just a moment but did not pause. He kept on with his sermon. As soon as she began shouting, Lydia left her seat, walked down an outside aisle, and exited the sanctuary, all the while continuing to shout "HALLELUJAH, HALLELUJAH, HALLELUJAH." As before, the congregation could still hear her from the lobby.

The very next week, Pastor Barnes did a sermon on worship. He began his sermon by discussing his Church of God in Christ experience and revealed that he "speaks in another language," which is usually called speaking in tongues. This was not something I had ever heard anyone do at the church, let alone the senior pastor, so it was a bit surprising. However, almost immediately after he revealed this about himself, he reassured the congregation by posing the question "Are things going to change at Crosstown?" He answered his own question with an unequivocal "No!" after which he announced that the church would be having a potluck dinner meeting the following month to discuss "Is there room for emotional expression at Crosstown?" He requested that people sign up in advance if they were planning to attend.

He continued with his sermon, drawing upon three sets of scriptures out of the books of Acts (chapters 9 and 13) and 1 Corinthians (chapter 2) in the New Testament. The 1 Corinthians passage discusses guidelines for congregational worship and mentions that everything done in a group worship setting should be done "decently and in order." The Acts passages were used to demonstrate how early Christians worshipped. Pastor Barnes made three key points in this sermon. One was that "every worship service needs prayerful planning that acknowledges God is our audience and we are multiethnic." The second was that, in order for people to come prepared for the service, "the congregation can pray for the service and be on time." His final point was that "maximum worship needs worship planning and preparation."

Pastor Barnes was expressing the values that those in leadership believed were central to worship services at Crosstown. One value was the interracial character of the church. Since the church was interracial, the worship service needed to be sensitive to the different cultural desires of the varying groups in the church. At least in part, the church was aiming to maintain its interracial status by developing a service that would facilitate this. Second, in each of the three points, the word "planning" or "prepared" was used at least once. And further, the "maximum" worship experience that a church could have required planning and preparation. Conversely, worship that was spontaneous or even impulsive would not produce the best kind of worship experience. The third value, in line with the second, was timeliness. The congregation was told that if they wanted a good worship experience, then they should, in addition to praying, be on time. Worship services were scheduled to begin at 10:30 A.M. and most often did. Less than a third of the regular attendees (a large majority of whom were white) would be present at 10:30 A.M. Others continued to trickle in until about 11 A.M. The church clocks were even set between five and seven minutes ahead to, I suspect, ensure timeliness.

These values were reinforced at the dinner meeting on worship expression the following month. The meeting was held on a weeknight in the church gym. The gym was about the length of a basketball court. Tables filled the gym, suggesting that there was an expectation for a large crowd. However, less than half of the available seats were taken. There were about fifty adults present at the meeting. About 80% of those in attendance were African American.

The potluck dinner was before the meeting. At 6 P.M., Michael, the head elder who presided over communion when Lydia shouted, prayed over the meal. The dinner was a self-serve buffet. The meal included baked chicken, store-bought biscuits, instant mashed potatoes, salads, broccoli, potato-and-cheese casseroles, and spaghetti, among other dishes. All of the desserts were store bought. During dinner, I was seated near the senior pastor. An African-American woman, who was also seated at the table and who had recently begun attending the church, asked him why the church was having this meeting. I learned from that conversation that Lydia's expressive form of worship was what had "initiated" the meeting. It led to people asking questions of the leadership and expressing some concerns. Factions were beginning to develop in the church. The purpose of the meeting was for the leadership to provide some guidance on this issue.

The meeting began a little after 7 P.M. Church literature reviewing the church's formal position on worship and a sermon on worship the pastor had given seven years earlier were passed out. After giving people several minutes to review the handouts, Michael opened the discussion. He asked if people had any thoughts, concerns, or questions on the topic of worship expression. No one said anything immediately. It wasn't until after several prompts and long uncomfortable pauses that people began to speak up.

One of the first questions of the meeting was from an African-American woman, Diane. She asked, "Why is the church having a meeting on whether there is room for emotional expression at Crosstown?" Michael explained that a few people had expressed concerns about expressive worship to him and other people in leadership. Another African-American woman, Ruby, asked a follow-up question. I had known Ruby to be a very polite, sweet woman who always had a smile on her face. But she expressed the most visceral opposition to the thought of limiting this kind of worship in the church. She often rolled her eyes during the meeting and asked direct, forthright questions. She asked what some of the concerns were. He explained that those concerned "used words like 'excessive,' 'not controlled,' or 'scary'" when describing Lydia's behavior. After his response, many African Americans began to snicker at these descriptions as if they were completely unwarranted. They gave each other knowing looks of shared disbelief. Ruby responded, "I haven't seen anything like what you are describing!"

Although it took some coaxing for people to participate, people began to share their thoughts on the topic and to ask questions of the leadership. The discussion lasted for over an hour. Most of the people who participated in the discussion were African American, the vast majority of whom expressed support of Lydia and the kind of expression she displayed. However, there were some African Americans who did not support shouting during the worship services. Among the few whites who spoke, half opposed shouting. Whites who were in favor of expressive worship were young, in their mid-twenties.

Similar to what I had heard during the informal conversations, people took one of two positions on shouting. No one said right out that shouting or waving hands was an inappropriate expression of worship. However, those who opposed shouting drew upon the "decently and in order" Bible passage in 1 Corinthians. One white woman suggested that shouting was inappropriate by simply asking, "Didn't the apostle Paul say do things decently and in order?" Others explained that the overall worship experience of the group should take precedence over the individual worship experience. Since shouting was disruptive and a distraction for those who were not a part of the experience, it was inappropriate for it to be done in the context of the worship service. One white attendee said:

Before Pastor Barnes, it was very orderly. It is very different now than what it used to be. I think there does need to be some kind of order. Pastor has to have control. You can't have someone disrupting the service.

This man went on to suggest that the church adequately represented diversity in worship expression, striking a balance between Charles Stanley's and Jimmy Swaggart's churches—both large, predominantly white congregations. Those in this camp also believed that the worship at Crosstown already sufficiently reflected the racial and cultural diversity of the church and that compromise was needed, suggesting that shouting was not a reasonable way of promoting compromise. An African-American woman told the group:

> What attracted me to Crosstown is that it was middle of the road.
> I came from a varied background. What appealed to me was
> the diversity on social levels and in manners of worship. I think
> the issue is not can we, but when we ... I know it is scriptural
> for us to compromise.

Unlike the white man above, she was apparently familiar with shouting and a greater breadth of worship expressions, but was willing to "compromise" to be in a diverse church.

The "pro" group's central position was based upon ideals of freedom, opportunity, and choice. People should be free to worship God as their spirit compels them. They should be able to just let go if they need to. Furthermore, they should have the opportunity to express themselves in church. One African-American woman explained: "I have a concern about bottling an emotional expression.... People have emotions they have to express as a result of the spirit. They can't control ... well, they can control it but do we want to prevent that?" Another African-American attendee shared a similar sentiment: "If I hit the lotto, I can hoot and holler. I should be able to do that when I feel it at church." A secondary position of those in the "pro" camp was that singing without effusive behavior did not constitute legitimate worship. One African-American attendee explained: "I don't see where there is a lot of worship time. There is a lot of singing, but not worship time. Why not provide five to ten minutes during the service to let people 'get it out.'" Her statement proposed that worship services should be structured to accommodate shouting, something Crosstown was not doing.

While freedom and opportunity were central to the explanations of "pro" African-American attendees, a primary reason that whites supported expressive worship was because it was a new experience for them that they appreciated. They did not explicitly state support for Lydia's form of expression, but rather mentioned things like raising hands during service. A twenty-something white woman put it this way: "As a young Christian, when I see people raise their hands and outwardly worship God, it teaches me how to worship God. Please don't hold back. I learn from you."

Lydia was present at the meeting, which I thought was rather brave given that the meeting was in many respects a response to her behavior. She stood up and gave her thoughts on the issue. She confidently explained:

> I think we should have permission to exalt and rejoice. I feel
> many times that the Holy Spirit is oppressed in the service.
> I recognize and embrace diversity and I want *them* to embrace me.
> All week, I am dealing with stress. When I come to the house of
> God, I should be free. I would think that my brothers and sisters
> would rejoice with me. I respect and love *them* when *they* are
> meek and quiet. I don't feel that I should have to be controlled.

Again, what emerges is a different frame for what worship ought to look like. The worship seemed oppressive to Lydia, and she believed that people who are a part of an interracial church should be accepting or at least tolerant of worship expressions that are different from their own. She felt that she was accepting of "them" with their meek and quiet form of worship expression, so they should have reciprocated this appreciation and respect. Furthermore, church was a place for her to honestly express how she was feeling, something she felt she was unable to do during the rest of the week. Here, at least, she should not need to put her feelings in check.

Other African Americans similarly used "us" and "them" language when explaining how they felt about expressive worship. While no one explicitly mentioned race, these frames signified that the lines of division that had emerged during the discussion represented not just diverging religious opinions, but collective values and perspectives rooted in shared experiences and understandings. The undertone of the conversation suggested that the differences were race-based, as did the racial breakdown of the supporters and opponents. Another African-American woman shared:

> We want everyone to have the understanding that they are free.
> I agree with Leslie, Crosstown is not going to become charismatic.

> We don't want to offend anyone, but we want *them* to understand.
> Let *them* know it is not false. It is something between [the indi-
> vidual] and the Lord.

Although this attendee supported expressive worship, much like Pastor
Barnes, she felt it necessary to reassure those who were concerned about
Crosstown becoming more expressive. Second, she did not want anyone to
be offended, but at the same time it was important for her that "they"
understand this form of worship. She, like Lydia, expressed a desire for
their acceptance and understanding.

The meeting ended with Pastor Barnes summarizing the position of
the church leadership on whether or not there was room for "emotional"
worship expression at Crosstown. The guiding principle of the leadership's
official position on the matter was that worship services were to be conducted "decently and in order." Pastor Barnes explained, "The principle is
to listen when everyone is listening and rejoice when everyone is rejoic-
ing." "It is biblical," he continued, for things to be done in order. The
congregation should take priority over the person, and individuals should
not be in competition with the communal activities taking place during the
worship service. In addition, as befits a church that God had called to be
interracial, sacrifice was required on everyone's part. The leadership did
not want to suppress people's expression. People could come and enjoy a
diverse experience. The final decree by the church leadership on emotionally expressive worship was that it was most appropriate for it to take
place during the twenty- to thirty-minute praise and singing segment of the
service. Pastor Barnes closed the meeting in prayer.

A month later, Lydia took the leadership up on their suggestion. She
began to shout praises during the singing and praise segment of the service. She again immediately excused herself and exited the sanctuary,
continuing to shout in the adjacent lobby. But her expression still evoked a
negative response. I spoke with two white members to get their opinion on
what happened. Both felt that people were uncomfortable with Lydia's
expression. One of them, a man in his early thirties who felt that her
shouting was out of place, described the experience as extremely uncomfortable, an elephant in the room that no one was acknowledging. Despite
the overwhelming discomfort, people avoided looking at Lydia and acted as
if nothing out of the ordinary was happening.

The Face of Race in Interracial Congregational Worship

Race is not the only social characteristic that informs people's religious and cultural preferences. However, when discord occurs over the worship practices and styles in interracial churches, these differences become freighted with meaning. They are imbued with a history of racial inequality, oppression, and segregation that has plagued American race relations. It is not just about one church faction's preferences versus another faction's, but acceptance, inclusion, and influence over defining who we are and what we do. When discord emerges along racial lines in interracial churches, dominant understandings of race are evoked, influencing the interactions and dynamics that dictate religious and cultural norms.

Crosstown's story, in combination with the results from the National Congregations Study, shows that interracial churches are not immune to white privilege and the normativity of white culture and beliefs. At Crosstown, African Americans' desire for more expressive worship was not accommodated. Instead, whites' primary beliefs about acceptable practices were reinforced. This was despite African Americans' broad support of shouting in the church, their numerical majority status, and an African-American senior pastor with roots in a black Pentecostal denomination. Although expressive worship was allegedly appropriate during the praise and singing segment of the worship service, the response of congregants to Lydia's shouting after the dinner meeting reveals that, even then, this was not the case.

Crosstown's African-American and white attendees possessed very different understandings of expressive worship. For whites, shouting and waving hands in church were extreme worship practices. To a certain extent, these practices were off their worship radar. This was, in part, the result of whites' limited knowledge of what worship looks like in black churches, as implied by one white attendee who drew upon predominantly white churches to illustrate the diversity of worship styles and practices. But also, whites' ideas of what constituted normative lively worship— which was the inclusion of contemporary praise choruses in the worship music repertoire, with some congregants clapping and raising their hands—did not include shouting.

Conversely, shouting during worship services in African-American churches is not unusual. The foundation of this worship practice has been traced to African culture.[10] DuBois argued that "the most characteristic expression of African character" is thought to be found among African-American congregations.[11] Services in many African-American churches are, in fact, structured to incorporate this kind of worship. The musicians, choir, and preacher work in concert to encourage shouting during worship services. According to Walter Pitts in his study of Afro-Baptist churches, "if one could attribute a single purpose to the service, it would be to 'bring down the Holy Spirit' or cause a possession like trance, called 'shouting.' "[12] African Americans at Crosstown concurred that shouting was not unusual for them. African-American attendees supported Lydia. They wanted a more upbeat service that accommodated shouting. They questioned the purpose of the dinner meeting on expressive worship and laughed at the implication that shouting was a problem, as if such concerns were unwarranted. Even African Americans who were in support of the "decently and in order" position were familiar with emotionally expressive worship and would have participated in more expressive worship if they felt that it would not be a cause for disorder in the service.

Additionally, churches have historically been places where blacks could share feelings and emotions they may have suppressed elsewhere.[13] Shouting was one way of expressing these emotions. African Americans at Crosstown agreed. Worship represented more than just a time for people to connect with God, but also a space where freedom and opportunity could be celebrated. The church was a place where people should be able to decompress and express themselves without restraint. White attendees at Crosstown, even the younger attendees who supported effusive worship, did not express this idea of worship. Rather, the foremost objective of worship for whites was to facilitate congregants' meeting God. So, in addition to having different understandings about what defined normative worship, African Americans and whites differed on what they believed the purpose of worship to be.[14]

The central position of the church leadership ultimately supported the position of the "con" group on shouting, and thereby the primary position of whites in the church. For the basis of the church's official position, church leaders evoked the New Testament, which says that all things should be done "decently and in order." But what does "decently and in order" mean, really? An African-American woman who had recently begun attending Crosstown inadvertently gave the most revealing insight into what is meant by this phrase. She explained during the dinner meeting:

There needs to be order and balance. When I first came to Crosstown, I raised my hands. But, then I looked around and noticed people were not raising their hands. So, I then stopped.

She previously had attended a church where effusive worship was common. However, after raising her hands at Crosstown, she realized that this kind of expression was not the norm for this church. She, therefore, stopped raising her hands during congregational worship and adapted to the normative (less effusive) worship culture of Crosstown.

Normative religious culture is not universal but rather varies by group and context.[15] Groups occupying particular social spaces at particular times decide what practices, styles, and rituals are acceptable. Therefore, decent and orderly worship is not an issue of what is theologically accurate, as this woman's story demonstrates, but is rather a standard set by those who wield the most power. In interracial churches, those who wield power affirm white privilege and culture. Congregational worship will appeal to whites in these congregations more so than African Americans. Consequently, African Americans will bear the greater burden of maintaining a racially mixed worship experience.

2

Bringing Race to the Center

Extrareligious Activities

Worship and religious practices are fundamental to the congregational life of churches. But American churches are not just places where people gather to pray and learn from the Bible, they are also significant social and cultural institutions. Churches uniquely provide groups with the capacity to collectively practice their own subcultures, organize for civic and community ends, and develop their own ideas about the world. This is especially true for racial minorities. Churches exemplify the utility of religion as an institution where subordinate cultural, social, and civic endeavors can be cultivated.[1] This is not to suggest that whites do not access the American religious structure for similar reasons. Rather, churches are especially important to racial minorities because they have often been the only institution through which they can effect change.

In this chapter, the extrareligious social and civic activities of interracial churches are examined. These types of activities inform our understanding of a church's culture and identity, revealing its values, priorities, and beliefs. I pay particular attention to racially salient activities, defined as those activities that either directly address issues of race or that are common in African-American churches. Understanding this area of congregational life in interracial churches will reveal if and how African Americans can draw upon an interracial church as a resource to reproduce their culture and generate social and civic changes that affect their community.[2]

Social and Civic Activities: How Do Interracial Churches Compare to Other Churches?

There has been considerable research addressing the extrareligious social and civic participation of white and black religious organizations. Research has consistently shown that African-American religious organizations are more inclined to participate in political and certain social and community activities than are white religious organizations.[3] Yet, no one has compared the extrareligious social and civic participation of interracial churches to that of other churches.

The social and civic activities considered from the NCS are community involvement; political involvement; participation in race-related discussions; and participation in activities that celebrate or preserve the culture of a particular racial or ethnic group (see appendix B for operationalizations). Community involvement measures churches' participation in community and socially oriented activities, such as feeding the hungry, building or repairing homes, and helping the homeless, among other community activities. Results show that, generally, churches' involvement in community activities is quite limited. Neither interracial, white, nor African-American churches have average community involvement scores higher than 1.8 on a 9-point scale (see table C-4, appendix C). Even after controlling for other congregational characteristics, interracial churches' community involvement does not differ from that of white or African-American churches. So, racial composition does not affect churches' participation in community activities (see table C-5, appendix C).

Political involvement measures churches' level of participation in political activities, such as voter registration, political discussions, and hosting political candidates, among others. Similar to community involvement, churches' average political involvement scores are low. However, as other research has shown, African-American churches are most inclined to draw upon religious resources for political endeavors.[4] African-American churches demonstrate the highest level of involvement in political activities. They have a score of 2.1 out of a possible 8, which means that, on average, African-American churches participated in at least two explicitly political activities over the previous year. White churches' average score for political involvement is 1.1.[5] For interracial churches, it is 1.6 (see table C-4, appendix C). When other congregational characteristics are taken into account, African-American churches' political involvement score is a full point higher than that of interracial churches, whose score is no longer higher than that of white churches (see table C-5, appendix C).

African-American churches are also most likely to have race-related discussion meetings. Twenty-nine percent of African-American churches had a race-related discussion meeting within the past year. This is compared to 24% of interracial churches and 20% of white churches (see table C-4, appendix C). After taking religious affiliation, church size, and class structure, among other congregational characteristics, into consideration, African-American churches are 2.6 times more likely than interracial churches to participate in race-related discussions. Again, interracial and white churches' levels of participation in race-related discussions are no different (see table C-6, appendix C).

Also considered is whether churches had an event that was intended to preserve or celebrate the cultural heritage of a particular racial or ethnic group. Results again show that African-American churches are the most inclined to offer this activity, with 35% of African-American churches hosting such an event. Still, about 15% of interracial churches hosted a racial or ethnocultural preservation activity. But only 4% of white churches had a similar kind of activity (see table C-4, appendix C). While the descriptive statistics may suggest that interracial churches are not too far behind African-American churches when it comes to racial or ethnocultural preservation, after controlling for other congregational characteristics, African-American churches are nearly seven times more likely than interracial churches to participate in this sort of activity, and white churches are 66% less likely than interracial churches to do so (see table C-6, appendix C).

While American churches are not particularly inclined to participate in extrareligious social and civic activities, some churches are more likely to participate in these kinds of activities than are others.[6] The extrareligious congregational life of African-American churches appears to be rather different from both white and interracial churches. African-American churches demonstrate a greater propensity than other churches to participate in racially salient social and political activities. Whereas interracial churches are more likely than white churches to participate in racial/ethnocultural preservation, in all other extrareligious activities they are the same. However, other factors besides racial composition matter for churches' participation in extrareligious activities. Church size and greater percentages of college-educated attendees are consistent predictors of churches' participation in the social and civic activities examined here. To the extent that larger and more-educated churches have more resources to expend on extrareligious activities, the relatively low levels of congregational participation in social and civic endeavors overall may be more a reflection of limited resources rather than a lack of interest or desire. Still, as with worship, it appears that interracial churches tend to adopt the congregational culture more common to white churches when it comes to participation in racially salient social and civic activities. A more in-depth look at Crosstown's extrareligious activities will help to show this.

Crosstown: Connecting with the Community

Even outside of the worship service, religious activities were central to the congregational life of Crosstown. This is not surprising given the church's conservative Protestant orientation.[7] Sunday school classes were held for children, teenagers, and adults before the worship services. There was also a weekly Bible study led by Pastor Barnes and several weekly prayer meetings. Still, Crosstown did support or participate in some community-oriented activities. The church contributed 10% of its annual budget (after operating costs) to outside organizations, including a Christian campground, a prison ministry, Youth for Christ (an organization dedicated to the evangelism of youth), and the Anderson Community Development Council (a not-for-profit community organization that was committed to improving the physical and social conditions of the town). However, most of Crosstown's community activities had an evangelical focus. The activities were not aimed at providing the local community with economic or social resources, but were instead intended to attract people from the neighborhood to the church.

One such event was "Movies under the Stars." During the summer, the church showed Christian and family-friendly secular movies, including *Jonah*, a Veggie Tales film, and *Like Mike*, which starred Lil' Bow Wow, a young African-American rapper. The movies were shown in the church courtyard, a grassy, outdoor space directly adjacent to the church. Posters

were put up in restaurants, grocery stores, and other businesses throughout Mapleton and Anderson to advertise movie dates and times. People
brought their own lawn chairs or blankets to sit on. Popcorn, candy, sodas,
and other snacks were available for purchase. Between thirty and forty
people came to each of the movie nights, many of them young children and
teens. I recognized most of the people who came as regular attendees of
Crosstown. However, there were some families whom I did not recognize
and who seemed to be newcomers from the local neighborhoods. Although
"Movies under the Stars" had an implicitly evangelical focus, I did not
witness explicit proselytizing. Beyond a brief opening prayer, there were
no other religious activities or rituals that took place. "Movies under the
Stars" ended with summer, but throughout the year, Crosstown continued
to host movie nights in the church gym.

Crosstown also organized a neighborhood walk campaign. This campaign had a more explicit evangelical emphasis than "Movies under the
Stars." The primary aim was to invite local residents to the church. During
the announcements at weekly worship services, regular attendees were recruited to volunteer for the neighborhood walk. Bright colorful door hangers
were professionally designed and produced for the event. The door hangers
invited readers to "Come Join Us! . . . at Crosstown where you'll find people
(just like you) that want to know God and grow in their relationship with
Him through Jesus Christ." A schedule of weekly church activities was
printed on the back. For several Saturday mornings in the fall, groups of
church volunteers walked the blocks surrounding the church and placed
these door hangers on the front door knobs of apartments and houses.

Although Crosstown's extrareligious activities were primarily evangelical, the church had expressed a desire to become more involved in
activities that directly serve the surrounding communities. Two years prior
to my study, the church held three meetings to identify future goals for the
church. A racially diverse gathering of approximately fifty people attended
each meeting. One goal discussed at length at these meetings was for
Crosstown to become more involved in local community endeavors like
mentoring disadvantaged youth or providing aid to poor families. Given
the community needs and challenges of Anderson, these activities were
apparently intended to reach out to Anderson residents. Yet, Crosstown
never implemented any of these ideas nor became actively involved in
Anderson in other ways. The church did participate in Mapleton community activities, though. One of these activities was a memorial service

for 9/11 victims. The other was a neighborhood-sponsored celebration of religious diversity called the "Walk of Faith."

The 9/11 memorial service was co-sponsored by eight churches located in Mapleton and other nearby communities; however, Mapleton Evangelical Church, a 1,000-plus-member, predominantly white church, was the primary organizer of the event. None of the churches that participated in the event was from nearby Anderson.[8] The service was held outdoors in one of the public parks in Mapleton. It was a weekday evening. The sky was clear and the temperature was still comfortable for outdoor evening activities. Attendees filled roughly a third of the park, which was about the size of a half city block. At least 300 people were present, about 90% of whom were white. The event reminded me of an outdoor concert. People brought their own seating for the service. They were sprawled about the grass on blankets and lawn chairs, facing a main stage. Music and singing were a large part of the program. A praise leader from Mapleton Evangelical Church led the crowd in several praise choruses, accompanied by a band with a keyboard, drums, and guitar. Solos and choir selections were performed. Interspersed between musical selections, encouraging sermonettes were given by pastors (including Pastor Barnes) from each of the sponsoring churches. During the program, casually dressed ushers passed out candles. By the end of the service, the sun was setting, and ushers returned to light the candles. With candles lit across the crowd, the service ended with a prayer and a moment of silence in remembrance of the victims of 9/11. The service lasted for about one and a half hours.

The "Walk of Faith" was part of the Mapleton centennial celebration. The purpose of the event was to celebrate the "diversity of faith" in Mapleton. Two dozen Mapleton organizations of various religious faiths participated. During a Sunday afternoon in the spring, participating churches hosted open houses for neighborhood residents to visit. Some churches presented historical displays, others performed musical presentations, and others offered church tours. Crosstown presented a historical display board that included information about the church's origins and previous pastors. Crosstown also offered tours of the church and refreshments to open house guests.

Crosstown did not participate in political events nor was there any explicit or implicit public support of a particular political party. The closest the church came to political participation of any kind was allowing voter registration pamphlets to be displayed on information tables located just outside the sanctuary. And it was no easy decision to allow these pamphlets to be displayed. To ensure that they had no political or social bias, Pastor Barnes carefully reviewed the pamphlets before allowing them to be placed on the information tables. There are two plausible explanations for Crosstown's limited political involvement. One explanation is that political participation was not something about which the people of Crosstown were particularly concerned. I asked attendees about their political party affiliations during the interviews. Their thoughts on politics suggest that attendees, regardless of race, did not have strong attachments to one political party or another. However, in the few cases when interviewees expressed strong political affiliations, African Americans tended to affiliate with the Democrats and whites tended to be Republican. In fact, one of the church's white elders was a staunch Republican who was active in local political campaigns. There was also the possibility that Crosstown was attempting to avoid cross-racial conflict by minimizing political discussions. Either way, Crosstown's lack of political involvement is consistent with that of other interracial churches in the United States.

Bringing Race to the Center?

We envision ourselves standing courageously at the intersection where race and class collide. . . . Aware of the differences that divide our community, we fearlessly confront our discomforts as we draw together to worship God and to share our lives with one another.

—Crosstown Community Church Mission
Statement

As evidenced by Crosstown's mission statement, the church's interracial character was central to its identity. The church purported to embrace racial and socioeconomic diversity and the challenges that go with it. Race and class divisions were very tangible for Crosstown with working-class, predominantly African-American Anderson to the north of the church and middle class/upper middle-class, majority-white Mapleton to the south. However, bridging this community divide proved to be a challenge for the church. The church's minimal involvement in Anderson community activities, when compared to its participation in Mapleton activities, is one indication of this. However, Crosstown attempted to bring issues of race closer to the center of congregational life. Before this, race was rarely discussed at Crosstown, not during the weekly worship services, nor during other church functions. At times, I heard church attendees talk about race-related issues in casual conversation, but this was not common. Explicit talk about race, particularly during church services, meetings, or other formally organized activities, was unfamiliar territory for Crosstown.

The new effort to tackle race-related issues was spearheaded by Pastor Barnes. He initiated the endeavor with a sermon entitled "Authentic Christian Community." The sermon was intended to provide the church with biblical guidelines for accomplishing its mission statement. Pastor Barnes acknowledged during the sermon that the church's mission statement was ambitious. But, as he put it, "crash potential" was intrinsic to the interracial and interclass interactions suggested by the statement. Successfully accomplishing the church's mission required that the church rely upon biblical principles.

Similar to his sermon on worship, the biblical perspective upon which Pastor Barnes based this sermon complied with the theological and social ideals common to white evangelicals, who use individualistic solutions to address social and racial problems.[9] Drawing upon scriptures from several books of the Bible (including Psalms, Matthew, Acts, Ephesians, James, and Revelation), he insisted that the primary way that Crosstown attendees could accomplish interracial and interclass unity was by possessing "Christ in their hearts." In other words, change would occur one heart at a time, as people adopted biblical principles in their own lives. This required committing to hearing and heeding the word of God; committing to principles of biblical unity; committing to appreciating and not just tolerating differences; and finally, committing to not giving deference to certain groups of people over others. Broader structural and social realities, such as racial segregation, racism, and social inequality, were not mentioned during the sermon.

Following the sermon, Pastor Barnes organized a nine-week seminar on racial diversity and Christianity. The seminar was loosely based upon the book *Divided by Faith*, a scholarly examination of why racial segregation persists among American evangelicals. Pastor Barnes persistently urged the congregation to attend the upcoming seminar. Every week, starting six weeks before the seminar was scheduled to begin, an announcement was made during the weekly worship service. Congregants were asked to sign up for the seminar in advance if they were planning to attend. Normally, the church administrative assistant would give the church announce-ments. However, Pastor Barnes personally announced the upcoming seminar on several occasions, encouraging people to read the book and attend. It was evident that the issue of racial diversity and religion was of great importance to him.

Thirty people signed up for the seminar, but ultimately forty people attended at least one of the nine sessions. The overall attendance reflected the racial composition of the church. Thirteen (33%) of the attendees were white. Twenty-five (63%) were black. A little more than half of the people who participated in the seminar attended on a regular basis, meaning they came to at least five of the nine sessions. African Americans appeared to be slightly more committed to the class than were whites. Among twenty-two regular attendees, seventeen were black and five were white. Additionally, nine of the forty people who attended the class held a leadership position in the church (i.e., pastor or lay leader). Six of the nine leaders attended the seminar regularly. However, only one of the nine leaders who attended was white, and he attended just one session. In fact, none of the eleven white pastors or lay leaders had signed up for the seminar, suggesting they never planned to attend it. Given that the leadership was racially mixed, this was a poor showing by the whites in leadership. Whites' relative absence from the seminar generally was rather curious given that Pastor Barnes personally planned the seminar and strongly urged people to attend it—a clear attempt on his part at moving the church toward engaging racial issues. And white leaders' absence from the seminar not only suggested a lack of interest in addressing issues of race but also a less than complete endorsement of Pastor Barnes' leadership, at least when it came to race-related issues.

A Christian not-for-profit organization that consults with churches on racial issues, the Racial Reconciliation Project (RRP), was hired to conduct the seminar. The seminar was held once a week on Tuesday evenings in one of the Sunday school rooms. The room was organized like a classroom. Folding chairs were placed in rows for seating. A whiteboard hung on the front wall. A television and VCR were set up at the front of the room. Each seminar session was scheduled to begin at 7:45 P.M. and to last for one hour, which it usually did. The sessions were structured to facilitate large group (the entire class) and small group (four to five people) discus-sions. Central themes of the seminar were evangelical religious history and culture; religious racial segregation among Christians; and blacks' and whites' responses to the recent racial reconciliation movement within evangelicalism (e.g., Promise Keepers). Seminar materials included the book *Divided by Faith*[10] and a discussion notebook that highlighted key concepts from the book. *Divided by Faith* was used during the seminar as a means of stimulating conversation. Clips from films such as *A Family Thing* and *Grand Canyon* and quotes from thinkers like Alexis de Tocqueville and Frederick Douglass were also used to facilitate group discussion.

Steve, a white, middle-aged man and a leader in RRP, led the seminar. Two African-American men, who were also part of RRP, periodically assisted Steve. At the beginning of the seminar, Steve laid out guidelines for the discussions. He explained, "We are going to work hard to not persuade each other to our points of view. We are going to listen to each other's stories . . . without putting a spin on them. Your pain is not more significant than other people's pain in the room." Steve also encouraged people to use the term "racialization," instead of "racism" or "racial prejudice" during discussions. This was problematic for some African Americans in the seminar. Steve asked people to share how they felt about this word, and one African-American woman shared that "racialization" didn't have any real meaning to her: "It is just a word on paper." An African-American man explained that he didn't like the term racialization because "it doesn't open up honest dialogue." Another African-American woman similarly felt that racialization didn't capture the real issues of race. In her opinion, using this term instead of racism limited the discussion. She asked Steve, "Why not [instead of using racialization] define racism accurately?" She went on to ask why they should accommodate whites by changing the word. She felt this "closed dialogue." As she was saying this, I heard an African-American woman sitting nearby say under her breath "sugar coating it," showing that she too felt that using a word like racialization instead of racism or racial prejudice did not allow the real issues of race to be confronted. Finally, one white woman shared her thoughts about the issue. She told the group that all her life she had heard that "whites are racists," so she felt like "why even try?" No one responded to what she said, but her comment confirmed Steve's implied reason for wanting to frame the racial discussions as he did. Whites in attendance could construe language like "racism" as offensive. Using less-offensive language and focusing on one's own racial story allowed whites to discuss race without feeling like they were being implicated in African Americans' racial experiences. Steve then closed this topic, entreating people to "bear with" the term racialization.

The class abided by the guidelines Steve proposed. The discussions during the remainder of the seminar were often characterized by people sharing isolated comments or opinions, rather than interpersonal dialogue. Little conflict about race or other related issues arose, which I suspect was another purpose of the rules. Yet, while these guidelines may have facilitated less-contentious interracial interaction, they also framed the discussions in such a way that limited African Americans' freedom to share their true feelings about race. The discussions concentrated on individual experiences. And, similar to the recent sermon on "Authentic Christian Community," the broader social realities of race were often elided. People, both African American and white, instead shared their negative personal encounters with people from the other race. For example, one woman shared the challenges she faced coming from an interracial background. A white man confessed that his family struggled with race. An African-American man told a story about how the window of his car was shot out while he was stopped at a rural Indiana gas station. Yet, none of these stories were framed within the larger context of American race relations.

Understandably, structuring the seminar around individuals' opinions and experiences left some with unresolved concerns. This was exemplified during the last session of the class. Steve gave people the opportunity to share any final thoughts. Samantha, an African-American woman, said that while she felt the seminar was beneficial, she also felt that "[the seminar] focused on whites' views of blacks . . . but we needed to also discuss blacks' views of whites." She admitted that she struggled with feelings of "us versus them" when it came to black/white relations. She further shared, "Whites don't understand our struggles. How can I have spiritual unity with someone who doesn't know what I have gone through?" Audrey, a white woman in her mid-thirties who had attended nearly every session of the seminar, also demonstrated how discussions of race based upon individual experiences and ideas didn't expose people to the structural nature of racial problems. Audrey adamantly expressed:

There is a myth in the black community that whites can change things if we want to because we all have power. But, most of us don't have power. There are whites in society, such as the president of my company, who can do something. I don't think it's true that all whites have power.

After she finished, her comment just hung in the air. There was silence for several seconds. No one, not even Steve, responded to what she had said. Her comment ended up being the final one of the seminar. Steve then made a few closing remarks and ended the final seminar session.

After the class, people continued to hang around and chat. I was gathering my possessions when an African-American leader in the church, Chester, came over to talk to me. He proceeded to tell me that he disagreed with Audrey. He told me that he did think whites had power and supported his claim by giving me an example of how he thinks white power manifests itself. He explained that, when he goes into a convenience store, the person behind the counter watches him suspiciously. However, if a white person walks into a convenience store, he is not automatically suspect. Therefore, to him, white power was a privilege that all whites possessed and benefited from. Although the volume of his speech remained appropriately low for a two-person conversation, his animus toward Audrey's comment was apparent. I was surprised by the timing of Chester's comment. Given his leadership status in the church, I would have expected him to feel empowered to share these thoughts during the session. I am not aware of others in the class who may have similarly disagreed with Audrey's comment about white power. However, blacks' personal experiences with racism and their opposition to how racial discussions were framed in the seminar lead me to suspect that others also disagreed with Audrey's sentiments.

The class was asked to fill out anonymous evaluations of the seminar. Since the evaluations were anonymous, I was unable to determine the race or gender of the evaluators. But nearly everyone reported that they had enjoyed the class and found it beneficial. Many also stated that they would like the church to have other classes on race-related topics. Several mentioned that they appreciated the "open and honest discussion," "hearing people's stories," and the "small group interaction." People also felt that they learned more about the experiences of the "other" racial group. One person, in response to the question "Do you think this class was helpful for you personally?" wrote, "Yes! [It] helped me understand blacks like I never did before." Another person wrote, "It has [helped] me to be more understanding of white evangelical Christians." Nevertheless, while the class was personally enlightening for those who attended, many felt that the benefit for Crosstown was limited. They expressed disappointment in the relatively low number of people who attended the seminar and seemed to imply that this disappointment was primarily with the limited number of whites who attended the seminar. One person wrote, "If there had been better re-presentation racially there would be better interaction and opportunities for growth within the church." Another person wrote, "I think the class helped those who have attended, but we still need the broader membership to be involved." Another evaluator specifically mentioned that one thing he/she did not like about the class was that "not enough of the white church of Crosstown had been a part of the class." Though this seminar was a breakthrough attempt by Crosstown at directly addressing race, it exposed a vulnerable fault line within the congregation. White and African-American attendees possessed different perspectives on race and different commit-ments to reconciling these differences. Under further duress, such a fault line could rupture and lead to a congregational split along racial lines.

Race and "Works" in Interracial Churches

For the African-American community especially, churches are both places of worship and places of social, cultural, and political significance. Unlike other American institutions, such as the workplace, schools, and housing, religion provides African Americans with an institutional vehicle through which they can preserve their culture and influence the world in which they live. However, a national comparison of churches' participation in racially salient social and civic activities suggests that, when blacks and whites attend the same church, the congregation is less apt to leverage the church for these extrareligious purposes. These results reinforce the notion that white normativity and privilege affect the congregational lives of in-terracial churches. Moreover, they suggest that African-American mem-bers of interracial churches pay the added cost of becoming less effective at preserving their culture, addressing race-related concerns, or creating so-cial change for their respective communities.

Crosstown was similarly disinclined to use the church as a resource for racially salient social or civic activities. Activities peripheral to Crosstown's weekly worship services were primarily religious, and the church's com-munity activities often possessed an evangelical objective. Both African-American Protestants and white conservative Protestants value religious activities and evangelism.[11] So, this area of congregational life would not likely evoke tensions between African-American and white Crosstown at-tendees. However, an examination of Crosstown's participation in extrareligious social and civic activities reveals the racial undertones that impact how interracial churches engage such matters.

For example, Crosstown was far more likely to participate in community activities in Mapleton than in Anderson. The church donated money to the Anderson Community Development Council, a commitment that demanded no direct investment from attendees. But it did not participate in any Anderson community activities. The church's tendency to favor Mapleton could be partially explained by Crosstown's physical location. While the church rested on the border between Mapleton and Anderson, it resided within the boundaries of Mapleton and, therefore, may have primarily identified as a Mapleton church. Nevertheless, Crosstown possessed strong ties to Anderson. At least half of Crosstown's regular attendees lived in Anderson, but more important, the president of one of Anderson's most civically involved and influential community organizations, the Anderson Community Development Council, was a member of Crosstown. Considering the church's stated desire to engage and bridge both communities, together with the church's ties to Anderson, it is reasonable to say that Crosstown had equal, if not more, opportunity to collaborate on Anderson community endeavors.

Additionally, politics were not central to the congregational life of Crosstown, which I attribute primarily to attendees' noncommittal stance on party affiliation. However, Crosstown made unprecedented steps toward addressing issues of race during the study. This is particularly relevant to our understanding of interracial churches' extrareligious social activities, given that about a quarter of them, according to the NCS, participate in race-related discussions of some kind. Crosstown's experience confronting race suggests that interracial churches espouse white Christian theology, ideals, and values. For conservative Protestant interracial churches, this means they draw upon the religio-cultural tools of white evangelicals—accountable freewill individualism, relationalism, and antistructuralism—to respond to racial and class problems.[12] This was most plainly demonstrated by Pastor Barnes' sermon proposing biblical direction on how the church could realize its mission. He advocated individual-level changes as the solution to developing a more racially and class-unified church. The seminar on race and religion did present a broader perspective on race in America. The relevance of history, socially constructed inequalities, and different racial experiences were acknowledged. Nevertheless, the way the class's discussion was structured emphasized people's personal experiences with and ideas about race rather than the structural realities of race, such as racial segregation and inequality. Therefore, a personal and individualistic perspective on social problems dominated the seminar, which stripped some African Americans of familiar tools for talking about race and left other people in the seminar, like Samantha and Audrey, without the tools to deal with their unresolved feelings about race.

Crosstown's efforts at addressing racial issues did not facilitate change in the church at the organizational level as predicted by those who attended the seminar. Race, in general, remained a marginalized topic at Crosstown. There were no other meetings, classes, or sermons explicitly addressing race-related issues. Nor were there any noticeable differences in congregational life. This is likely due to the church's individualistic approach to the subject. And because Crosstown relegated race-related discussions to events outside of the core church activities (i.e., the worship service, Sunday school, or quarterly church meetings), only those attendees who were particularly invested in engaging racial issues and willing to sacrifice an hour or so once a week during a weekday evening did so. If a person was not invested in the issue, he or she could easily avoid engaging it. The seminar was also ineffective because whites, especially the white leaders, acted as a silent opposing constituency. By disengaging from the effort, they voiced their lack of support. And, since any successful effort at dealing with race in the church required their involvement, they in effect thwarted any potentially lasting organizational or cultural changes from the seminar.

Extrareligious activities are not central to the congregational life of churches. Nevertheless, if secular society does not provide opportunities for racial minorities to equally stake their collective interests in civic society and to celebrate their cultures, the evidence from the NCS suggests that racially diversifying churches, as they are currently structured, could be a detriment to their capacity to do so. Furthermore, despite the peripheral importance of extrareligious activities, Crosstown's experience reveals that racial tensions still emerge over these kinds of activities in interracial churches. Where both whites and African Americans actively engaged in the racial conflict over worship practices described in the previous chapter, whites were more likely to disengage from the racial conflict that subtly underlay the church's community and race-related activities. As with worship practices at Crosstown, white attendees' interests and proclivities ultimately governed this area of congregational life as well. Race returned to being a subtext to Crosstown's congregational discourse.

3

Spiritual Affirmative Action

Leadership Structure and Characteristics

The congregation was shocked when it heard the news that
Crosstown would be losing two of its three pastors. It was during
a Sunday morning worship service. Pastor Raymond Barnes invited Pastor Dave McPherson, the assistant pastor, to join him at
the pulpit. Pastor McPherson, a white man in his early thirties,
approached the microphone and announced that he had been
offered a pastoral position at another church, located out of state.
He told the congregation that this was a difficult decision for
him and his wife, Julie, but they ultimately believed that God
desired for him to take the position, and he did. They would be
moving in a month. Many in the congregation gasped at the news
and sighed with disappointment. Pastor McPherson was something of a staple at Crosstown. He predated Pastor Barnes and had
been a leader in the church, in one capacity or another, for over
ten years. After sharing the news of his imminent departure,
Pastor McPherson returned to his seat. Then, Pastor Barnes invited Pastor Andrew Smith, the youth pastor, to join him at the
pulpit. The congregation was told that he, too, would be step-
ping down from his position. Although he was unsure of God's
specific direction for his life, he believed that he was not to remain
a youth pastor. This announcement similarly elicited gasps and
sighs of disappointment from several people in the congregation.
Pastor Smith was also white and in his early thirties and also
predated Pastor Barnes.

The departures of Pastor McPherson and Pastor Smith initiated a new era at Crosstown Community Church. With two pastoral positions vacant, Pastor Barnes had an opportunity to influence the hiring of other key leaders at Crosstown and to further establish his agenda for the church. However, Pastor McPherson's and Pastor Smith's departures also presented a challenge. Crosstown had demonstrated a capacity to defy the normative racialized order of things by hiring an African American as senior pastor at a time when the church was still majority white. Nevertheless, while Pastor Barnes was welcomed by most at Crosstown when he first became senior pastor, according to a long-time member and leader of the church, several white families left soon after he assumed this position. With a history of white flight that was seemingly triggered by the addition of an African American to the pastoral staff, the loss of two influential, visible white leaders would further challenge Crosstown's openness to African-American structural power in the church.

Leadership Structure and Characteristics of Crosstown

As an interracial church with an African-American senior pastor, NCS analysis reveals that Crosstown was in limited company. A large majority (68%) of the head pastors of interracial churches in the United States are white. This may be due, in part, to race matching between the congregation and the head pastor, as about two-thirds of adult attendees of interracial churches, on average, are white.[1] Crosstown provides further insight into how the leadership of interracial churches is structured and the extent to which race matters for leadership more generally.

Crosstown's leadership consisted of several positions, including pastors, elders, deacons, and coordinators. The church had three full-time pastor positions: senior pastor, assistant pastor, and youth pastor. Pastor Barnes, as senior pastor, was responsible for supervising the assistant and youth pastors and the office staff. Other primary responsibilities of the senior pastor included planning the Sunday morning worship services, religious teaching, and community relations. The senior pastor conducted the majority of sermons. He also counseled attendees and performed religious ceremonies, such as dedicating babies to God and marriages. The assistant pastor supervised adult ministries (e.g., adult Sunday school, small groups, etc.) and lay leaders (excluding the elders) and was responsible for the maintenance and use of church property. The youth pastor was responsible for all children's activities from infancy through adolescence, including the nursery, children's church, and youth group. Both the assistant and youth pastors provided family counseling and periodically did the sermons during weekly worship services. The remaining leadership roles were lay positions. Crosstown had four elders (one of whom was the senior pastor), ten deacons, and eleven coordinators. Elders were responsible for the overall direction and governance of the church. All church activities were first approved by the elder board. Deacons were responsible for various church functions. These included, for example, music, prayer, and marriage and family support. The coordinators organized worship service activities, such as ushering, greeting, and welcoming visitors.

Crosstown's leadership was racially diverse, closely approximating the racial composition of the church. Of the twenty-eight pastoral and lay leader positions, whites filled eleven and African Americans filled the remaining seventeen. Although the church had an African-American head pastor, whites were slightly overrepresented among the higher leadership positions at Crosstown. The coordinators were the least balanced racially, with eight African Americans and three whites. There were four white and six black deacons. And, including Pastor Barnes, there were two African-American elders and two white elders. In this regard, whites had a slight structural advantage at Crosstown relative to what would be expected given the proportion of whites who regularly attended the church. If the leadership were completely representative, whites would hold about one-third of each category. Instead, whites comprised 27% of the coordinators, 40% of the deacons, and 50% of the elders. The greater the authority of the leadership position, the greater the proportion of whites holding that position. So, while the racial composition of leadership, as demonstrated from the NCS and my study of Crosstown, may be due, in part, to the racial composition of the church, the story of Crosstown's pastoral replacement process reveals that other factors are also at work.

Meeting Pastor Barnes

Crosstown was, indeed, unusual in that it had an African-American senior pastor. However, Crosstown was unsuccessful at accommodating shouting during worship services, despite Pastor Barnes' familiarity with more effusive worship. And Pastor Barnes received limited support from the white leadership when he attempted to bring racial issues to the center of the church's congregational discourse. This suggests that having an African-American senior pastor does not necessarily mean that the preferences and social interests of African-American attendees will be served to their satisfaction.

I sat down and talked with Pastor Barnes to gain a better understanding of his perspective on being a senior pastor of an interracial church and the challenges that come with such a position, as well as to learn more about his religious heritage and experiences. We met in his office at the church. The interview was semistructured, lasting for a little over an hour. Pastor Barnes answered questions cautiously, careful not to indict Crosstown or any person or group in the church. He often spoke in generalities and rarely strayed in his responses to questions. Nevertheless, his answers were thorough and provided insight into who he was as a pastor, his religious persuasions, and the ways in which his past religious experiences influenced his current social and religious ideas.

Pastor Barnes was raised in a predominantly African-American, urban, working-class neighborhood. Although his paternal grandfather was a pastor of a Presbyterian congregation, his spiritual heritage is rooted in the black church. He attended an African Methodist Episcopal (AME) church with his extended family during his early childhood. Then, as an adolescent, he began attending a Church of God in Christ (COGIC) church after experiencing a spiritual conversion at a church revival. During the interview, Pastor Barnes fondly reminisced about his time in COGIC and considered this part of his spiritual heritage to be the most central to his spiritual development. There, he had become familiar with "gifts of the spirit" and was exposed to godly men whom he respected. He also experienced and appreciated the effusive, experiential worship at this church. He recalled "joyful testimonies" being delivered during the worship services. There would be, he described:

> hand clapping, dancing, rejoicing for sometimes hours. . . . [There was] congregational call and response [and] a lot of call-response kind of music and singing. . . . You had the freedom to sing your own song and people would get on board with you.

However, although Pastor Barnes' religious and spiritual heritage was rooted in the black church, as an adult he became increasingly affiliated with white evangelicalism. After receiving the "call" into ministry, he attended Dallas Theological Seminary, a predominantly white and particularly conservative evangelical seminary. He apprenticed at Dallas Metropolitan Church, a predominantly African-American congregation with a substantial white attendance. The pastor of Dallas Metropolitan Church was popular within white evangelical circles, regularly featured on evangelical radio programs. After receiving his master's degree, Pastor Barnes became an assistant pastor at Anderson Evangelical Church (AEC). Anderson Evangelical Church was a largely African-American, yet interracial church and a member of a white evangelical denomination. He described AEC as "inclusive." The worship was similar to the worship at Crosstown. He explained, "the worship was not a 'let it all hang out' kind of worship service as what may characterize some predominantly black churches." Pastor Barnes worked at AEC for five years. His next pastorship was at Crosstown where, at the time we spoke, he had been senior pastor for eight years. He was not only the first African-American senior pastor of Crosstown Community Church, but the only racial minority to ever hold any pastoral position in the church. Pastor Barnes' appointment was, therefore, a historic event for the church. As such, Pastor Barnes was poised to initiate changes in the church, which he did. The most evident change was the introduction of upbeat music. In addition to hymns and melodious Christian choruses, praise choruses and gospel music were added to the church's musical repertoire. The church also got a set of drums. Some attendees, particularly the senior white members, objected to some of these changes. However, they were welcomed by the younger white generation at Crosstown and signaled better things to come for African-American attendees.

Nevertheless, even with the changes that Pastor Barnes initiated at Crosstown, it did not reflect the worship environment in the COGIC church for which he had expressed such respect and appreciation earlier in the interview. I asked him if he missed this kind of worship. He explained:

> I still have a measure of enjoyment of that. But I found other ways to enjoy God. Certainly that is a legitimate way of enjoying God. But there are different and other ways because in some

regard, there were extremes to the neglect of certain other
things.... I was definitely fully nurtured in that regard [i.e.,
worship, music, singing], [but] there were some other things
that had less emphasis that would have made for a more well-
rounded kind of growth and development both as a Christian
and as a man and as a black man.

While Pastor Barnes still appreciated the worship style of the COGIC
tradition, he had apparently become less enamored with not only the
worship, but other religious practices of this tradition. The spiritual heritage he had experienced growing up was no longer central to his theology
or religious identity.[2] Pastor Barnes elaborated on two areas in the COGIC
church that he believed impeded people's spiritual and personal development. The first was the leadership structure. It centered around one
"central recognizable leader." As Pastor Barnes described it:

You recognize that, you honor that, you support that, but there is
not necessarily the leadership development of other people....
It could have been more than just honoring them [but] seeing and
recognizing the societal pressure that is on African-American
men in particular and the church sort of putting things in
place that could counter the societal perspectives in helping to
build men up and helping in a greater degree to define biblical
maleness.

In his opinion, this kind of leadership structure was a particular dis-
service to black men because of the dearth of African-American male socialization outside of the church. The church was a vital place where men
could be trained, respected, and developed, but the COGIC church did not,
in his opinion, provide these tools. Except for the head pastor, African-
American men were not developed nor respected to the degree they ought
to have been. Paradoxically, Crosstown also did not have any formal programs or structures with the explicit purpose of building up African-
American men. I did not ask Pastor Barnes about this, but found it curious that the church did not have such programs, given his strong feelings
about their importance. It could be that the largely middle-class black
men in the church found opportunities for male socialization outside the
church or that Pastor Barnes did not have sufficient influence to develop
such programs.

Pastor Barnes also took issue with religious teaching in the COGIC tradition. It was relevant to everyday life, but as he explained, it "did not necessarily [put a] major [emphasis] on explanation, which helps build a case for why you do what you do." He said:

> That was the strength of [the COGIC tradition]. It's really life oriented—how God relates to you in your everyday living. Now sometimes the weakness of that is that [leaders] may have gotten that or try to get that from a text [in the Bible] that wasn't necessarily saying that.... they could take the exhortative part of a sermon and build on that but not necessarily do what preceded that as far as the explanation and leading into that.... It wasn't as God-centered as it could be.... The character of God was somewhat assumed, but not necessarily explained.... It seemed like there was a lot of buy-in and not necessarily "convince me of this."

Pastor Barnes' characterization of the teaching style in the COGIC church as "not as God-centered" and weak suggests that not only did he believe that the COGIC church was not adept at properly interpreting biblical scripture, but that he placed greater value on intellectual religious engagement than on experiential religious engagement. He recognized the importance of religious teaching having real-life applicability, but blind faith or assuming the "character of God" without understanding or desiring to be "convinced" of the theological underpinnings of the faith was an insufficient approach to religion. This perspective was reflected in his and the elders' response to Lydia's shouting. They placed less spiritual significance on "gettin' the spirit," or experiential religious engagement, than on more controlled, contemplative religious practices.

Pastor Barnes' rejection of some of COGIC's practices and beliefs and his adoption of those more consistent with white evangelicalism made him "theologically compatible" with Crosstown. As he told me, "generally speaking, it was not a major leap for me to come here as far as what I believed." His theological and religious beliefs, in addition to his "multicultural" experience, made him a viable candidate for senior pastor of the interracial, yet majority white, congregation that voted him in as senior pastor.

In addition to his religious beliefs and interracial experience, his race and cultural familiarity made him attractive to Crosstown. A long-time attendee and elder board member at the time of Pastor Barnes' appointment explained that Pastor Barnes was:

the most qualified by far. . . . He had connections with the community. He was working at Anderson Evangelical Church at the time. He had articulate speaking. He was a man of prayer and I think the pulpit committee sensed that it was the timing of the Lord to bring a person who had a mature ministry experience [and] for an African-American guy to come in at the time of the transition that the church was in, it was like the Lord said, "Wow, this is great."

Later in the interview, he clarified that while Pastor Barnes' race was "relevant," he was offered the position of senior pastor because he was the most qualified. However, it would appear that race was more important than the former elder may have wanted to admit. Several candidates were considered for the position, including Pastor Barnes, and they were all African American. Crosstown was in a fragile stage at the time of Pastor Barnes' candidacy, still recovering from a rather severe church conflict over theology. It made a decision to reach out to African Americans at this point in its history. Hiring an African-American senior pastor could further ensure the church's stability. In fact, it may have been essential to the church's survival, greatly facilitating the church's recovery process. Additionally, as an "articulate" person, Pastor Barnes apparently possessed the cultural skills palatable to Crosstown's members.

If interview participants' attitudes about Pastor Barnes are any indication, he also appealed to the significant African-American population that had developed at Crosstown by the time of his appointment. Without being asked specifically about their thoughts concerning Pastor Barnes, several African Americans I interviewed mentioned that Pastor Barnes was one of the things they appreciated most about the church. They considered him to be a good leader, caring and genuinely interested in congregants. One African-American family continued to attend Crosstown despite deep frustrations with the church out of their "respect for him, [their] love for him." Others shared similar sentiments:

Pastor Barnes was there for me and he visited me on several occasions. He would call me and I thought that was fantastic, I really did, and I've never had that happen to me at any other church that I've attended.

I truly think Pastor Barnes has a calling for the ministry and I think he is believable. I think he's passionate, I think he's a good leader.

Pastor Barnes, him being a pastor. I think that's really what has been our whole force for being there.... I think he is very caring, I always think he is a very good shepherd.

Several people (most of whom were not African American), while they did not mention characteristics of Pastor Barnes specifically, often shared that they enjoyed his sermons. An Asian man appreciated the way he explained Bible passages, saying: "I really like Pastor Barnes' preaching a lot.... He does a good job of actually explaining the Bible as opposed to sort of just giving his opinions on random things." An African-American woman felt similarly: "We liked his delivery style, we liked the content of his message, we felt his message was godly, he was using the Bible and not making stuff up as he went along." One white woman told me that Pastor Barnes' sermons were a primary reason for her attending Crosstown. She said, "I really enjoy the pastor's messages and that was the big draw." Another white woman noted the structure of the service, in particular: "I think [the services are] well ordered and organized. I like that there usually is a theme that kind of runs through."

Ironically, Pastor Barnes' attempts to move away from what he perceived as deficient in the teaching and presentation style he learned in the COGIC tradition alienated many African-American attendees at Crosstown. Despite their appreciation and respect for him, some African Americans possessed a certain ambivalence about Pastor Barnes. So while many attendees, non–African Americans especially, appreciated Pastor Barnes' teaching style, his style was a hindrance to some African Americans and left other African Americans spiritually detached from the worship services. Not only were his sermons too bookish, they did not integrate the expressiveness and collective engagement that are often fundamental to the delivery style of preachers in African-American traditions. For example, one African-American woman who described Pastor Barnes as an "eloquent speaker" talked about the difficulty she had with his sermons. She explained:

The way Pastor Barnes delivers his sermon, sometimes it goes over my head, and I have to recap and think, what did he mean by this or what did he say?... Some Sundays, I do come away from Crosstown and I'm not real sure about what was said sermon-wise, and I think it's mostly because of the vocabulary, speaking the bigger words.... A lot of times I don't know. I need a dictionary or something. But you don't want to take a dictionary to church, you don't want to feel like you are in school or you are in the classroom. You want to come away, like some of the older folks will say, "I've been fed."

This woman's assessment of Pastor Barnes concurs with other African Americans' feelings about his teaching and presentation style. Additionally, her feelings about Pastor Barnes were compounded by the relatively un-expressive worship style. She saw Pastor Barnes as the primary agent for creating change in the worship style in the church. She implied that Pastor Barnes should speak to the spiritual and religious interests of African-American attendees. To some degree, she considered it his responsibility as the pastor to address these issues. This added to the alienation of African Americans from the worship experience. She continued:

> I think that people tend to follow a leader, and I've always looked at a pastor of a church as a shepherd. . . . There are some Sundays that I come to Crosstown and I feel like I'm back at the Catholic church with the sitting and the standing and the hymn singing. There's not a whole lot that's gained from [the service] or a lot of feeling or emotion, and I think a lot of times when I go to church, I want to feel like I'm at church. . . . I think if there was more emphasis put on people not being afraid of being expressive . . . the church might be a little bit more upbeat . . . but I know it has to come probably from the top down instead of from down to up.

Another African-American attendee, who had begun attending Crosstown before the arrival of Pastor Barnes and whose spiritual heritage was also rooted in the COGIC tradition, was initially excited about Pastor Barnes' candidacy for senior pastor when she found out he was inter-viewing for the position. However, her excitement waned soon after he arrived. She expected Pastor Barnes to effect change in the church's wor-ship style. However, he did not produce the kinds of changes for which she had hoped. She said:

> Because I know he's from the Church of God in Christ, I know he's quite familiar with some of the other styles in worship. And actually when I heard that he was from the Church of God in Christ, you know, a little joy leaped in my heart. But, it hasn't been . . . I don't want to say it's a real big issue for me because I've

stayed there all this time and not until recently had I really started feeling like I missed that.

Later in the interview, she admitted that she recently began periodically attending a COGIC church to compensate for what she was missing at Crosstown.

Nonetheless, African Americans realized that the church had a decidedly interracial identity. They expressed empathy for Pastor Barnes as, they imagined, he likely faced many challenges as an African-American senior pastor of an interracial church. While they expressed frustration with Pastor Barnes' sermon style and the church's worship style, they acknowledged a need to appeal to the religious tastes of white congregants. One African-American attendee said: "Sometimes I think the worship service is a little sterile.... I think part of that could be because Pastor Barnes is trying to appeal to both races so I think that his delivery has to be in such a manner." Another put it this way: "I really give it to Pastor Barnes. He tries to minister to his congregation and not make one [group] feel not as important as another. I know it's difficult for him at times to balance things out, to try to keep everybody happy."

Pastor Barnes admitted having challenges as an African-American pastor of an interracial church. These challenges became more apparent *after* he was appointed as senior pastor. He felt that the idea of being an interracial church and having an African-American pastor was appealing on the surface, but the majority-white congregation at the time was not prepared for all that meant. Pastor Barnes explained:

There probably was a certain amount of both novelty and naïveté on different people's part—probably a measure of that even for me.... [But] the novelty of we're worshipping together as black and white, the novelty that we've got a black pastor begins to wear off. You see the more cultural and idiosyncratic kind of things. [People realize,] "Hey this really is a brother here!" or that "we really have to work here" or that "so-and-so is this." These things come to the surface.... When the novelty wears off, you really see the price that you are going to have to pay to [be an interracial church].

The congregation was fine with the idea of hiring an African American as long as it did not have any major impact on the church. But once his

African-American identity became more evident (i.e., that he really was a "brother"),[3] the idea of having an African-American pastor was less attractive. Furthermore, congregants did not hesitate to make their concerns about various practices, styles, or activities known to him and the elders. Although people had similar religious beliefs and appeared compatible culturally, their varying religio-cultural, socioeconomic, and life experiences made racial integration far more complicated than originally anticipated.

Pastor Barnes filled a particular need for Crosstown. His African-American heritage and his support of and familiarity with the religious, theological, and cultural perspectives of Crosstown made him a likely candidate for further bridging and stabilizing the African-American and white attendance in the church. His blackness endeared him to African-American attendees. They remained supportive of him despite frustrations with the church and his "nonblack" worship and preaching style. Whites appreciated him for what many African Americans did not, his intellectual religious orientation. He emphasized understanding spiritual things more than experiencing them. Yet, he was also caught between two worlds. He was not fully embraced by either African Americans or whites. Many African Americans respected and appreciated him, but it was difficult for some to accept that he was ineffective at introducing more African-American religious culture in the church. On the other hand, whites, at least according to Pastor Barnes, accepted him conditionally. As long as those parts of his identity that were particular to his black experience remained concealed, he was acceptable.

Leadership Changes and White Flight

During Pastor Barnes' tenure at Crosstown, the church became increasingly African American, going from 70% white when he arrived to 65% African American while I was there. Many white families left to go to other local white churches. Other white families relocated to predominantly white suburbs. The announcement of Pastor McPherson's and Pastor Smith's impending departures precipitated the loss of several other white families. Within seven months after this announcement, at least four other white families also left the church. This amounted to a loss of roughly 15% of the regular white attendees. Each of these families was actively involved in the church, with most of the parents serving in some kind of leadership capacity, such as coordinator, Bible study leader, or Sunday school teacher. Nearly all of the families, similar to Pastor McPherson and Pastor Smith, were given the chance to say their good-byes and to share their future plans with the rest of the congregation during weekly Sunday worship services. The reasons these families provided for leaving the church were usually grounded within a spiritual framework. That is, people said they were leaving Crosstown because they believed that God was "leading" them to do so.

Both white and African-American attendees shared concerns about the racial transition taking place at the church. For some African-American attendees, the racial transition at Crosstown was particularly discouraging because they had believed that church was one place that racial difference could be overcome. They expressed sadness, frustration, and disappointment about the loss of the white families and the potentially lost opportunity to worship in a racially diverse context. One African-American woman told me:

> The more white people I see leave the church ... the more I'm
> feeling like, well maybe, you know, what's wrong? Why are they
> leaving? At one point, it seemed to be very nice ... whites, blacks,
> a couple of Hispanic families, some Asian families and singles
> but now it's beginning to become all African American and
> it's sad in a sense because I feel as though Christian people
> have such an obligation to break down racial barriers and ...
> such an opportunity [to show] people that there are churches in
> this part of the world who could care less what color you are.
> But ... here we go again. The same thing happened in our
> neighborhood. ... It's just sad. It gives the impression that
> they are running as we come in. And I could be wrong, God
> forgive me.

This woman had hoped that, in a Christian context, race would not be an issue. She believed that whites and people of color would strive together to bridge racial divides. However, as whites left, her faith in religious racial integration weakened.

Although the reasons that white families gave for leaving the church were not explicitly racial, African Americans reluctantly suspected that the underlying reasons were. Though they were suspicious of whites' true motives, they wanted to believe otherwise. Their suspicions were rooted in past experiences and a history of racial exclusion and segregation in other contexts:

> I hope it doesn't go any farther than what it is, where all the white people leave and then the church becomes all black.... The neighborhood where I raised my kids was all white.... And in about four to five years' time that all changed. Most of the white families had left.... So you see... it's a common thing and I guess it can happen in the church. I'm starting to see it happen at Crosstown. (African-American woman)

> I'm very sad and frustrated that a lot of the Caucasians are leaving. I didn't want to see that happen. I know it happens when we move in their neighborhoods, they begin to move out. I was just so happy to see blacks and whites praising the Lord together, worshipping together. (African-American woman)

> When blacks show up in dominant numbers in the school system, whites leave. For whatever reason, these things that prevail outside of the church just carry themselves over into the church, and at Crosstown I really don't see it being any different than what I have experienced in the past whether you are a Christian or non-Christian. (African-American man)

Whites I interviewed were far less likely to be concerned about the loss of other white families at Crosstown and its impact on the racial diversity of the church. And those who did share concerns were not particularly disheartened by what seemed to African Americans as a potentially failed attempt at overcoming racial barriers. Instead, they were more worried about the inability of the church to successfully attract other white families and their families', especially their children's, relational compatibility with the remaining or new (perhaps African-American) attendees. A married father explained:

> We've [i.e., he and other church members] talked about the number of Caucasian families with [older] kids who have left. There weren't that many to start with, but there have been a few obvious examples and I guess in a way that has bothered me. We're a white family and when our kids get to be in high school, will we be dissatisfied enough with the youth program that we'd pull

out too? I mean, you think about that sort of thing. . . . I don't want that same thing to happen with the young [white] kids that are growing up now and for us to make the same decisions that some of these other white families have already done before us.

Among the whites who left Crosstown, most were families with children still in the home.[4] The loss of these white families especially challenged this attendee and his family's commitment to the church. He had begun to wonder if he too would leave once his children reached adolescence. What is most intriguing about his concerns was that both his children were under five years old and he was already worried about whether or not there would be white families in the church when they reached adolescence. The mere possibility that his family's future interests might not be met led him to consider leaving the church. This contrasts with African-American attendees who, despite frustrations with the church, remained committed to Crosstown.

Other white attendees, similar to the father above, were apprehensive about remaining at Crosstown in the face of possible racial transitioning. Indeed, they had witnessed other white families leave the church for this very reason. Former white attendees I interviewed corroborated these speculations about why white families had left Crosstown:

> By the time he got [to the youth group], he was about the only white kid. They were really reaching out to the Anderson area kids. And so, it was geared for sort of non-Christian kids. . . . And to be honest, he felt very out of place. And it wasn't necessarily a black/white issue. It was an inner city/suburban issue. . . . And so we really had to take into consideration his needs and felt like if we wanted to keep him growing spiritually, we had to do something for him. So we began to look and found a place where he was much more happy. (white mother)

Interestingly, according to the youth pastor, a large majority of the African-American youth involved in the youth programs at Crosstown were the children of families who attended the church. So, while a large majority of the children were from Anderson, these were usually children of other church families.[5] This misconception about the youth group reflects segregation within the church. If white and black families regularly interacted, the white parents would know that the "Anderson teens" were children of black parents in the church. It also suggests that class and race (as all the children in question were African American) were more salient for white parents than religious similarities. Another former attendee of Crosstown had the following to say about why his family left the church:

> Well, one of the primary things was our oldest daughter. . . .
> I mean, she stopped coming [to church] a lot of times. . . . Most of my life I looked forward to Sunday mornings. And it reached a point now that I just wasn't looking forward to Sunday mornings. It was just a great fight to get [our daughter] to come. . . . I can recall when she was younger that she was like the one white kid amongst a bunch of black girls. . . . And in the younger years, I felt that they [i.e., black children] sought to include her. They really did. But something had happened to her. . . . A friend of hers [from the church] really turned tail on her, who she [also] went to school with. . . . So, if anything else, I felt that I needed to find a situation in which she felt comfortable. (white father)

While this father recounted other reasons for leaving Crosstown, the main reason he and his family left the church was because one of his children had a bad experience with an African-American youth in the church. It was important for him to find a church with a youth group where his daughter would feel at ease.

Both of these parents told me earlier in the interviews that they had intentionally been searching for an interracial church when they found Crosstown. They apparently valued racial diversity at some level. However, they had not pondered the potential cost of racial diversity for them and their families, as Pastor Barnes implied. Moreover, although they tried to evade race as the key motive for leaving the church, race was evidently a factor in their decisions, whether consciously or not. After leaving Crosstown, both families began attending predominantly white local churches with predominantly white youth programs. While neither parent said as much, a former leader in the youth group noted an underlying pattern among white families who left Crosstown. Their departures tended to coincide with their children reaching adolescence, the time when dating usually begins. Concerns about interracial dating may have contributed to their decisions to leave the church.

People of Crosstown, across race, valued worshipping in a racially diverse church. People hoped that the church would remain racially diverse. However, the racial transitioning that ensued after the change in pastoral leadership weakened attendees' faith in interracial community. It also heightened people's sense of the vulnerability of the church's interracial status and impelled them to secure the church's racial diversity. The potential loss of more white families was of utmost concern to some attendees, both African American and white. As one African-American woman declared during a church business meeting, "Crosstown has experienced white flight, and we need to recognize that." Because the loss of white families seemed to follow the loss of white pastors, many wondered if and how race would factor into the selection of the new pastors.

In Search of New Pastors

Crosstown initiated hiring processes for new assistant and youth pastors soon after Pastors McPherson and Smith announced that they were leaving. In the interim, Pastor Barnes took over their responsibilities. To minimize these additional burdens, lay church leaders took on additional responsibilities, and the church invited several guest speakers to give the sermons at Sunday morning services. The guest speakers were both African American and white. However, consistent with the church's white evangelical leanings, they were all affiliated with white evangelical organizations or institutions. Some were pastors of other interracial or predominantly white evangelical churches in the area. Others were professors or high-level administrators from predominantly white evangelical seminaries.

People at Crosstown were quite invested in who was going to fill the recently vacated pastoral positions. According to the church constitution, church members, who all went through a formal membership program, voted on pastoral, elder, and deacon candidates.[6] Candidates needed 75% of church members' votes before they could be confirmed in their respective positions. Crosstown first attempted to fill the assistant pastor position. Applicants for the position were recruited through the Internet and the personal networks of Pastor Barnes and other church leaders. One month after Pastor McPherson left Crosstown, a candidate for assistant pastor emerged: Floyd Winston. He was an assistant pastor over praise music and singing at another interracial church in the area. This church was considerably larger than Crosstown, with nearly 1,000 regular attendees and multiple church services. Winston had also worked as a director of a Christian social service agency located in Anderson. He was college educated at a predominantly white evangelical college. And he had worked with Pastor Barnes at another church and was his close friend. During a church business meeting, Pastor Barnes attested to the "mutual respect" he and Winston had for one another and their ability to work well together in the past. It was evident that Pastor Barnes strongly supported the candidacy of Floyd Winston. Winston was also African American. If he were elected, African Americans would fill Crosstown's two most influential paid positions.

When it became known that Winston was being considered for the assistant pastor position, rumblings about his candidacy surfaced almost immediately. During informal conversations, people expressed both strong support for and adamant disapproval of his candidacy. There seemed to be little middle ground on the issue. People who were in favor of Winston's candidacy were largely African American, but there was a select group of whites who also supported his candidacy. Those who had concerns about Winston's candidacy were both white and African American. African Americans who did not support his candidacy were usually married interracially or had close racially integrated social networks within the church. These attendees arguably had the most to lose by way of social support if Crosstown experienced a complete racial transition.

Proponents of Winston's candidacy were impressed with his resume. His familiarity with the local community and past work experience as a church worship leader and directing a Christian social service agency in Anderson were characteristics that made him an excellent candidate for the assistant pastor position, in their opinion. Plus, he and Pastor Barnes had an established relationship. Supporters felt that a senior pastor needed an assistant pastor whom he knew, trusted, and respected. Additionally, since Crosstown desired to be more involved in the local community, some felt that his long-time residency in Anderson and previous work in the community would help the church to reach this goal. Finally, as he was a long-time resident of Anderson, many people in the church knew and liked him and were quite supportive of him joining the church as assistant pastor.

Opponents of Winston's candidacy, however, were far more vocal about their opinions. Several people met with the church leadership to voice their concerns. Additionally, many attendees mentioned their concerns about the potential changes in pastoral leadership during the in-depth interviews, although I did not ask about the assistant pastor candidacy specifically. The characteristics that made Winston attractive to some members made him unattractive to others. Some were concerned about the degree of openness in the selection process. Since Winston was a close friend and colleague of Pastor Barnes, several members perceived that he had been hand selected before the application process was opened to other potential candidates. People referred to the way in which this candidate was selected as "secretive" and exclusive, implying that the leadership was playing favorites. One African-American respondent, who was a lay leader and involved in the selection of assistant pastor candidates, shared his frustration about how this candidate was selected. He adamantly explained:

> One of the frustrations that I currently have is the process
> that we're going through to select our next assistant pastor....
> I thought the process could've been done much better than what
> it was, at least what it was said to be and what it actually is.

He went on to say how he thought the search should have been conducted:

> I would match up our [goals as a church] and a person's quali-
> fications. [We] would get the best person to help the church move
> in the direction which the church has identified.... And, in my
> opinion, we haven't done that job or done a good job of that.

For this leader, not only were the recruitment methods for the position exclusive, but they did not yield the best candidate. Winston, in his opinion, was not poised to help the church meet its identified goals. And he did not believe that Winston was the most qualified.

Others were also concerned about his qualifications. While this lay leader emphasized the incompatibility of Winston's previous experience with the church's goals, others questioned how well he balanced Pastor Barnes. Many believed that the church needed an assistant pastor who would "complement" Pastor Barnes. Instead of their similar backgrounds and close relationship being an asset, it was a detriment. Several people with whom I spoke, both during the interviews and informally, perceived Winston and Pastor Barnes as having similar personalities, both being rather reserved and introspective. People also spoke of the similarities in their past work experiences as problematic. In their opinion, this candidate would not bring anything new to the church. It is important to note that those who felt

Winston did not best complement Pastor Barnes often contrasted this supposed lack of balance to how well the previous assistant pastors had balanced Pastor Barnes. Since all of the previous pastors who worked with Pastor Barnes were also white, these concerns may have been confounded with issues of racial balance among the pastoral staff. In other words, complementing Pastor Barnes implicitly meant having a white assistant pastor.

The final concern, and the most delicate, was Winston's race. Given the recent loss of white pastors and the subsequent loss of white members, his election could pose a threat to the remaining diversity at the church. Many believed that since Crosstown was an interracial church and identified as such, the leadership should also be interracial. Having senior and assistant pastors of the same race did not represent the church. A white interviewee told me:

> When I first thought of that, I thought, oh man, we need to have diversity in the leadership and I still believe we do, I really do. I agree you choose a man based on his beliefs in the Lord, of course, and I think we found a real gem with the guy that we found. But I guess now knowing that he may be the assistant pastor, now I'm wondering if the Lord will lead us to have an African-American youth pastor too. . . . I'm kind of hoping that they would choose a Caucasian there to keep the diversity in the leadership.

Additionally, Crosstown attendees did not want to see the church become a predominantly African-American church. If the church did not hire a white assistant pastor, some suspected that whites would continue to leave. An African-American attendee shared his concerns about white people's willingness to remain in the church with two black pastors:

> I think the thing that is bothersome to me is what message it might send to other white people who are like, possibly, you know, on the fringes, not knowing which way to go with things and if they see certain positions in the church becoming too black or something like that, they might decide to leave too.

Several meetings were arranged so that the congregation could be formally introduced to Winston and learn more about him. However, by the time these meetings were organized, people's concerns, feelings, and opinions about Winston had already been circulating among members and the leadership. Winston was first presented to the congregation during a Sunday morning worship service. Pastor Barnes introduced him. During the introduction, he told the congregation that he was "compelled to commend Winston as a candidate for assistant pastor." He explained that he had known him for fifteen years. He was "musically gifted" and had a "shepherd's heart" (evangelical code language for "he would make a good pastor"). After Pastor Barnes finished his introduction, Winston moved to the piano and taught the congregation a contemporary praise chorus. He struck me as an upbeat, relatively captivating, yet casual person. I could agree with Pastor Barnes. Winston was a talented singer and musician, and he did not strike me as similar to Pastor Barnes, at least in his personality. Winston also gave the sermon during this service. In this, he was similar to Pastor Barnes. His presentation style did not reflect spontaneity or bold movements. His speech remained even throughout. He stayed behind the podium for most of his sermon and regularly referenced his sermon notes. His sermon was drawn from the book of Ephesians in the New Testament. He explained it line by line.

It seemed that the leaders made a special effort to provide members with forums to become acquainted with Winston. Three separate meetings were organized for congregants to ask him questions. This was largely, I suspect, because several people had already presented their concerns about Winston's candidacy to the leadership, and it was hoped that these concerns could be addressed before the official vote. One of the meetings was held after the Sunday morning worship service where Winston gave his sermon. The other two meetings were held on weeknights. Close to a hundred people in total attended these meetings. The meetings were like a group job interview, except that nearly one hundred people could potentially ask Winston questions about anything. And, one after another, people did. Their questions touched on a wide range of topics, including his theological beliefs, long-range goals, thoughts on racial diversity, and how he balanced family and work life. It appeared that people took the pastoral selection rather seriously. Many people brought pads of paper to the meetings to take notes.

Opponents of Winston's candidacy used these meetings to gain some clarification about their concerns. One of the central issues brought up was the candidate's race. During one of the meetings, an African-American woman asked Winston how he felt about the church having an African-American senior pastor and now possibly an African-American assistant pastor. She prefaced her question by explaining that she had several white friends in the church who were concerned about this, although she did not specify why. Others concurred with her question with nods of their heads. Given that he was the candidate in question, it is no surprise that he did not have a problem with this possibility. More important, however, her question gave Pastor Barnes and the elders at the meeting the chance to clarify what they felt. Michael, the chair of the elder board, explained that he, Pastor Barnes, and the other elders discussed the importance of considering the candidates' racial backgrounds and how they might affect the church. They concluded, however, that they should rather choose to "follow God's leading." They did not believe it was right to practice, as he put it, "spiritual affirmative action." In the interviews and other informal conversations I had with regular attendees of Crosstown, I heard others similarly struggle with considering race as a criterion for the assistant pastor. Despite their desire to have a white assistant pastor, they explicitly explained that they did not support affirmative action–type policies.

The Sunday after Winston was first introduced to the congregation, Crosstown voted on whether to extend Winston an offer for the assistant pastor position. The vote was held after the worship service. Ballots were passed out. Only members were allowed to vote. People marked the ballots and then passed them across the pews to ushers, who collected them in the aisles. The church secretary and one of the deacons left the sanctuary to count the votes in another room. In the meantime, other church business was addressed. The new church budget was voted on. New members were voted into the church. Michael updated members on various church maintenance projects. After a while, people began to get restless, and Michael officially adjourned the meeting. Still, most people stayed to hear the results of the election. Finally, the church secretary and deacon returned with the results. The sanctuary had become a bit chaotic with people standing in the aisles, others walking around, and the chatter of several conversations. The noise was so loud that Michael had to shout the results of the election. The vote was "affirmative." Winston received 83% of the vote. After Michael made the announcement, several African Americans demonstrated their own affirmation of the results with loud resounding "amens."

However, that was not the end of it. During the next Sunday worship service, Michael announced that there was a discrepancy between the quorum and the actual number of people who voted during the election last Sunday. In other words, they believed that nonmembers had voted. The elders decided to have a revote to ensure accurate results. The second vote on Winston's candidacy for assistant pastor took place two weeks after the first, again after a Sunday morning worship service. This time, the elders took particular care to ensure that only church members voted. Ballots were handed out to people individually only after they were verified as being on the membership roster. Members dropped their votes in a ballot box before leaving the sanctuary. The meeting was quiet, orderly, and structured compared to the first election. And it was quite brief, lasting no more than twenty minutes. Before I left the sanctuary, an older African-American woman approached me and spouted with a reserved anger in her voice and dogged look in her eyes that she didn't think the revote was necessary. "They" (whom I took to be white members), she explained, wanted the revote because they were not satisfied with the original election results.

Pastor Barnes announced the results of the second vote during the following Sunday morning worship service. The second vote had barely affirmed Winston's candidacy with 76% of the vote. Pastor Barnes and the elders did extend Winston the offer to be assistant pastor. However, he declined. Pastor Barnes gave Winston's reasons for not accepting the offer. Among them was that Winston felt that the closeness of the vote did not reflect enough confidence in him as an assistant pastor. He was also aware of members' concerns about the assistant pastor selection process which, in his opinion, reflected a lack of confidence in Crosstown's leadership overall.

The church next searched for a new youth pastor. The search process for a youth pastor had a far different outcome than that for the assistant pastor. The position was advertised on Christian youth and youth pastor–related Web sites, among other advertising outlets. The ideal candidate, according to the church leadership, would be between the ages of thirty and forty-five with experience in a multicultural setting. The top candidate that emerged for the youth pastor position was John Lewis. Lewis was white and in his late thirties. He was currently the youth pastor at another interracial church in the local area and described himself as having a "burden for discipleship of young people through the local church." Lewis was introduced to the congregation during a Sunday worship service. He struck me as rather shy and unpretentious. During his introduction, he told the congregation that he attended Moody Bible Institute and had worked for ten years at Urban Contact, an outreach program to urban, predominantly African-American youth. Except for the brief introduction, Lewis did not participate in the service.

The congregation did have the opportunity to ask Lewis questions, as they did Winston, during a meeting following the service. A racially mixed group of about fifty people attended the meeting. Those in attendance were given a copy of Lewis's profile and resume. Similar to Floyd Winston's congregational interview, people were free to ask him anything they wanted. The questions addressed the candidate's work experience and ideas for youth programs, family life, and racial diversity, among other topics. Lewis was very focused when answering questions. He often paused and considered his answers before responding.

A few weeks later, Lewis was affirmed almost unanimously by the congregation, with a vote of 91–1. The process was remarkably uneventful compared to Winston's vote. I personally hadn't interacted with anyone who expressed any concerns about his candidacy. People's thoughts and opinions about Lewis were consistent across race. I did speak to one African-American member and leader in the church about the pastoral searches, and he thought the difference between the congregation's responses to Lewis's and Winston's candidacies was primarily an issue of race. As he put it, "the 'brothers' can't get a break." He may have had a point. Two other candidates were considered for the assistant pastor position. Both of them were African American, and neither ended up filling the job. One withdrew his candidacy and the other was not considered sufficiently qualified for the position. The final candidate considered for the assistant pastor position was white. At least on paper, his qualifications for the position did not surpass those of the African-American candidates. He had a master's degree from an evangelical seminary. He had worked on the staff (not as a pastor) at a predominantly white church in the suburbs. He had also worked overseas as a missionary. By the end of my time there, an election on his candidacy had yet to take place. However, I learned later that the congregation strongly affirmed his candidacy. He is now Crosstown's assistant pastor. Unlike with Winston, there was no resistance or apparent objections to his candidacy. After all of the positions on the church staff had been filled, Pastor Barnes remained the only racial minority in the church office. Even another position that was created, part-time assistant to the youth pastor, was filled by someone who was white.

Leadership and the Problem of Race

Whites disproportionately fill positions of power in nearly every arena of American life, including politics, education, and business. However, religion is unique in that there are opportunities for racial minorities to ascend to the highest authority positions in racially homogeneous religious organizations and, to a lesser extent, in interracial churches. However, a closer look at the leadership structure of interracial churches provides a clearer picture of how race remains integral to who holds leadership positions and suggests that race is central to the processes that dictate how people are selected for these positions.

Pastor Barnes' appointment was historic for Crosstown. As such, he was poised to initiate changes in the church, and he did. The most obvious change was the introduction of more upbeat music, for which older white attendees had little appreciation. However, in most other areas, Pastor Barnes was amenable to the culture of Crosstown. His theological education was from Dallas Theological seminary, a particularly conservative, predominantly white evangelical seminary. His previous pastoral experience was with another interracial church that was a member of a white-controlled evangelical denomination. While he appreciated some aspects of his spiritual heritage in the black church, he no longer espoused many of the religious beliefs and practices that characterize some denominations within the black church tradition. Indeed, in Pastor Barnes, Crosstown found an African-American pastor who suited its theology and worship style. This is not to suggest that Pastor Barnes did not identify with his African-American heritage. His concern for African-American men and gratitude for his COGIC roots are examples of his attachment to the African-American community. Nevertheless, his religious, theological, and cultural orientations were consistent with those of white evangelicalism. Consequently, he ensured the church's stability during a precarious time in its history, while not posing a threat to the religious and cultural predilections of white attendees.

Yet, the proportion of whites at Crosstown still steadily decreased during his tenure as senior pastor. The racial transition that occurred at Crosstown can be attributed partly to changes in the racial compositions of Mapleton and Anderson. Crosstown was nearly 30% African American when Pastor Barnes came on board as senior pastor in 1994, but according to the 2000 U.S. Census, Mapleton and Anderson combined were about 65% African American and 30% white. By the time I arrived, Crosstown had transitioned to reflect its surrounding community. As a church that identified as a neighborhood church, the parallels between the church's racial composition and that of the local community should not be surprising. Still, congregations are voluntary.[7] People choose congregations that meet their desires and needs. Other factors affect where people go to church besides where they live. Several white families left Crosstown soon after Pastor Barnes was appointed as senior pastor. The more recent loss of two white pastors appears to have further initiated racial change at Crosstown as about 15% of the regular white attendees left Crosstown within seven months after Pastors Smith and McPherson announced their departures. The reasons they gave were not explicitly racial.[8] Yet, a pattern had emerged. A threat to whites' structural advantage in the church was followed by losses in white regular attendance.

Additionally, excluding Pastor Barnes, the pastoral and office staff of Crosstown Community Church remained all white. This does not mean that the people who filled the pastoral positions were not competent, qualified people. However, the assistant pastor and youth pastor searches illustrate that race was central to leadership selection. Winston's assistant pastor candidacy was paved with tension and division from the time his candidacy was suggested to the final vote on whether or not the church would extend him an offer. Arguably, he was more than qualified to be Crosstown's assistant pastor. Nevertheless, his qualifications, the way he was selected, and his race were points of considerable dispute. Other African-American candidates experienced similar resistance. In contrast, the paths of both white pastoral candidates were smooth. There was little, if any, resistance to either of their candidacies. And both were ultimately offered and filled the vacant pastoral positions.

A primary reason that African-American and white candidates' experiences were so different was because some members had concerns about racial transition at the church. Changes, even the threat of changes, to the racial composition of pastoral leadership precipitated a noticeable loss in white attendance, as well as angst about racial transition among the remaining attendees. Recognizing the effect that a loss in white pastoral leadership had on white attendance, some Crosstown members, African Americans included, acquiesced to concerned whites' desires in order to maintain the church's racial diversity. Members who were particularly invested in maintaining a racially diverse congregation believed that it was imperative for Crosstown to hire a white pastor to combat the racial transition at the church. Their concerns about white flight are supported by research,[9] but this perspective reinforced dominant understandings of white social advantage and ultimately reestablished whites' structural dominance in the church.

When it comes to leadership structure in interracial churches, race matters both symbolically and culturally. That is, the actual race of key leaders in interracial churches is important, but so is leaders' possession of and investment in white cultural capital.[10] Research has shown that the procurement of cultural capital yields social dividends for its possessors.[11] In the United States, people have negotiated the edges of white society, including Jews, Irish, and Southern European immigrants,[12] by exchanging their proficiency in white cultural capital (dominant white attitudes, beliefs, behaviors, networks, credentials, etc.) for access to desirable resources.[13] Similarly, African-American leaders' access to Crosstown was contingent upon their proficiency in white evangelical attitudes, beliefs, behaviors, and credentials. Pastor Barnes was, in his own words, "theologically compatible" with Crosstown. He was also "articulate," and at least at the time he was initially brought on board as senior pastor, he was not seen as a threat to the remaining white attendees. People were not aware of his connection to his African-American identity. Furthermore, Floyd Winston and even African-American guest ministers at Crosstown were either trained at predominantly white evangelical seminaries, held positions at these seminaries, or pastored interracial churches affiliated with white evangelical denominations. This further suggests that possessing white cultural capital was important in order for African Americans to gain access to leadership roles in the church.

Nevertheless, the possession of white evangelical cultural capital, while a necessary qualification for potential pastors at Crosstown, was not always sufficient for filling a pastoral position. Cultural capital is contextual and can vary based upon a particular social setting.[14] Furthermore, the institution or organization in which an individual is attempting to exchange his or her credentials and cultural knowledge to facilitate access to a position of power (in this case, a pastoral position) must be complicit in the exchange.[15] In other words, the organization must accept the offer of cultural capital in order for the transaction to be complete. Winston's candidacy as compared to those of white candidates exemplifies this. Regardless of his possession of and attempt at exchanging his credentials and familiarity with the normative attitudes, beliefs, and behavior of white evangelicals for a pastoral position, they were not enough for him to become the new assistant pastor of Crosstown. His race mattered in this context as well. It played a key role in the pastoral hiring processes. Although Crosstown had an African-American senior pastor, every other person on the pastoral staff was white. And thus, whites continued to be structurally dominant on the pastoral staff.

Success within the religious marketplace is not necessarily dependent upon people's possession of white cultural capital or their race, as it may be in other institutions. Groups are able to develop their own separate religious organizations and institutions where varied forms of cultural capital are valued and where racial minorities can be structurally dominant. However, the experience of Crosstown suggests that, for interracial churches, where presumably race is inconsequential and various kinds of cultural capital could provide people access to leadership, race and white cultural capital are important resources that give people access to leadership.

4

Racial Identity

Material for Cross-Racial Bridging?

The homophily principle, simply put, says that people like to hang out with others who are like them.[1] This suggests that people attend interracial churches because identities other than race are more important to them, to how they think of who they are, trumping their racial identities and creating a bridge between them and people from different racial groups. But what role does racial identity play in people's decisions to attend interracial churches?

Identities are socially constructed, meaningful categories that people use to describe themselves.[2] They dictate behavior and provide people with a sense of who they are in relation to others. People possess a repertoire of identities that are organized hierarchically based upon their level of salience to them.[3] Included within these repertoires are three types of identities: personal identities, role identities, and collective identities.[4] Personal identities are based upon one's biology or unique individual experiences, like one's family lineage or belonging to a certain church. Role identities such as mother, manager, or teacher are personal self-conceptions of the particular positions people occupy in society.[5] And collective identity, which includes racial identity, is "that part of an individual's self-concept which derives from [one's] knowledge of [one's] membership of a social group (groups) together with the value and emotional significance attached to that membership."[6] Where role identities are largely constructed by interpersonal interactions and expectations, collective identities are informed by intergroup relations. People develop a sense of their collective identities based upon real or perceived interactions of their group with other groups. The salience of these identities varies based upon a person's commitment to a particularly important social network (e.g., family, work colleagues), interactions with similar or different others (e.g., different racial group, gender, class), and understandings about broader intergroup relations.

Research has shown that the racial identity of whites is peripheral to their sense of self. Mary Waters revealed the contradictory nature of white identity.[7] She argued that whites choose from a variety of symbolic ethnic identities (i.e., Italian, Irish, German, etc.) that conveniently and simultaneously provide them with both a sense of belonging and individuality.[8] Because these identities are "costless," meaning they do not affect their social or economic status, whites can select them without concern for the consequences of these identities for their lives. In other words, unlike racial minorities, whites are able to live anonymously and unencumbered by their race and ethnic identity. However, Waters goes on to argue that the reality of whites' power to choose their ethnicity reinforces their racist attitudes and dominant ideologies. Their experiences inform their perceptions about the social circumstances and opportunities of racial minorities. Consequently, whites do not or are unwilling to recognize the oppressive and constraining consequences of racial identities for racial minorities. More recent works on white identity support Waters' assertions.[9] Whites benefit from being white but do not recognize it.[10] They do not experience themselves as living within the racial realm and are unaware of the privileges their race affords them.[11] Therefore, white identity, as a racial identity, is unacknowledged as real and consequential for whites' lives.

Three major factors consistently affect the salience of African-American identity: educational attainment, early childhood interracial interactions, and participation in the black church. African Americans with lower educational attainment feel closer to other blacks than those with higher educational attainment.[12] African Americans who experience regular interracial contact have a very positive evaluation of African Americans as a group, but they also have a weaker sense of closeness to their black identity.[13] Moreover, interracial contact during childhood weakens racial identity among African Americans.[14] Last, participation in the black church positively affects African Americans' racial identity so that those who regularly attend a church in this religious tradition report feeling closer to blacks than those who do not.[15]

These findings suggest that African Americans who attend interracial churches will have a relatively weak racial identity, while simultaneously possessing a high regard for their racial group. Moreover, if they have at least some college education, their racial identity might be even less salient. While there is consistent evidence that racial identity for whites is not salient for them, there is limited research that discusses the impact of interracial interactions on the identities of white Americans. We do know, however, that whites who regularly interact with African Americans possess racial attitudes that are more sympathetic to the subordinate social conditions of African Americans.[16] It is plausible, then, that whites who attend interracial churches may at least be more aware of the privileges their race affords them.

Racial Identity: Salience and Meaning

Drawing upon other research, I conceptualize racial identity as having multiple dimensions to ensure a more comprehensive understanding of interracial attendees' racial identities. These dimensions include the salience and awareness of one's racial identity; one's feelings and ideas about what one's race means; and one's perspective on racial inequality between African Americans and whites.[17] In an attempt to find out what was most central to people's sense of self, I asked attendees, "How would you describe yourself?" I intentionally began with this broad, open-ended question to avoid prompting them to respond with identities they believed should be relevant to their sense of self. If race were, indeed, a salient identity, it would be one of the first identities they would mention. Responses to this preliminary question demonstrated that this was the case for African-American attendees. African Americans mentioned race as the first or second identity when telling me how they would describe themselves. One man described himself as "African American, male, middle class, formally educated, veteran, Christian, follower of Christ." Another responded with a confident and firm "I am a strong black woman!" Whites, on the other hand, were not inclined to describe themselves in racial terms. A couple mentioned race, but whites usually drew upon other identities when describing themselves.

Admittedly, for most interviewees, this initial question did not elicit information about their social identities. Instead, I often received responses about personality characteristics. For example, people described themselves as "an outgoing person" or "reserved." However, I followed up with a series of other questions about interview participants' identities to further understand the salience of race for them. With the initial question, interview participants could draw upon any identity they felt was relevant to describing who they are. Using this second method, interview participants were given the opportunity to consider race as an important identity for them and to consider the relevance of race to their sense of self.[18]

I handed interview participants a stack of cards. On each card was listed an identity. Examples of identities listed include mother, father, Christian, middle class, African American, white, Democrat, and Republican, among many others.[19] I asked them to go through the stack of cards and pull out every card they felt applied to them. I also gave them blank cards to add any identities that I had not included in the stack. After people finished perusing and selecting the applicable identity cards and adding any custom identity cards, I asked them to stack the cards so that the top card revealed the identity to which they felt the closest and the bottom card of the stack revealed the identity to which they felt the least close.[20] Few people added custom identity cards to the stack. When they did, they usually placed them toward the bottom of the stack. I expected this second method to encourage white attendees in particular to reconsider the importance of race for them personally. If prompted to think about it, I thought they might reevaluate their race as a more salient identity. However, this second approach produced similar results as the first. The average number of identity cards people selected was eighteen. On average, race ranked fifth within the identity repertoires of African Americans, behind religious identities and family roles (which whites also ranked highest). On average, whites ranked their race fourteenth.

Next, I asked interview participants to explain what some of the various identities they selected meant to them. I wanted to understand how they believed race was relevant to their lives without implying that I was only interested in their ideas about race. The responses revealed that not only did white and African-American interview participants vary in the centrality of race to their senses of self, but also they varied in their understandings of what it means to belong to their racial group.

African Americans, for the most part, did not distinguish between "African American" and "black." They provided three explanations for what it meant to be black or African American. One group gave ethnicity-oriented responses. That is, being African American meant that someone was American with African ancestral roots. One woman put it this way: "My ancestors (some of them) came from Africa, and I live in America so now I'm considered, according to this world, African American." Another group focused on cultural characteristics, such as eating certain foods or speaking a particular dialect. As another African-American woman explained: "I have Afro-American traits, characteristics, traditions. My whole life is Afro-American. I can't put it in exact terms. It's the whole being of myself—food, even talk, language."

Most African Americans, however, perceived being black as a subordinate social position. That is, blackness had less to do with culture, traditions, and their ethnic heritage and far more to do with where they were located within a social hierarchy. Even if an interview participant had not defined blackness in terms of subjugation or social location, nearly everyone with whom I spoke had a personal story of racism, demonstrating that while they did not cognitively relate blackness to occupying a disadvantaged social location, they personally understood it as such. Being black or African American meant exclusion, discrimination, and having to struggle. The capacity to persevere and endure the oppression that accompanies being African American was also central to what being black meant to them. And the ability to endure these hardships provided them with a sense of pride.[21] Some interview participants described being black or African American:

> What it means to be black is to understand what it is to be on the outside looking in [in] America or other places in the world.... We have to deal with things that other people don't have to deal with.

> It means struggle, that's the first thing it means.

> I would say, for me, to be black is to have a legacy and a struggle historically in this country and part of that legacy is persistence.... The ability to persist and overcome social inequities.... To be able to maintain your sanity, a good sense of self, and be

able to enjoy your life in spite of challenges that exist socially and institutionally.

There were a few white interview participants who described what it meant to them to be white in structural terms. These interview participants were young adults, still in their early twenties, or attended a racially diverse high school with African Americans. This suggests that early interracial interactions and age or cohort effects may be factors in whites' beliefs about what it means to be white in America. One young woman attributed most of her recent understandings about whiteness and race in America to her college education. Racial diversity was often discussed in her classes, and this challenged her to consider how race affected her as a white person:

> It's something I'm realizing more and more. . . . Obviously, I'm part of a majority in this country currently, and therefore there is a lot of privilege afforded to me. I don't have to think about my race, it's just there. When I was growing up, I was taught the best thing to be is to be color blind, which is basically a form of racism in itself. . . . It's an interesting thing to look at and see how privileged I can be without noticing how much I've just done that. How I've just lived and not noticed for so long.

However, nearly all of the white interview participants found it rather difficult to explain what it means to be white.[22] Any kind of lucid response often completely eluded them. Several admitted to never having thought about it before. Some had to think about it for a long time before they finally produced a response. In these cases, the responses were quite varied and somewhat incoherent. They really did not understand what being white meant to them, or they did not understand how race was potentially consequential for their lives. It was apparent that they had never been asked to ponder how their whiteness affected them. But still, they felt compelled to give some kind of answer. For example, after a long pause, one person ventured this explanation:

> Not just my blood, I guess. I guess I put it last but still it's very fundamental to who I am and the way I think, just be [the] default I guess. But I didn't put it last necessarily because I'm ashamed of it, it's just . . . because I'm sure in some ways being white predisposes me to . . . I don't know, I'm going to stop talkin'. I guess it affects the way I act in a lot of ways that I don't realize,

you know, in very subtle ways. It affects the way I think in a
lot of ways so it's last but not central to who I am because I see
other things as superseding that.

As can be seen from this response, he found that it was difficult to decide
which explanation best described what being white meant for him. He had
a vague sense that being white was more than his physical heritage, yet
he was incapable of clearly articulating just what that extra something
was. He seemed to stumble upon one key attribute of what it means to be
white, cultural normativity: as he tentatively put it, being the "default." Yet,
he was not committed to this explanation and continued to search for a better
one. He further suggested that being white "predisposed" whites to certain
kinds of outcomes. But what exactly those outcomes were also escaped him.
So, while he intuitively believed that his race afforded him certain kinds of
privileges, he was not convinced that this had any real consequences for
him. In the end, all other identities "superseded" his racial identity.

Another white Crosstown member similarly possessed a vague understanding of what it means to be white. He admitted having never considered this before, but after pushing himself to think about it, he was able
to recognize the advantages inherent in whiteness. Yet, again, he seemed
to be grasping for any acceptable explanation as he ended his response with
"I don't know. I've just always been [white]":

I suppose I never really think of it. To be white . . . [thirty-second
pause] . . . when I stop and think about it, people are probably
watching me less if I'm at a store, for shoplifting, you know.
Maybe they do that. There are just some intrinsic advantages that
I have never been without but it's kind of like, what's it like to
have two arms? Well, I've always had two arms. And I've always been white and that's not a high thing that I identify with
because it's kind of inbred. I don't know. I've just always been.

Interestingly, this man was one of the most aware whites I interviewed
when it came to issues of racial inequality.

These ideas about racial identity reveal that African Americans and
whites at Crosstown had very different levels of connection to their racial
group, different conceptualizations of racial identity, and different ideas
about what belonging to a particular racial group means. Close, regular,
voluntary interracial interactions did not have an effect on the salience of

racial identity for white attendees of Crosstown, nor did these interactions affect how they understood what racial identity meant for their own lives. They had a lot of difficulty presenting any kind of explanation for the meaning of whiteness. On the other hand, race was central to African-American attendees' senses of self. Blacks chose to draw upon race as a primary way of describing themselves without being prompted. Additionally, African-American attendees saw their blackness as consequential for their life outcomes. For them, being black meant structural subordination, social exclusion, and struggling to overcome these barriers.

Racial Identity: Perspectives on Race as a Social Hierarchy

People's perceptions of and connection to their racial identities are informed by their understandings about broader interracial relations. So, I tried to dig deeper by asking people for their thoughts on the existence of racism, racial inequality, and possible solutions.[23] In many ways, white and African-American attendees' perspectives on racism were rather similar. For example, to the question "Does racism still exist in the United States?" all interview participants, across race, said they believed that racism did still exist.[24] People were particularly firm in their responses, saying, "Heck, yes!" or "Oh, without a doubt," or "Oh yeah, definitely." One African American asked me, in response to the question, "Is that a trick question?!" After I told her it was not, she responded with a resounding "Absolutely, yes!" When asked why racism still existed, "sin" was a common answer given by both African Americans and whites. As one African-American woman put it, "Man is just evil." Furthermore, everyone with whom I spoke tended to use structural frames (i.e., racial segregation or lack of opportunity) more than individualistic frames (i.e., biological differences or laziness) to explain racism and racial inequality.

White Attendees' Thoughts on Racial Inequality

There were points at which white and African-American attendees' views on racism and racial inequality diverged. This was most evident in the particular reasons they gave for *why* racism and racial inequality existed. White attendees often said that racism was due to ignorance. And ignorance stemmed from whites' limited cross-racial exposure. With this understanding of racism and racial inequality, white attendees were apt to see racial integration as *the solution* for racial problems in the United States. One man proposed that, because people choose to interact with those with whom they feel most comfortable, they lead racially isolated lives. Racial isolation produces ignorance, which then fosters racism. He explained:

> I think that maybe some of it kind of goes back to getting out of your comfort zone and being exposed to different groups. I feel like there are a lot of whites that only, when you look at their circle of influence or the areas where they go, they hardly ever encounter people outside of their groups. . . . I feel like those are the kind of people that have the most potential . . . to kind of have some of these racist thoughts.

Another woman similarly believed that ignorance and, subsequently, racist attitudes are the result of racial segregation. As she explained:

> Sometimes I just think people don't know better or don't know any differently. I think they should know better. It's not right but I don't think that they have been exposed to different groups of people. What they've learned is not right. . . . Other than the fact that it's just the way that they've grown up and the things that they have been taught and never had anybody challenge it.

If whites had the opportunity to interact with African Americans and were provided with more accurate knowledge about them, whites would not be racists. She does not question why whites do not interact with people of other races in the first place.

Some white attendees affirmed the importance of racial integration by drawing upon their personal experiences. One man explicitly attributed his ideas about race and racial inequality to his interracial experiences at Crosstown. Before developing cross-racial friendships with African-American attendees, he didn't believe that black/white socioeconomic inequality still existed in America. It was not until he had been regularly attending Crosstown for two years that he began to recognize the subordinate condition of African Americans in the United States. His conversion came not just from regularly interacting with African Americans, but from more intimate relationships with African Americans. As a result of these relationships, he became aware of the racial lives of his African-American friends and recognized a difference in how whites and African Americans are treated in America. He now attributed racial inequality to racial prejudice. When asked why racial inequality exists, he said:

> Because there's prejudice still, very high in American society.... I guess if you would've asked me that question five years ago, no, I would say even three years ago, I would say, "Well, you know, I don't know that I would agree with that."

> INTERVIEWER   *Agree with what? the statement?*

> Yeah. I would say, "Oh, you're just kind of having that same attitude and you're just thinking back in the past, you know, there was prejudice but we have come so far and nobody looks at your skin color any more when they hire you or when they serve you." And it's like, that is such a lie! I mean, I've been with people, been in a restaurant or a store where I'm in there with all whites and I'm treated one way, and if I'm in with a predominantly black group, I'm treated an entirely different way, and so I see that this is not in the mind of black people, this is reality. It's sad, but it's reality. So it's prejudice.

Another white attendee believed that neighborhood racial segregation was the cause of racial inequality. And, further, the proliferation of drugs and gangs in predominantly African-American neighborhoods was ultimately due to white flight. He continued:

> The same people who have moved way out probably go "Oh, there is so much crime and awful things in the inner city and all those black people." You know, there's more to it than that. I mean, if people would've stayed, if people would've understood, if business[es] would get back in there and people would contribute and distribute . . . we would be definitely a lot better off. But my opinion would be to not necessarily have the government lead that, I mean, the government should push that but not necessarily control the money but have faith-based initiatives to really get that stuff going, get that money back in there. Not that money is going to solve it either, but faith-based institutions with money backing [them are] very important.

Despite this man's awareness of the structural processes that contributed to racial inequality, he was not committed to macro-level structural solutions.

He, rather, believed that religious organizations should bear the responsibility of reducing racial inequality. His strong preference for faith-based
evangelical programs to reduce racial inequality demonstrates an anti-
structuralist approach to social problems. This kind of opposition to government initiatives, which over the past century have been most effective
at reducing racial inequality, stymies progress toward racial equality at institutional levels and acts to sustain the status quo.[25]

Whites also stressed past racialized social structures and discrimination when talking about racism and racial inequality. For example, one
man believed that the lingering effects of slavery and white Americans'
unwillingness to recognize the problems that have stemmed from slavery
are what developed and perpetuate racial inequality:

> I think part of [it] may be related to the history of the U.S. When
> you think about blacks, for 300 years [there was] slavery in
> this country. I think that was an enormous detriment. . . . It still
> has an effect on the American culture. . . . And then I feel like,
> in some sense, the white culture has kind of abandoned and
> tried to pretend that the problem doesn't exist and [is] very un-
> willing to try and make some changes in that.

A woman similarly noted historical discrimination and the perpetual effects of these forces on racial inequality. However, she did not think that
contemporary racial discrimination was prevalent, implying that modern-
day discrimination does not impact the social outcomes of African
Americans. She said:

> I think because there was a lot of discrimination further back
> with black people and not wanting them to have good jobs or just
> discriminating against them. I think that's still . . . just a reper-
> cussion of that. . . . I think now people don't try to discriminate as
> much but just the repercussions of all that when it was hap-
> pening, to have caused that.

Similar to the white evangelicals who attended interracial churches
in Emerson and Smith's work, white attendees most often used solely
structural explanations for racial inequality.[26] Yet, a few provided veiled
individually oriented reasons for racial inequality. They would begin with a
structural reason for racial inequality, but their responses focused on individually based explanations. In other words, while they were aware that

social structures play a part in racial inequality, individual-level attitudes and characteristics are most responsible for the existence of racial inequality today. For example, here is what one white woman, who had been attending Crosstown for several years, had to say:

> [Blacks] are still having to fight an uphill battle. So I think historically they have always had that. And . . . I [also] think some people have become content in that—lower jobs, etc. And that sounds bad, that they are very content in that, but you know what? I'm very content to be middle class. You know what I mean? Like, I don't think really poor black families are content, but I think, you know, it's kind of scary [in thinking of her own middle-class position] to think about making $100,000 instead of $40,000 because it's different.

She went on to claim that she thought African-American teens who wanted to advance in life were "going to have to work harder . . . because there is a stereotype of black people being lazy, there just is." This woman recognized that African Americans were disadvantaged in America. However, the reason for persistent racial inequality is because some African Americans have become content with their lower social status. Moreover, she compared African Americans' social situation to that of middle-class whites, drawing parallels between her contentment with middle-class life and the supposed contentment of African Americans with their social status. In this, she revealed a limited grasp of racial inequality, suggesting that blacks' lower social status is primarily a matter of choice and that racial subjugation is not reason enough for economic inequality between whites and African Americans. She further implied that African Americans were primarily responsible for their persistent social disadvantage. As she said, African-American youth just need to work harder.

African-American Attendees' Thoughts on Racial Inequality

While white attendees were more likely to emphasize ignorance, racial segregation, and discrimination as explanations for racism and racial inequality, African Americans were more likely to provide explanations that focused on power, opportunity, and economic reforms. For example, one woman explained the reason that racism exists:

It's a power struggle, and power concedes nothing unless there
is a demand placed upon it. I think the face of racism has
changed because of the demands that African Americans (and
others too) have placed upon the system, but it doesn't mean
the power struggle goes away; it continues but just doesn't
go away.

Her perspective on race was broader than individual attitudes or even
ecological situations, such as neighborhood racial segregation. She believed that race was rooted in group-based, macro-level power dynamics.
Another African-American attendee pointed to African Americans' limited
access to and knowledge of opportunities, professional socialization, and
important social networks to explain why racial inequality persists:

Lack of opportunity, lack of preparation [to take] advantage [of an
opportunity] if there is an opportunity, and lack of networking
or associations with people who can help with some of the written or nonverbal tangibles that tend to be important in excel-
ling or advancing whether it's in the corporate world or
nonprofessional.

African-American attendees also believed that solutions for racial
inequality needed to take place at the institutional or national levels. Providing equal opportunities was the most common response. Others suggested more radical solutions. One man called for reparations:

Having an equal and level playing field. I think many Anglos
need to acknowledge what this country was and what effect it had
not only on African Americans but also [on] other people of
color. . . . I think white America in many ways does owe African
Americans something. . . . I mean, I believe in reparations and
I don't know what models of reparations, but at the very essence
I do believe in reparations.

An African-American woman pointed to separatism as a possible solution
to racial inequality:

I guess, if I were to think of any solution, I think it might be for
people of color to develop their own institutions, and that's much
bigger than just developing your own company.

Moreover, unlike for white attendees, race was a personal, lived reality for African Americans. Their ideas about race and racial inequality were often informed by these personal experiences, both their own and experiences they heard about from other African Americans. One man shared his experience with racial profiling:

> [Racism] happens to me every day for no other reason than I'm black. I'm driving my car in Carlsberg [a predominantly white suburb] or whatever. For no reason, they'll say, "Sir, we're just doing a check because you were doing thirty-four [miles per hour] in a thirty[-mile zone]." Well, that is a reason and that is speeding, yes, . . . and it could very well be [they pulled me over] because I'm going thirty-four in a thirty. But, the way I'm approached after the cop comes over, and the fact that it was a thirty-four in a thirty, I think the only reason, in my opinion, is because I'm black.

As discussed above, many of the African Americans I interviewed at Crosstown used structural frames when discussing racism and racial inequality. This is consistent with other research, which has found that conservative African-American Protestants (like those who attend Crosstown) are most likely, when compared to whites and other African Americans, to rely upon structural explanations for racial inequality.[27] Yet, past research has not focused upon the perspectives of blacks who choose to regularly interact with whites in intimate, personal, and sacred contexts, such as Crosstown. I found that African-American attendees at Crosstown were actually more inclined to use individually oriented explanations for racial inequality than were white Crosstown attendees. Nearly a third of the African-American interview participants drew upon individualistic as well as structural explanations for racism and racial inequality.

The most common of these was a belief in a meritocracy.[28] In their opinion, some African Americans did not possess the desire to achieve. They had developed an attitude of victimization that impaired their ability to excel. They did not strive to achieve more in their lives because they felt that white society was indebted to them. The following woman, who employed both individual and structural explanations for racial inequality, recognized that institutional racism affects African Americans. Nonetheless, she emphasized individual responsibility:

Part of it is institutionalized racism, but part of it is accepting institutionalized racism. I mean, some of it is just true—that jobs and things are set up where blacks are not treated the same way.... Some of it is that some people have stereotypes about black people. You know, black folks are lazier, they don't work as hard.... I think too that some of it is that black people can fall into the victimization thing and what society owes them and so they don't take opportunities that are there. And some of it is just oppression, it's just simply years of oppression and generational, you know, "this is just what we do." The people who "get out" are the ones that say, "No, I'm gonna push you further, better, harder," etc.

Another African American who had been attending Crosstown for several years at the time of the interview had a racially diverse network of close friends in the church. She believed that racial inequality in modern society was a consequence of choice. Although blacks were disadvantaged in the past, the obstacles that used to impede black progress no longer existed. When asked why black/white racial inequality still existed, she told me:

Historically speaking, one would say that [racial inequality is] because of the advantages that are given to whites. That they have these opportunities. Well, here in the twenty-first century, I can honestly say that it is the comfort of blaming someone for [blacks] not being able to do what they need to.... There's always something around them that will just bring them down, and it's a choice and sometimes they don't know that the choices they are making [are] the wrong choice.

In short, racial inequality has persisted because African Americans make poor decisions that perpetuate their subordinate status.

Paradox of Racial Integration

For African Americans at Crosstown, race was central to how they thought about themselves. Furthermore, most African Americans included ideas of social disadvantage and oppression in their conceptions of what it means to be black. They said that African Americans had to "struggle." They were on the "outside" of mainstream society and experienced social and institutional challenges. Other African Americans' explanations relied upon culture and ancestry to define what it means for them to be black, but they still related to the experience of racial subordination personally.

African Americans possessed varying ideas about why blacks are socioeconomically disadvantaged. All African Americans I interviewed believed that racism still existed. Yet, more than a third drew upon individualistic explanations, particularly belief in a meritocracy, for racial inequality. Relative to other conservative Protestant African Americans, African Americans at Crosstown demonstrated greater susceptibility to the dominant white (particularly white evangelical) ideology about racial inequality in the United States. It is unclear whether they had these ideas before coming to Crosstown. Nevertheless, their incorporation of white evangelical cultural tools in their cultural toolkits suggests that some African-American attendees at Crosstown would not be disposed to challenge white normativity and privilege.

Race was not a salient identity for whites at Crosstown. Unlike most African-American attendees, who drew upon concepts of structural disadvantage to explain what it means for them to be black, most whites did not relate what it means to be white to the analogous concept of structural advantage. Some were able to stumble upon concepts of privilege and cultural normativity. Yet others limited their explanations of whiteness to cultural and ancestral traits. And still others didn't believe that being white had any real meaning for them at all. There were a couple of whites who had evidently contemplated how race affects their lives before I prompted them. They had recognized that they belong to a socially and culturally dominant group and that this group membership affords them privileges that others do not experience. Nonetheless, for nearly all of the white attendees with whom I spoke, race was not a salient identity. This supports other work which has shown that not only is race not a salient identity for white Americans, but that whites are unaware of how it affects their lives.[29]

However, whites' beliefs about racism and racial inequality seem to contradict their feelings about their own racial identity and its impact on their lives. All white attendees believed that racism still exists in the United States, and most white attendees attributed racial inequality to solely structural forces. Since I, the interviewer, am African American, it could have been that whites were giving answers that they thought were socially acceptable. Instead, their true thoughts on racism and racial inequality were consistent with their views on white racial identity. However, their ideas about racial inequality and racism are congruent with other findings, which suggest that white conservative Protestants who experience regular interactions with African Americans are more likely to see racism as persistent and racial inequality as the result of social structures.[30] White Crosstown attendees exemplified a paradox that exists in whiteness. They understood how race places African Americans at a social and economic disadvantage, but they were unable to comprehend how being white privileges them. Despite their regular interactions with African Americans, they did not recognize how their whiteness affords them advantage in U.S. society.[31]

What can be learned from this exploration of racial identity among interracial church attendees is that people of different races can worship together, even when the salience of racial identity drastically differs across racial groups. Social group identity theory proposes that interracial churches can be created and sustained by reducing the salience of racial identities among group members and promoting an identity that encompasses multiple subgroups. Interracial churches attempt this by emphasizing a social identity that is common among church attendees, generally a religious identity, and deemphasizing racial differences.[32] For example, Mosaic, a racially integrated congregation in Los Angeles, intentionally emphasizes congregants' identities as "followers of Jesus Christ" as a strategy for successfully unifying members of diverse backgrounds.[33] This strategy renders ethnicity in this religious organization "irrelevant."[34]

In the case of Crosstown, religious as well as family identities were salient for both African Americans and whites. Are these identities acting as social bridges that connect people across racial lines? Possibly. But we must recognize that the content of what it means to be of a particular faith or family structure is informed by groups' cultural tools and specific experiences. White and black evangelicals, for example, have different religio-cultural toolkits. Adherents draw upon the resources in these toolkits to construct their distinctive understandings of what it means to be evangelical.[35] This is evident with whites' and African Americans' ideas of normative worship and the role racial discourse should have at Crosstown. Motherhood and fatherhood also tend to be lived out differently for whites and African Americans, with single parenthood being far more normative among African Americans.[36] This was no exception at Crosstown. A majority of the African-American families with children in the church were headed by women. I was aware of only one white family with this kind of structure. And further, white and African-American parents apparently did not interact much. An identity which was not particularly salient for attendees was their class status. By standard indicators, most attendees at Crosstown would be considered middle class. To the extent that middle class blacks are familiar with the dominant middle class culture through experiences at, for example, school or the workplace, class provides blacks and whites a common cultural ground. Yet, as with family and religious identities, the meaning of middle class for blacks is qualitatively different from that for whites. Middle class blacks occupy less prestigious, marginalized jobs, live in more socioeconomically diverse neighborhoods, and are less wealthy than their white counterparts.[37] Further, unlike middle class white attendees at Crosstown, middle class black attendees often identified as *both* middle class and working class. For instance, one African-American woman who was an engineer explained that she also identifies as working class because "as opposed to someone who has things pretty much given to them ... I have to get out there and work for it." Therefore, even when certain identities are equally salient within the identity repertoires of African Americans and whites, or there are other important identities, like class, that African Americans and whites have in common, these identities do not necessarily have similar meanings. Any cross-racial ties based upon these sorts of racialized identities, then, are fragile ones. The promotion of a broader, inclusive identity can end up submerging the real, everyday consequences of living life in the United States as a racial minority, reducing racial issues to personal prejudice or a problem of social interaction, rather than attributing them to structural realities.

Finally, the findings in this chapter suggest that, while interracial interactions have the capacity to influence the racial attitudes of whites, they do not necessarily impact how they view their own location in the social structure and the consequences of that location. In other words, interracial interactions, for whites, do not affect the salience of their own racial identities. Race continues to be about other people. And the linchpin of race remains intact.

5

Why Do They Come?

If race is a salient identity for African-American attendees and if
interracial churches lean toward adopting the cultural practices
and structural characteristics preferred by whites, why do African
Americans continue to attend? One reason might be that people who go to interracial churches are most comfortable in racially diverse settings. Other research suggests that people who
experienced regular interracial contact during their childhood,
particularly in high school, are more likely to have interracial social networks as adults.[1] People also prefer social settings to
which they are accustomed, leading them to choose similar kinds
of environments in the future.[2] I suspected, then, that people
who attended Crosstown experienced sustained interracial exposure as youth and came to prefer being in racially diverse environments as adults.

I asked attendees about the racial compositions of their
high schools, neighborhoods (when they were adolescents), and
childhood churches (if they attended one). About a quarter of the
African Americans I interviewed had all-black social existences
during their youth. That is, their neighborhoods, schools, and
churches were all predominantly African American. In one
woman's words, her "entire young experience was totally black."
However, the remaining 75% of African Americans with whom
I spoke had, in one social environment or another, experienced
regular cross-racial interactions with whites as teenagers. All of

these interviewees attended a predominantly white or interracial high school. And more than half of them lived in predominantly white or interracial neighborhoods. Moreover, it was not only the younger people who had this kind of cross-racial exposure, as might be expected. These experiences spanned generations. People from their twenties to their sixties had regularly interacted with whites in their youth. So, most African Americans who attended Crosstown were accustomed to interacting with whites.

Conversely, for most of the white attendees I interviewed, interracial contact during adolescence was the exception rather than the rule. Whites had little to no interaction with African Americans in their neighborhoods. Nearly all of them attended predominantly white churches. However, about a quarter of whites went to high school with African Americans. This is not to say that African Americans constituted a large proportion of their schools' populations. African Americans usually made up no more than about 10% of the student body. So, even these white attendees' exposure to African Americans was relatively limited.[3]

I also asked about the racial compositions of their close social networks during high school. A little more than half of the people who experienced regular interracial contacts while teenagers also had close interracial friendships during this time. Half of the African Americans who regularly interacted with whites as youth had a close white friend. Although whites were less likely to have interacted with people of another race growing up, at least among those who had experienced some kind of interracial exposure during high school, half also had a close friend of another race (although not necessarily African American). Therefore, those who were accustomed to interracial interactions were comfortable enough with persons of another race to forge intimate cross-racial relationships.

Spiritual Heritage of Crosstown Attendees

People's past religious experiences affect the kinds of religious choices they make as adults.[4] So, I also spoke with Crosstown attendees about their religious experiences while growing up. Nearly everyone I interviewed attended church regularly when they were young. I asked interviewees to describe the racial compositions, worship styles, and religious practices of their childhood churches. All but one of the African Americans I interviewed told me that they were raised in predominantly black churches. Yet, the religious backgrounds of African-American interviewees were still somewhat diverse, including, among others, Baptist, Pentecostal, Catholic, and Seventh-Day Adventist.

I asked attendees to recall what the worship services were like at their childhood churches in order to gain an understanding of their religio-cultural socialization. A few African Americans described the worship services at their childhood churches as quite liturgical and staid. The one woman who attended a predominantly white Catholic church as a child told me her church was "boring." She said: "[We would] sit down, stand up, get on your knees, sit down, stand up, get on your knees. We said the same prayer all the time. They sang the same songs all the time. It was just boring." Another African-American attendee, who recalled her experience at a predominantly black Seventh-Day Adventist church, had this to say:

It was mostly hymns, mostly dead. It was very solemn. . . . [And the sermons were] just very preachy, like, what you don't do. The Old Testament, everything was heavily laden on the Old Testament doctrine—the Thou Shalt Not's and all the punishments people would get for being disobedient to God.

However, these characterizations of African Americans' religious experiences growing up were rare. Most African Americans with whom I spoke grew up in the black church. And their childhood church experiences were quite different from those of the African-American interviewees discussed above. People described the worship services as "very participatory." They were even "entertaining," as perceived through some of their eyes as young children. They admitted that, as children, they did not really understand the purposes behind certain kinds of religious practices, such as shouting or call and response. Additionally, church lasted for several hours on Sunday afternoons. As one woman put it, "[My church growing up] was what I like to call the 'traditional black church.' By traditional, I mean we started early, we ended late—an all-day deal." Yet, despite the length of the services and their limited understanding of some of the religious practices, they enjoyed their experiences growing up in this church environment:

The music was great, I mean, lots of singing, choirs. . . . As [the minister] was wrapping up the service, one of the sisters in the church would start hoppin', you know, those old standard gospel songs, and everybody in the congregation would join in.

> [The church] was Missionary Baptist, African American. So
> [there was] preachin' and good worship. They are very enthused.
> There was a lot of family there. They have high energy, high
> charisma, a lot of passion in preaching. The music was very gospel
> oriented, older. I would say old gospel compared to what's out
> now.... People spoke not only from the word but from their ex-
> perience. Very practical—hands on.

These interviewees' childhood church experiences suggest that many
African-American Crosstown attendees were personally familiar with wor-
ship styles and religious practices commonly associated with predominantly
African-American churches.

The religious backgrounds of whites were also varied. They included
Presbyterian, evangelical Congregational, Baptist, and nondenominational.
None with whom I spoke grew up in Pentecostal or charismatic churches.
The worship at white attendees' childhood churches was also not mono-
lithic. About half attended churches where mainly hymns were sung and
only the piano was used for accompaniment. One interviewee described the
church he attended as a youth as "pretty conservative. We would sing
hymns primarily, a couple of choruses." Another explained that, at her
childhood church, it was "always hymns out of the hymn book. And then
preaching, once a month communion, offering. There was nothing that
would, like, interest a teenager now." But several whites I interviewed attended churches that were intentionally aiming to attract younger attendees
by creating more contemporary worship services. These churches used
multiple instruments, like guitars and drums, and sang hymns as well as
contemporary praise choruses. One attendee said:

> When I was younger, it was more traditional. We mostly sang
> hymns.... And then through the years, it eventually has gotten a
> little bit more contemporary and ... the songs are probably a
> mixture of hymns, contemporary praise songs. We try to get the
> youth involved a lot during the worship ... and we have quite a
> few instruments ... guitar, drums, keyboard, piano, and some-
> times flute or other random instruments.

Yet, despite the inclusion of more contemporary worship, white attendees
did not describe their childhood churches as particularly interactive or
effusive, like the African Americans with whom I spoke. There was little

clapping or hand raising. And, unlike the worship services at African Americans' childhood churches, the worship services were relatively short. As one white interviewee explained, the worship services at his childhood church "were pretty consistently an hour. An hour fifteen was a really long service."[5]

I also asked people to tell me about the church they attended right before coming to Crosstown. I wanted to know if Crosstown attendees had a pattern of attending interracial churches. This would begin to give me an idea of how important interracial worship was to them. Only eight of the people I interviewed were attending interracial churches before coming to Crosstown. Most of the churches that African Americans were attending before coming to Crosstown were predominantly black. Although many of the pastors of these churches had adopted a modified, more modern version of the traditional black preaching style, call and response and effusive worship were still common. One person who attended a traditional black church as a child was attending a predominantly African-American Baptist church before she came to Crosstown, which she described as follows:

It was a Baptist church that was similar to the church that I grew up in but a little bit different in that I think that the minister . . . I think his sermons were a little bit more thought provoking and a little bit more applicable to life situations. It wasn't so much telling you what you should do [but] helping you to understand life and your responses to different things.

Another African-American attendee with whom I spoke had similar sentiments about the worship and preaching at the church she was attending before Crosstown. This church was a predominantly black, "very interactive," nondenominational church where, according to her, call and response was common. People responded to the pastor with such sayings as "Can I get an amen," "Preacher, amen," or "Say that, preacher!" She compared the sermon style to that of Crosstown:

It wasn't like how right now we do, like a study, learn the word. It was more like take a passage, relate it to real-life experience, what happened to be going on in the community and then . . . why you should follow God's word. So it was more of a story telling. Not so much whoopin' but because old school Southern Baptist was [the pastor's] background . . . sometimes it would [be] intertwine[d].

The African Americans who were attending interracial churches before coming to Crosstown explained that similar to Crosstown, these churches were majority-black with whites being the second largest group. One African-American man, who hadn't grown up attending church but experienced a religious conversion during college, told me that the music at his previous church included hymns, contemporary songs, and some gospel music, but the sermon was the focus of the service. He explained:

> Oftentimes there would be a person or a small group, like [Crosstown's praise team] that would often [lead worship]. Bulk of the time was for the ministry of the word. Quite often, there was a challenge from the pulpit and an altar call to the believers and the unsaved alike. So it was pretty much parallel to Crosstown's church fellowship and adult Sunday worship.

Another African-American interviewee who attended an interracial church before coming to Crosstown similarly described his previous church. He recalled: "The services were two hours long. It had a charismatic flavor to it on occasion, a lot of contemporary singing, [but] a mixture of hymns and also contemporary praise songs."

Most whites I interviewed had attended predominantly white churches before coming to Crosstown, but three had attended interracial churches. The churches varied in size and denominational affiliation. Some of the churches were located in the suburbs, while others were in the city. But all were evangelical. Additionally, the worship services incorporated traditional hymns or contemporary praise music or a bit of both. One white attendee, similar to what some African Americans reported, explained that she particularly liked the applicability of the sermons at her previous church. The church was predominantly white and located in a suburb. She said:

> We had a time of worship, not very many hymns, more of the chorus-type things with a band, probably about twenty-five minutes of that, and then announcements and then the speaker would come up. He was a really good speaker. His speaking was good because it was very applicable to daily life.

Another white attendee, who had formerly attended an interracial, but largely white, church before coming to Crosstown, explained that the worship services at her previous church included hymns, but over time the church had begun to integrate contemporary praise music as well:

> The church was fundamental, evangelical.... When we first
> started going there, there were two hymn books and those were
> the only two hymn books that we ever sang out of.... Then
> they started to try to draw more people, younger people in, so they
> started trying out choruses and more of the modern singing,
> using other instruments other than just piano and organ.

I did interview one white attendee who had made a personal commitment to cross-racial worship while in college who attended a predominantly African-American church before coming to Crosstown. The church was a nondenominational, independent church. The services at this fifty-plus-person church were longer than he was accustomed to, lasting about two hours. But he eventually adjusted: "After I got used to [the length of the service], then it was like, okay, this church is longer. It was just a way of life in a sense." This church also incorporated a variety of music styles, including contemporary praise, gospel, and hymns. In his opinion, the worship songs at this church were "pretty similar to what we sing at Crosstown——'Integrity,' 'Hosannah,' or whatever. They were trying to mix different things, trying to get different styles of music there to kind of blend." He also described the people in the church as "kind of with it." I asked him to explain what he meant by this. He told me:

> Reasonably intelligent. Most of the people went to college and
> graduated and now are working in some professional kind of
> environment.... So it made it a little easier to relate to people
> because the main dimension ... the diversity was really on just
> the skin color.... Mostly in age and economics, we were similar.

In many ways, he was similar to others who attended this church. He had a graduate education and held a professional position in a Fortune 500 company. In his opinion, these similarities made the racial differences unimportant. As he put it, the diversity really was "just the skin color."

Attendees' spiritual heritages, as children and as adults, were not, it seems, a factor in why people attended an interracial church, as nearly everyone I interviewed came from racially homogeneous, culturally familiar religious backgrounds. However, the religious experiences of whites were more consistent with the worship style of Crosstown, particularly in the types of music and instruments, than those of most African Americans I interviewed.

Why Crosstown?

The cross-racial experiences of Crosstown attendees reveal that sustained interracial exposure as youth may have been an important factor in why some people, particularly African Americans, decided to attend the church. Furthermore, Crosstown's worship style and religious practices reflected more closely the religious backgrounds and experiences of white attendees. So, for white attendees, Crosstown was, in many ways, familiar religious territory. These findings provide some insight into why people attend interracial churches. In order to gain a more complete understanding of why people attend interracial churches, I asked people what attracted them to Crosstown and what characteristics they particularly enjoyed about the church.

Nearly everyone with whom I spoke said that the quality they most enjoyed about Crosstown was the friendliness and warmth of the church. It was apparently one of the church's greatest strengths. People explained that the church made them feel welcome. People were approachable, and they knew their fellow congregants by name. The greeting time during the Sunday morning worship services exemplifies this. Every week, visitors were asked to stand so the congregation could recognize and welcome them. After visitors would stand, several people from around the church would spontaneously rise from their seats, walk over to the visitors, and give them a hearty, enthusiastic welcome, with a smile, a handshake, and a "Great to have you!" or "Welcome to Crosstown!" After visitors had been greeted, everyone was invited to stand and greet one another. At this time, those who were still seated got out of their seats and walked up, down, and across aisles, shaking hands, giving hugs or pats on the back as they greeted their fellow congregants with a "Good morning!" or "How are you doin'?" or "God bless you." I can attest that the welcome I experienced when I first attended Crosstown was one of the warmest and most genuine I had experienced from a church. These qualities encouraged a more recent attendee I interviewed to consider becoming a member of the church. He explained: "I just liked the feeling of Crosstown, the sincerity that seemed to be there in everybody that I came in contact with, and I told Pastor Barnes that I would become a member."

Ironically, although Crosstown attendees felt that the church was a very welcoming, warm place, a majority of the respondents reported that their closest friends did not attend the church. I asked interviewees the races of their three closest friends who attended the church and the races of their three closest friends who did not attend the church.[6] I then asked them to rank order all six friends according to how close they felt to each friend. The closest church friends of African Americans at Crosstown tended to be of their same race. About three-fourths of African-American respondents reported that both their closest and second-closest church friends were African American. Among whites with whom I spoke, a slight majority reported that their closest church friend was white. When considering both friends who attend the church and those who do not, people's closest friends continued to be of their race. But they usually did not attend Crosstown. People explained that, while they had good friends in the church to whom they felt close, they were closer to those friends whom they had known longer, particularly those whom they had known since they were of high school or college age.

The church's racial diversity was also a quality that most attendees said they enjoyed. Among the whites I interviewed, racial diversity and the church's warmth and friendliness were tied for the top characteristic that whites enjoyed about the church. Racial diversity was less important for the African Americans I interviewed. Still, most reported that racial diversity was something they enjoyed about Crosstown. The characteristic most often mentioned by African Americans was the warmth and friendliness of the church.

People gave various reasons for why racial diversity was important to them. Some mentioned that interracial worship was a good evangelism tool to non-Christians because, as one person explained, racial diversity demonstrated that the church had "taken an interest in the community, that [the church] really care[d] and want[ed] to reach out to everybody and not just one particular group." Several people said that they believed the church should reflect the diversity that exists in society. This is how God intended it to be. One African-American woman put it this way:

> It's the real world. We live in an ethnic, diverse world. We live in a global world. We've got all kinds of people, and I think the church needs to reflect the world that we live in, and so I think ethnicity in the church is a good thing.

Yet, overall, Crosstown's racial diversity was appealing to different groups for different reasons. For example, the church had at least ten interracial families. People from interracial families explained that the church's diversity provided them with a level of comfort that they often did not experience in other contexts. For these families, interracial churches were a refuge from a racially segregated world. A man in an interracial marriage told me why he enjoyed the diversity at Crosstown:

> No one stared at us. . . . We felt very welcome. We saw other interracial couples. We felt at home. We didn't have to explain anything or, like, when you go to the grocery store and they ask if [my wife and I] are together—that happens a lot. So we felt welcomed.

Whites explained that attending an interracial church enhanced their religious lives. It added a little extra something to their worship experience or filled what felt like a void in their spirituality. They also felt that attending an interracial church broadened their world view. One white attendee told me:

> There was something that was missing in my faith growing up in all-white churches when I was little. It just feels like something was missing, I'm not really sure what, but it would be very hard for me to go back to an all-white church.

Another white attendee said:

> It really enhances your background and perspective on things. Anytime you get somebody from a different perspective, different upbringing, or just a different way of doing things, you learn a lot, and I really enjoy that.

Moreover, the church's racial diversity was the primary characteristic that initially attracted whites to Crosstown. Several white attendees intentionally chose Crosstown because of their desire to worship in a racially diverse congregation. One man said: "We wanted a diverse church where they would do Bible exposition where it's [a] more biblical-based style of preaching. . . . you know, where the pastor would take some scripture and expound upon it." Another white attendee told me: "I knew the ideology of the church, was excited about things that were going on at the church, and wanted to be in a church that was more diverse. I shouldn't say just more diverse but really had African Americans in it."

A small number of white attendees I interviewed told me that they had developed an interest in interracial relations as youth. As they explained, their exposure to African Americans was very limited growing up, and consequently, they had not realized the extent of racial segregation in America. When they were exposed to African Americans as young adults, their curiosity was piqued. They experienced an epiphany about racial segregation, which led to a desire to improve race relations, particularly between whites and African Americans. As a result of this experience, they made personal commitments to racial diversity in their own lives. One interviewee described when he first became aware of the extent of racial and socioeconomic segregation and his subsequent social conversion about racial issues. It happened when he was a youth, driving from the white suburb where his family lived to the predominantly black neighborhoods in the city:

> When you got downtown, it felt like a totally different world.
> You got interaction[s] with other groups of people that you didn't
> see at home, out in the suburbs. So kind of through that, I felt
> something pulling at me about being involved in this issue.
> I wanted to live in a more diverse area when I finally got out
> of college. . . . I felt like I wanted to go to a church that was more
> diverse.

Racial diversity was also important to African-American attendees. For many, Crosstown was the first environment they had experienced where cooperative interracial interaction was the norm. Therefore, interracial worship was a unique experience for several of them. Through their experiences at Crosstown, they had come to believe that skin color was of little consequence. As one person told me:

> [The diversity at Crosstown] helped me to develop relationships
> with people outside my race where I felt they were my friend
> and we share Christ in our life and that they have the same
> struggles as I do and all of that. . . . I've gotten to know other
> people on that more personal level where I've said, wow, you
> know, it's not that much of a difference.

However, unlike white attendees, racial diversity was not the primary characteristic that initially attracted African Americans to Crosstown. One

African-American interviewee did tell me that, when he first came to Crosstown, he "saw a mixed group of people, and it made [him] feel at home." But this was not a typical response from most African Americans. Other factors were what made them choose to make Crosstown their church. In addition to the friendliness and warmth of the church, several people mentioned the church's location. It was convenient and in easy walking distance to their homes. And, as mentioned in chapter three, some really appreciated Pastor Barnes.

However, in addition to these pull factors (that is, characteristics which attracted them to the church), there were also factors that pushed some African-American attendees away from the African-American churches to which they had been accustomed. Most of those who were "pushed" from African-American churches mentioned that they still would appreciate a more interactive, effusive worship style at Crosstown. Nonetheless, religious practices such as long worship services were not appealing. As one woman put it, "I didn't like being in church all day." Others told me that they did not want to have to dress up every week to go to church. They appreciated the freedom to come to church dressed casually, which they could at Crosstown. There were also a few African Americans with whom I spoke who did not appreciate the worship and preaching styles that are common to African-American church tradition. One African-American man I interviewed was specifically looking for a church that was anything but a traditional black church. He did not grow up attending church regularly. Nor was he attending a church before he came to Crosstown. He did not like the preaching style of the African-American ministers he witnessed nor was the worship experience in the traditional black churches he attended "believable" to him. He told me:

> I wanted to be in a church that was different from what I was
> accustomed to in a traditional black church and that was really
> the bottom line and that's what I have found appealing about
> Crosstown, more than anything else.... [I didn't like] the hem-
> min' and hawin' from the podium. The catching the Holy Ghost,
> so to speak, and people running around the church and all
> those kind[s] of different things. I had a difficult time believing
> the way the sermon was delivered. It wasn't believable to me
> in many instances. It was more show and tell, and like I said,
> I was looking for something that was scripturally sound, that the

church had a sound body, and I felt like I was being led instead of being talked down to and just, it wasn't believable from the pulpit.

Given his distaste for traditional African-American Christian religion, I asked him if he could attend a majority-white church. He responded, "probably not. . . . I'd probably feel more comfortable attending a church that's all black." Therefore, his distaste for African-American religion was not connected to a desire to interact with whites or to assimilate into the dominant culture. And, although he did not appreciate the worship style distinctive to many African-American churches, he mentioned later in the interview that he would still like the worship style at Crosstown to be a bit more upbeat. The perspective of this interviewee was the most extreme. Yet his sentiments were shared by a few other black attendees.

Another person shared that she had encountered a string of bad experiences with predominantly African-American churches before coming to Crosstown. These experiences poised her to be open to other religious alternatives even though most of her religious background was rooted in predominantly African-American churches. She explained why she left the most recent church she had attended before coming to Crosstown: "There were not a lot of genuine things that were done there as far as praise of the Lord but rather praise of man, praise of money, and after I became aware of that, naturally I didn't want any part of that." She had actually assumed, before first attending Crosstown, that the church was predominantly black. When she was greeted at the door by the white assistant pastor, she was a bit apprehensive about staying. However, the open, warm welcome she received from the church made her return.

Then, there were African Americans with whom I spoke who appreciated the worship style they experienced in the traditional black churches they had attended, but who had not participated in the worship with the same level of fervency as others. For one woman, her lack of fervency led her to ask why she was different. In discussing the church where she grew up, she explained:

Honestly, some of it was very uplifting but I always wondered why I didn't get excited like many of the people did. I never felt that same level of excitement in terms of standing up and shouting and that kind of thing, although, you know, like I said, some of it was uplifting. You definitely had your spirits lifted after listening, but I never really, I can't say I ever got to the emotional frenzy that some people did, and I always wondered why I didn't.

Her less-engaged personal style of worship seems to have placed her on the fringes of the worship experience at her childhood church.

The Past in the Present

When it comes to understanding why people attend interracial churches, childhood interracial interactions matter for African Americans, but do not matter so much for whites. African Americans at Crosstown regularly interacted with whites as youth in their high schools, and sometimes in their neighborhoods and churches. Many African Americans' closest friends as youth were white, which likely led to greater familiarity with the dominant culture. A large majority of white attendees I interviewed at Crosstown did not interact regularly with people of another race as youth. Therefore, racial socialization as children does not explain why whites attend interracial churches.

Childhood religious socialization does not inform our understanding of why people attend interracial churches as adults. Nearly all Crosstown attendees who went to church as children attended racially homogeneous churches. African Americans tended to go to predominantly black churches, often those associated with African-American denominations. The predominantly white churches that most white interviewees attended as youth were rather liturgical and reserved. It was not until people became adults that they developed preferences, or at least an appreciation, for worship styles and practices that were different from those they experienced in their childhood churches. Whites desired to worship in interracial environments. And African Americans began to appreciate certain religious practices that were not commonly present in the African-American churches they had attended.

Nevertheless, despite both whites' and African Americans' newly acquired religious interests, Crosstown's worship services, with the exception of some gospel music, did not incorporate the kind of worship style and religious practices with which African Americans were most familiar. Instead, Crosstown's worship services looked more similar to what whites were already accustomed to, with a minimally expressive worship style and a predominance of contemporary praise choruses and traditional hymns. Their interracial exposure and religious experiences likely made African Americans more willing to accommodate the religio-cultural preferences of whites, rather than the converse. The acculturation of most African Americans into the white dominant culture during their youth, in combination with their appreciation for diverse religious practices, would make them more inclined to do so.

6

Reproducing White Hegemony

Beverly, an African-American woman who had a racially diverse friendship network at Crosstown, told me:

> I remember somebody saying to me, a white person,
> "Crosstown is becoming an African-American church."
> I said, "When was the last time you have gone to an
> African-American church? Because Crosstown is
> in *no way* an African-American church."

Another woman, a Latina named Yolanda who had been attending the church for about a year, presented a similar assessment: "I feel like [Crosstown's] more Caucasian to a degree than it is black even though there are black people." The stories discussed in the preceding chapters affirm Beverly's and Yolanda's perceptions.

The survey results from the National Congregations Study and the experiences of Crosstown show that interracial churches are impacted by whiteness. The cultures and structures of interracial churches emulate those more commonly observed in white churches. Interracial churches tend to cater to the predilections of whites. The worship styles and practices mainly suit the desires of whites. Most interracial churches are also led by whites. And in Crosstown's case, where an African American heads the church, proficiency in and support of white religious culture is vital. While interracial churches, like Crosstown, are inclined to have some discussions about issues of race, whites may be disinclined to participate in such discussions. Furthermore, these discussions will not likely reflect the structural concerns and interests of African Americans. All this may happen despite whites' firm support of racially integrated churches and African Americans' advocacy for changes that would reflect their religio-cultural preferences.

How does this happen? How do purposeful racially diverse churches succumb to whiteness and end up contributing to the reproduction of white hegemony? How is it that they continue to attract and keep people from diverse backgrounds under these conditions? The answer lies in whites' embodiment of whiteness as well as racial minorities' (sometimes inadvertent) affirmation of whiteness. But conditions external to these churches that limit religious opportunities for racial minorities are also important. These factors together create an environment that sustains white hegemony. To frame this process, I elaborate on two theoretical approaches—homophily and hegemony—that are useful for understanding interracial churches.

Homophily

The *homophily* principle says that people prefer to interact regularly with others who are like them.[1] This principle has often been used to explain why voluntary organizations, including social clubs, professional organizations, and churches, are homogeneous. The central point is that voluntary organizations tend to be homogeneous because people are recruited into voluntary organizations through social networks mainly made up of people who are similar to them.[2] In order for organizations to attract and retain members, they need to specialize in particular "niches" of the population.[3] This is not necessarily intentional. But because people's social networks are homogeneous and people learn about voluntary organizations through their networks, these organizations attract and serve segments of the population that are made up of people with similar sociodemographic characteristics, such as gender, age, or race.

Other dynamics also facilitate homogeneous voluntary organizations. People who are atypical or members of the numerical minority of a voluntary organization do not remain in the organization as long as typical members because they do not feel as connected to the organization, they tend to have fewer friends in the organization, or they may not be treated as well as others. Conversely, those who are typical members tend to be more connected to and have more friends in the organization, which helps to keep them in the organization longer.[4] Additionally, voluntary organizations exist in a market-driven environment where they compete for the time and energy of potential members. Voluntary organizations depend on these resources. When multiple organizations specialize in a particular sociodemographic group, the people in these groups are in greater demand than others. They have more options and because of their own limited time and energy will have to choose where they want to expend their resources. People who are in demand like this leave voluntary organizations sooner than those who are not. When we consider these dynamics, we can see that people who are both atypical members and in demand by multiple organizations will be the most likely to leave an organization.[5]

Religious organizations are clear examples of these dynamics. Not only is religion voluntary, but religious organizations are the most common type of voluntary organization in the United States. In some neighborhoods, one can find a church on every corner. With such a saturated market, religious organizations need to be all the more competitive when vying for members. This has resulted in many different kinds of churches that specialize in different niches, especially denominational, ethnic, and racial ones. Yet, while denominational and (to a lesser extent) ethnic lines have become more blurry over recent decades, racial lines remain salient.[6]

Emerson and Smith[7] draw upon the homophily principle to explain the persistent racial divide within evangelical Christianity. They argue that the organization of American religion, as a pluralistic and voluntaristic institution, creates and perpetuates homogeneity within religious groups. The disestablishment of religion in America has made religion a matter of choice. And this marketplace structure requires religious groups to specialize in a niche to appeal to a certain type. Due to the principle of homophily, individual members of religious groups recruit other members who are similar to them, which, given the salience of race, leads to the development of racially homogeneous religious groups. Consequently, religious life is separated along racial lines, "reducing the opportunities for intergroup relations and social ties" among evangelical Christians in particular, ultimately producing racially segregated churches.[8]

Because people like to be around others who are like them, it is important to understand how atypical members manage in interracial churches.

Relying upon in-depth interviews with respondents from a multiracial congregation, Brad Christerson and Michael Emerson found that typical members, or members of the numerical majority group in the church, are more likely than atypical members to have same-race friendships.[9] Over 80% of atypical members in the congregation expressed frustration with their inability to develop close relationships within the church. This is compared to just over 20% of the majority group's members. And about 80% of the atypical church members believed that diversity made interrelations and organizational practices more difficult, while few typical church members shared this belief. This suggests that people who are not core to the church, as represented by the relative size of their group, are likely to be less connected to and less satisfied with their experiences. They are also not likely to stay with the organization as long as core members, especially if they have other options where they can have their needs met.

The homophily principle is applicable to our understanding of interracial churches and of racially diverse voluntary organizations generally. However, the conceptualization of the "atypical" member may need revisiting. According to the homophily literature, the relative size of one's group is what makes a member atypical. For racially diverse voluntary organizations, this is problematic. Other factors matter. At Crosstown, for example, whites left in noticeable numbers while still holding numerical majority status when Pastor Barnes became senior pastor. Even after whites became the numerical minority in the church, they were culturally and structurally advantaged. The church was inclined to adopt the religio-cultural preferences of whites. This outcome is consistent with that of other interracial churches in America. Therefore, the social dynamics that govern membership processes and the culture and structure of racially diverse voluntary organizations are not limited to the relative size of groups. If, in addition to relative size, we think of atypical members as those who are social minorities—that is, people who belong to an economically, politically, or culturally subordinate group—then African Americans would be atypical members at Crosstown. Given that African-American Crosstown attendees were not able to use their numerical majority status to hire another African-American pastor, create a religious space that accommodated shouting, or move race-related discussion toward the center of congregational discourse, this appears to be the case. Social factors external to Crosstown, such as the broader black/white relations and meanings of racial categories, affected the inner-workings of the church.

Hegemony

Hegemony is a form of rule where the dominant group's status is based primarily upon the consent of subordinate groups.[10] Subordinate groups perceive the dominant group's rule as legitimate and acknowledge its beliefs, values, and practices as "common sense." Consent can look like full endorsement of a dominant group's culture and status, or like a passive, uneasy acceptance that it is the only doable means of organizing society. Either way, subordinate groups are embedded in society and perceive no other truly viable alternative.[11]

Antonio Gramsci, an early twentieth-century Italian philosopher, brought the concept of hegemony to the forefront of sociological and political thought.[12] According to Gramsci, there are several key components operating within any hegemonic system. Coercion, which is executed by political entities, including the police, the military, and the courts, is needed to gain power. It is also used during moments of threat after consent has been achieved in order to maintain power.[13] Consent is necessary to sustain power over the long term. Nations, for instance, may use force to take over other nations. They will continue to use force periodically after establishing rule. But, in order to have a settled new society, the conquering nation must indoctrinate the conquered with the belief that its way of life is better for everyone. Civil entities, which include schools, media outlets, and churches, are responsible for generating consent.[14] They construct "common sense" and provide a moral basis for the social order. Religion is one of the key civil entities in this process.[15] In the antebellum South, white pastors of slave churches emphasized the importance of obedience, duty, and heavenly rewards to their parishioners, values that reinforced the system of slavery.[16] It made sense to do your work and obey your master because that is how you would make it to heaven.

Of course, not all minorities completely buy into the dominant way of life. For example, while some slaves followed the teachings of their white pastors, others followed slave preachers, like Nat Turner, into rebellions against their masters or participated in organizing the Underground Railroad.[17] Hegemonic societies inevitably have "counterhegemonies," like these, which consist of bands of leaders who form movements that oppose the normative way of life. However, those who are already in power have a supreme advantage in preserving their status over any opposition. They can rely on existing structures (i.e., patterns of rule) to their benefit and more easily gain the ear of the people to make a case for their claims and to build consent. Still, a sustainable hegemony is one that incorporates certain cultural elements of subordinate groups, those that do not disrupt the status of those in power, into the broader culture.[18]

White Hegemony

White hegemony is a form of rule where whites dominate society with the consent of racial minorities. Racial minorities acknowledge whites' dominant status as legitimate and affirm (if only passively) the culture and structures that sustain it. In the United States, consent is organized primarily around three dominant ideologies: democracy, the "American dream," and color blindness. Following Gramsci, a true democracy would be a nation where all racial and ethnic groups have an equal ability to disseminate their ideas and beliefs to the masses through the civil entities in society. If certain groups' ability to engage the democratic system is largely restricted to political entities (voting, for example), as it is for most racial and ethnic minorities, democracy is diminished to an "effective means for creating an illusion" that those in power are there because of popular opinion.[19] Individualistic explanations, like the American dream, that tie success to people's hard work rather than to structural realities, are used to make sense of racial minorities' perpetual disadvantage.[20] They are not as well off because they do not work hard enough. Color blindness is the most commonly used explanation for the status quo.[21] Race is deemed inconsequential because there are very few explicit racists any more. Or because people naturally want to be with others who are like them. Color blindness says that to even acknowledge racial differences is in itself racist and that any kind of disparities that do exist are not because of racialized structures but poor cultural habits, making it difficult to address racial inequalities.[22]

While racial minorities do not fully embrace these dominant ideologies, it is common for them to incorporate certain themes into their world views. Eduardo Bonilla-Silva and David Embrick studied if and how blacks use color blindness to explain racial issues. They found that African Americans acknowledge the impact of racist structures, but also assert that people's situations are linked to personal decisions.[23] One of their interviewees answered a question about how often discrimination affects the everyday lives of African Americans by saying: "You might have to deal with it but you have to keep going. I don't think it really puts an impact...on your day or inhibits anybody from doing what they want to do or being what they want to be. That's up to the individuals."[24] What this demonstrates is that, even where racial minorities have developed ideologies that challenge the status of whites, they still operate within the parameters of white hegemony and inevitably sustain it.[25]

Subordinate racial groups develop counterhegemonic movements in an effort to challenge the meaning of racial categories and to improve the status of racial minorities. But these movements, despite their impact, have been effectively absorbed into the dominant culture, with whites retaining their dominant status.[26] For example, the Civil Rights movement, which was an indigenous and religious movement—one that was born within the African-American community and organized around the structure of the black church—led to major reforms in the United States, including the collapse of Jim Crow and the end of discriminatory voting laws.[27] Yet, it became ineffectual at eliminating racial disparities because it splintered into competing movements after these concessions were made and, more important, because the movement drew upon hegemonic themes of racelessness, equality, and democracy. People should not be judged by what they look like, but by their abilities. People should be given equal opportunities to get a good job, eat in the restaurant of their choosing, or gain a sound education. Obstacles to voting need to be removed. These rights had previously only applied to whites, but the Civil Rights movement demanded that they be expanded to include African Americans and other racial minorities and that structural reforms were needed to make these changes happen. While these objectives were clearly needed and desirable, they broadened the hegemonic base. And ideas like racelessness and equality were eventually redefined to mean that race does not matter (i.e., color-blind ideology), and the elimination of race-based laws and policies places people on equal footing. While the explicitly racist laws and policies that had been in place for centuries were eliminated, the racialized structures they had constructed were not addressed, leaving the existing racial order intact.

Michael Omi and Howard Winant, in their theory of how race is constructed in Western societies, call this pattern of conflict within racial hegemonies "racial formation."[28] It is a process by which racial categories are created, changed, and potentially eliminated from the racial landscape.

This process is composed of multiple "racial projects," the "building blocks" of racial hegemonies.[29] These are interpretations or explanations of race relations and of how race should be reflected in society. They occur at the macro-level, in court decisions on the role race should play in policy making, and during everyday experiences, like dinner discussions about how race matters for athletes, and anywhere in between. Racial projects that aim to sustain an existing racial order are hegemonic. Those that intend to disrupt it are counterhegemonic.

The idea of racial projects is a useful one because it can be applied in a variety of contexts. Omi and Winant only focus on macro-level racial projects, particularly those within political institutions. But churches are important sites for understanding how white hegemony is reproduced. They are civil entities, places where consent is constructed. But they are also places where oppositional cultures are fostered. I have already talked about the Civil Rights movement, a prime example of religion acting as a means for counterhegemony. But there is also the abolitionist movement, a religious, moral, and political coalition of African-Americans and whites who relentlessly and fervently struggled for the emancipation of slaves—and Cesar Chavez and others, who drew upon the tenets of Catholicism as a source of legitimation and support for the farm workers' strikes and racial/ethnic segregation protests in California.[30] Interracial churches, in particular, are places where people could voluntarily interact across racial lines to build a religious community that worships God and challenges racialized structures. Instead, they embrace their racial diversity while at the same time affirming the status quo. Interracial churches are a powerful domain of consent building within the broader American social structure. They are appealing because they are inclusive of racial minorities. However, this inclusiveness conceals their tendency to embrace whiteness. Thus, interracial churches are not without conflict, if Crosstown is any indication. The power of white hegemony is most evident during these moments, which show how racial minorities in interracial churches attempt to stimulate change and how those with power, by drawing upon the tools of hegemony, organize life to their benefit.

White Hegemony at Crosstown

During the conflict over shouting at Crosstown, African Americans and whites held competing ideas about the purpose of worship. Both groups recognized worship as a means of connecting with God, but African Americans also viewed it as an opportunity to freely express themselves. Whites did not. Their primary view was that worship expressions should benefit everyone. Shouting interfered with some people's ability to have a fulfilling worship experience. This stance is a religious articulation of a dominant ideological theme in Western society: individualism. Individuals have the right to do what they want as long as it does not interfere with the goals of others. This is not a legal or political prescription, but rather a moral one that governs how people are expected to behave. But individualism was inherent in African Americans' position as well. Their main emphasis was freedom. The distinction was in each group's understanding of what scholars of individual rights call a person's "recognized personal sphere," which is the "circle around every individual human being which no government, be it that of one, or a few, or many ought to be permitted to overstep."[31] What best defines someone's recognized personal sphere is a topic of constant debate among philosophers. But at Crosstown, whites' understanding of the boundaries of individual worship expression was reestablished by those in power. This was largely because they held the authority to sanction church culture, and the people chosen to be in leadership were supporters of white evangelical religious culture. As in any context where hegemony prevails, though, church leaders incorporated African Americans' ideas about worship into their final proclamation. A symbolic provision for shouting was made. Although informal norms dictated otherwise, shouting was permitted during a particular segment of the worship service.

Where African Americans were less accepting of dominant ideologies was in their views of race. While some affirmed individualistic solutions for racial inequality, nearly all experienced and/or articulated blackness as a structurally subordinated status and recognized race and an identity that affected their lives on a regular basis. At the seminar on the role of race in Christianity, African Americans held to this view, expressing discontent with a discussion that, in their opinion, avoided the real issues of race. Yet this counterhegemonic view could not gain any real leverage at Crosstown because the existing structures limited its influence. From the pulpit, congregants did not hear structural reasons for poor race relations. Race was an individualistic matter, one that required people to make personal changes that reflected tolerance of other groups and did not give deference to certain groups over others. There was no place of prominence in the church for dissenting voices to make their claims about the meaning of race. The only site was the race and religion seminar, which limited how people could talk about it. Still, white attendees, particularly white leaders, were conspicuously absent from the seminar, demonstrating that they were not invested in dealing with racial issues in the church. Therefore, race-related activities were not only individualistic but were marginalized by whites.[32]

A hegemonic system's effectiveness is bigger than one single person or small group of people. It lies in the pervasiveness of the dominant culture and structure, which makes it very difficult for threats to power to rise up. Hence, Pastor Barnes was unable to bring Floyd Winston on as the next assistant pastor and make race more central to the church's congregational discourse. He was embedded in a structure that dictated that people in positions of power affirm white evangelical culture, facilitate white structural advantage, and assuage white transparency. Pastor Barnes used his position to endorse Winston. Still, despite this endorsement and Winston's cultural compatibility with the church, a substantial portion of the congregation did not support him, and many were dead set against his candidacy. Similarly, Pastor Barnes strongly advocated for the church to engage discussions of race. But white leaders and attendees did not follow his lead. The church's populist approach meant that Pastor Barnes needed the support of others in leadership and the members to enact his agenda. However, as one member highlighted during a members' meeting at Crosstown, other churches often give senior pastors the sole power to hire their staff, including other pastors, and to provide guidance to the church. Crosstown did not entertain this suggestion to expand Pastor Barnes' breadth of authority.

This more monocratic form of leadership is common in other churches, particularly those within the black church. Aldon Morris noted that the black minister "oversees the workforce of the church and delegates authority throughout its organizational structure. The minister, more than anyone else, determines the goals of the church and identifies the causes to be supported by the congregation."[33] This feature of the black church was paramount to the success of the Civil Rights movement. Pastor Barnes' power as an African-American pastor in an interracial church was, therefore, limited compared to some of his counterparts in African-American churches. However, it was not only the dominant structure and culture in which he found himself, but his full consent to it, that limited his power. His reproach of the black church leadership structure and his adoption of white evangelical culture left him with very few options to make changes in the church. And the democratic approach, while useful in many contexts, restricted his authority and influence in this context.

How Do Interracial Churches Work?

Hegemony is often used to describe how an entire society is controlled. But hegemony is the outcome of many micro-level projects taking place across society. These projects together sustain hegemony. Even projects that have macro-level outcomes, such as federal laws, have their origins in micro-level situations. Crosstown offers examples of micro-level projects. They do not represent how all racial projects transpire, but they do reveal white hegemony in action and point to how groups with diverse and even competing ideas, motives, and behaviors can work independently and still, together, perpetuate white hegemony.

Hegemonies depend upon subordinate groups perceiving no viable alternatives. This is the case for African Americans at Crosstown. Although whites at Crosstown were more likely to tell me that they were committed to interracial churches, African Americans were more likely to stay. They remained at the church in the face of structural change, conflict, and unmet desires. This is because even though African Americans may have been in demand by black churches, they saw Crosstown as their best option. Crosstown was one of the rare places where voluntary, cooperative, and friendly interracial interactions could occur. Several African Americans told me that they hadn't been in this kind of environment before. Since coming to Crosstown, they were able to develop friendly relationships with whites. They came to believe that there were far more similarities between whites and African Americans than differences. They valued these experiences and what they added to their lives. Perhaps most important, African-American churches did not appeal to most African Americans with whom I spoke at Crosstown. They preferred certain religious and cultural practices that were not commonly practiced in the African-American churches with which they were familiar. There may have been African-American churches that could have met more of their preferences, but these African-American churches were few and far between.

The limited options for African Americans who attend interracial churches place them at a disadvantage. They cannot have all of their preferences met. They need to choose a church that meets those select religious and cultural needs that are most important to them. For example, many African Americans told me that they did not appreciate the relatively staid worship style at Crosstown. Yet, the African-American churches of which they were aware engaged in other practices they did not prefer, such as formal dress codes and longer services. They had to choose, then, between their preference for, say, effusive worship and their preference for shorter worship services. It was apparently difficult for them to find a church that satisfied both of these desires.

On the other hand, whites perceived white churches as viable alternatives. This was despite their stated desire to worship in a racially diverse religious community. And for most, their sense of connectedness to the church was fragile and dependent upon the church's affirmation of whiteness. All this was true whether whites were in the numerical minority or majority. Their greater likelihood to leave, combined with African Americans' limited options elsewhere, gave whites leverage. They may or may not have been consciously aware they had it, but they still accessed it. There was a real threat that whites would leave if African Americans did not make the necessary sacrifices. And it was ever present.

Yet, this does not fully explain why the congregational life of interracial churches ends up adopting the religio-cultural preferences of whites. It is not simply that whites will leave unless their demands are met. The voluntary nature of churches rules this out. Whites can make demands, but African Americans can choose not to comply and/or leave. Nor is it enough that African Americans are aware that whites may leave. Instead, two complementary processes must be in place for interracial churches to cater to the predilections of whites. Whites need to be more likely to leave the church than African Americans, and African Americans must care that they might. An interracial church doesn't need most African Americans to care whether whites leave, just a critical mass. From my observations at Crosstown, the critical mass amounted to no more than than 10% of all African-American attendees. The complicity of this core group provided sufficient support for a congregational life that favored the desires of white attendees.

Archetypes of Black and White Attendees of Interracial Churches

Church attendees can be placed into six categories. These categories are broad and fluid. Depending upon the particular context, a person in one category may temporarily assume some of the characteristics of another category. Moreover, people may shift categories over time. These categories apply to interracial churches where African Americans and whites are the two largest groups. As these are constructed from a single case study, I offer them as archetypes to be tested in future studies of African-American and white attendees of other similar types of interracial churches.

The three categories for white attendees are defined by how they respond when whiteness is threatened. Of course, not all white attendees may perceive that their interests are being threatened, but evidence from Crosstown suggests that most will. Additionally, whites' responses to conflicts differ depending on the centrality of that activity to congregational life. For example, when it came to worship, arguably the most central activity to congregational life and that area of congregational life that most represents the identity of a church, white attendees directly engaged threats by vocalizing their position. White attendees' opposition to less-central church activities, like the seminar on religious racial segregation, did not require such a direct approach. Rather, white attendees were able to perpetuate whiteness by disengaging from the seminar. Their absence, particularly that of the white leadership, delegitimized the importance of the seminar and limited its potential impact. White attendees were most likely to remove themselves from congregational life altogether when white structural dominance was threatened. Both when Pastor Barnes was appointed as the first African-American pastor of Crosstown and when there was potentially a second African American to be appointed, whites left the church.

The largest group of whites who attend interracial churches fall into a category I call *experimenters* (see table 6-1). Experimenters find that interracial worship broadens their spiritual perspective and improves their religious experience. They have some, albeit limited, tolerance for different ways of doing worship and structuring congregational life. But their tie to the church is the weakest. They want to attend an interracial church, but it must be one where their preferred practices are dominant. If the possibility emerges that their desires may not be met, they are inclined to leave. They will not engage conflicts to rectify differences.

There are three groups of experimenters. One group is whites who left around the inauguration of Pastor Barnes and after the announcement that the two white pastors would be leaving. The appointment (or potential appointment) of an African-American pastor signaled changes that they did not support. Other experimenters are young adults, in their early twenties who have recently graduated from college. These attendees are interested in experiencing a diverse worship environment, in part because of exposure to racial diversity or classes on racial issues during college. Yet while they demonstrate a genuine enthusiasm for diversity, their commitment is tenuous, based more on their interests in personal fulfillment than creating bridges across racial lines. From my observations, they only attend the church for about two or three years. The third group is married couples with no or young children. After this group has children or once peer relationships become important for their children, they leave the church. These parents are not willing to sacrifice the white privilege of their children in order to attend an interracial church. Former attendees of Crosstown highlighted this. The parents of adolescents especially acknowledged that one of the main reasons their families left Crosstown was because of their children's relationships with African-American youth in the church.

The second type of white attendee is a *conditional believer*. Conditional believers strongly support interracial churches and have strong interracial ties in the church. Although they may not be most comfortable in interracial environments, they value interactions with racial minorities. But, more important, they believe that interracial worship is morally right. However, conditional believers do not necessarily support a pluralistic church where the preferences of African Americans and whites are equally represented. Similar to experimenters, they want the best of both worlds— an interracial church where their preferred practices are prevalent. Nevertheless, while they may eventually leave, they are willing to engage conflict in an effort to sustain integration. The conditional believers at Crosstown are the whites who expressed deep concern about shouting during worship services and about Winston's candidacy, but still stayed at the church and engaged the conflicts that arose over these issues.

The smallest category of white attendees is the *activists*. Activists have usually experienced a kind of epiphany regarding American race relations, recognizing racial injustice and black/white inequality. They consequently have a strong commitment to interracial churches. They support the inclusion of distinctly African-American religio-cultural practices into congregational life, at the risk that their religio-cultural preferences may not be met. Activists at Crosstown supported the candidacies of African-American pastoral candidates and more effusive worship in the church. Their close social

TABLE 6-1. Archetypes of White and African-American Interracial Church Attendees

Whites	African Americans
Experimenters	Defectors
• Largest group	• Largest group
• Curious about racial diversity	• Preferred religious culture and structure
• Weakest tie to church	is the priority, not racial diversity
• Likely to leave when whiteness	• Engage conflict when preferred religious
is threatened	culture and structure is at risk
Conditional Believers	Disillusioned Integrationists
• Believe in racial integration	• Used to be defectors
• Engage conflict when threats	• Come to appreciate racial diversity but
to whiteness arise in core church	also ambivalent about it
activities	• Less willing to make sacrifices to sustain
• Desist when threats to whiteness	racial diversity
are minimal	
• Inclined to leave if they "lose	
out" after conflicts	
Activists	Advocates
• Smallest group	• Smallest group
• Commitment to religious racial	• Used to be defectors or have had limited
diversity based upon a "revelation"	connection to African-American churches
• Have strong interracial ties and	• Most comfortable in interracial environments
sometimes come from interracial	• Have strong interracial ties and sometimes
families	come from interracial families
• Affirm religio-cultural preferences	• Willing to acquiesce to whites to keep them
of African Americans	in the church

networks are usually racially diverse, and they are often single or young. Sometimes, they are members of multiracial families. This category of whites might be the most promising for developing more culturally equal and structurally representative interracial churches. However, their numbers alone would not be sufficient for sustaining an interracial church. I estimate that less than ten percent of white attendees at Crosstown were activists.

Despite the salience of their racial identity, African-American attendees were complicit in the perpetuation of whiteness as well. The three categories for African Americans are based upon their level of consent to whiteness. African Americans' consent was needed for Crosstown to be a stable church. While they may not have perceived that they had other church options, they could have continually caused conflict in the church. But this was not the case. Still, African Americans were not all equally complicit. Most African-American attendees' consent was passive. They were not particularly concerned about whether or not whites' interests were satisfied, nor were most especially committed to interracial worship. But there was a consistent core of African Americans who did support whites' interests and who were willing to acquiesce to white attendees' desires during conflicts.

A majority of the African-American attendees I interviewed explained that they were not drawn to Crosstown because of the racial diversity, but because they preferred its religious culture and structure over that of African-American churches. I call this first category of African-American attendees *defectors*. Defectors appreciate some of the practices distinct to the black church experience, but not all. This encourages them to look elsewhere. Furthermore, while they appreciate interracial worship, they are not especially committed to it. Consequently, defectors are not concerned about whether an interracial church remains racially diverse. They are not interested in retaining white attendees during conflict, nor are they motivated to support a particular practice or church agenda to keep them in the church. If they are concerned about anything, it is about whether or not the church is going to participate in those religious practices they prefer. If it happens that their interests align with the interests of most white attendees, then so be it. For example, a defector who strongly prefers timeliness might advocate for shorter worship services, a practice often preferred by white church attendees. However, the defector's intention would not be to sustain racial integration, but to maintain practices he or she favors.

During interviews and informal interactions, some African-American attendees confessed their disappointment with the loss of white attendees. As one African-American attendee shared: "I'm very sad and frustrated that a lot of the Caucasians are leaving. I didn't want to see that happen." This second category of African-American attendees I call *disillusioned integrationists*. Disillusioned integrationists are originally defectors. However, over time, they come to value interaction with whites in the church. They are persuaded that whites who attend interracial churches are different from other whites. They believe that these whites would be comfortable with practices that were more common to their religious experiences. However, when they realize that white flight also happens in churches or that whites are unsupportive of the desires and preferences of African Americans, they become disillusioned about the possibility of racial integration in any context. They doubt the viability of truly pluralistic, racially integrated environments. Therefore, despite their support of racial integration, these African Americans are not inclined to sacrifice those beliefs and practices they prefer in order to sustain racial integration.

There was a stable contingent of African-American attendees who supported whites' interests and who were willing to acquiesce to white attendees' desires. This final category of African Americans I call *advocates*. Advocates are that critical mass of black attendees essential for interracial churches to affirm whiteness. They strongly support interracial churches. They are more comfortable in interracial environments, and interracial interaction is important to them. And they often have strong ties with whites in the church. Advocates have two origins. Some advocates are originally defectors. However, unlike disillusioned integrationists, they come to value interracial interaction enough that they are willing to make sacrifices to sustain white attendance. The other type of advocate was both socialized in interracial environments as a child and was raised outside of the influence of the black church. Not only do these advocates prefer interracial environments, they have not developed a particular taste for religio-cultural practices that are more distinctive of the black church. This makes them candidates for advocating racial integration because they do not need to sacrifice as much as other African Americans in order to keep whites in the church.

Contributing to White Hegemony

Both white and black attendees help to reproduce white hegemony in interracial churches. The archetypical categories of attendees become most salient during conflicts. Categories tend to work together in pairs. Defectors (i.e., blacks with the least attachment to racial diversity) and activists (i.e., whites with the strongest commitment to racial diversity) are often on the same side of conflicts. They affirm religious and cultural practices preferred by most African-American attendees. Conditional believers (i.e., whites who engage conflict when threats to whiteness arise) and advocates (i.e., blacks who are most consenting to whiteness) tend to be on the other side of conflicts. They affirm a religious culture and structure that primarily suits the preferences of whites. Disillusioned integrationists (i.e., blacks who are ambivalent about religious racial integration) and experimenters (i.e., whites with the least tolerance of threats to whiteness) play supporting but separate roles during these times. Of these six categories, advocates and, to a lesser extent, conditional believers are most central to this process.

When conflict arises, defectors and activists support religious and cultural practices that compete with those preferred by the majority of whites (specifically, experimenters and conditional believers) in the church. They do not fervently fight for their position by, for example, expressing their concerns to leadership directly. But they do hold firmly to it. This is particularly threatening to experimenters, so much so that they may leave the church. Yet, even though experimenters do not engage conflicts, their discontent or departures provoke advocates and conditional believers to act. Their role then, though indirect, is still important.

When experimenters become restless and uneasy about potential changes in the church, the role of advocates and conditional believers becomes vital. These two groups work in tandem to increase the proportion of people who support the preferences and interests of most whites. With increased support for their religio-cultural preferences, this can serve to retain any remaining experimenters and attract new ones to the church. In a congregation like Crosstown, where church members vote on important matters, advocates' support is all the more important, maybe even essential. For example, advocates contested African Americans' candidacies for assistant pastor. It is likely that, without their disapproving votes, Floyd Winston would have become the second African-American pastor of Crosstown. Additionally, since leadership is also inclined to affirm the religio-cultural practices and beliefs preferred by most whites, the backing of advocates and conditional believers gives them added support to sustain a church culture and structure that privileges whites. Advocates and conditional believers also use the threat that experimenters will leave unless their preferences are met to gain an added advantage during conflicts. During a church meeting at Crosstown, advocates, with evidence provided by conditional believers, brought to light whites' concerns about hiring a black pastor and introduced the threat of white flight in an effort to gain support for their position. Finally, advocates—as African Americans who support the preferred practices of whites—provide legitimacy to the idea that the religio-cultural practices preferred by most whites *should* be normative. They can also imply that practices common in African-American churches are only for blacks or even that they are unacceptable.

Disillusioned integrationists are more peripheral in this process because they are ambivalent about racial diversity. During conflicts, they are
not clearly on one side or the other. They tend to side with defectors and
activists. But, if a disillusioned integrationist is feeling connected to whites
during a conflict, the threat of whites leaving could work to enlist him or
her to the cause of conditional believers and advocates.

Racial Integration, Religion, and Broader Sociological Lessons

The premise of this study extends beyond the black/white dichotomy and
beyond religion. Although race is endemic to the American social system,
structuring all institutions, it is first manifested in the everyday, routine
activities and interactions of life—where we live, work, and, for many
Americans, where we worship. Crosstown's story shows how whiteness
can govern interracial organizations generally and perpetuate white hegemony. There are several lessons to be learned as we look to better understand the effect of whiteness on racially diverse places. These lessons
have implications for our understanding of how whiteness operates in
other contexts.

Throughout this book, I have focused on the experiences of African-
American and white interracial church attendees because black/white relations in America have proved to be most challenging. However, while
I have emphasized the experiences of black/white interracial churches, I
suspect that similar racial dynamics will be evident in Christian interracial organizations of other racial compositions where whites have a
presence. Whiteness is a ubiquitous force in the United States. And its
ultimate outcome, white hegemony, can persist regardless of which racial
minority group is subjected to it.[34] It is only the particular ways in which
whiteness manifests itself that will differ across racial minority groups. But
the critical issue is that whiteness sustains an existing social hierarchy that
privileges whites. So, in the case of interracial congregations where Native
Americans, Latinos, or Asians are the largest racial or ethnic minority, I
suspect that similar issues over the control of structural and cultural space
will arise. The predilections of whites will be paramount if the church
wants to retain white attendees. Other studies of interracial churches
where Latinos and Asians are the larger racial minority groups provide
support for this proposition. For example, at Wilcrest Baptist Church, a

multiracial church in Houston with a large proportion of Latinos, several whites, including white leaders, left the church after Latino cultural practices were introduced into the weekly worship services.[35]

Crosstown confirms that you don't need racists to reproduce white hegemony. Other research has demonstrated this as well.[36] However, this study extends our understanding of this phenomenon by revealing the processes that dictate how whiteness prospers in an environment that portends to be racially diverse, inclusive, and egalitarian. I have no doubt that the people of Crosstown, whites and African Americans, were well intentioned. Their mission stated that they aspired to create a religious community that "courageously" and "fearlessly" confronted racial division. However, dominant, covert beliefs and norms about race and culture undermined the church's ability to realize this mission. This suggests that racial hierarchies are dependent upon latent ideologies and group interests, not on overt missions or policies. These ideologies and group interests will prevail even in cases where there are contrary policies in place. This may explain, for example, how socially and politically liberal communities, organizations, or administrations can perpetuate a culture and structure that privileges whites. A first step in rectifying racial inequalities, therefore, is exposing and addressing those latent ideologies and interests that sustain white hegemony.

White transparency can help to sabotage anything that could potentially produce racially egalitarian communities. If whites do not recognize that, by virtue of their racial identity, they are in a superior position in the social hierarchy, they are not apt to recognize underlying ideologies that run counter to egalitarian principles. Again, this can also be evident among people who are socially liberal on issues of race. White Crosstown leaders and attendees believed strongly in racial integration and understood the structural nature of racial inequality. However, they failed to acknowledge their role, as benefactors of whiteness, in hindering the fulfillment of the church's mission. They were largely unaware of their privilege. Subsequently, they were passive about actively engaging race so that when an opportunity to discuss race arose, they did not take advantage of it.

Over the past few decades, we have witnessed an increase in the number of racial minorities holding visible, top-level positions in some of the country's most powerful organizations and institutions as CEOs of Fortune 500 companies, governors, and members of presidential cabinets. We celebrate racial minorities who gain access to high positions. And rightly so. This is an indication that progress has been made. However, as we have seen, having racial minorities fill top positions in an organization does not preclude white hegemony. White dominance can be sustained even under these conditions. Pastor Barnes held the highest formal position of authority in the church and was, in many respects, good for Crosstown. Nevertheless, he was unable to garner sufficient support for his agenda. Floyd Winston, his preferred candidate for assistant pastor, did not receive strong support from the congregation. The race and religion seminar he initiated was relegated to the periphery and received virtually no support from white church leaders. If Pastor Barnes had accomplished his goals, African Americans' power and influence in the church may have increased.

In an ideal meritocracy, the qualifications listed for a job directly reflect the skills needed for that position. However, merit is a contested concept. Floyd Winston's candidacy highlights how job credentials are intertwined with a group's interests (stated and unstated) and its ideas about what benefits it and supports its organizational mission, rather than specific job responsibilities. Depending upon the interests of the opposing groups, retaining and attracting white attendees or extending Pastor Barnes' agenda for the church, Winston's credentials were viewed quite differently. It would appear, based on the stated goals, that he was indeed qualified for the assistant pastor position. However, he ultimately received weak support from the congregation, suggesting that other factors were at work. Churches are not synonymous with business organizations. People in senior positions in these settings are generally only accountable to their superiors. Pastors are accountable to their superiors in the denomination, if they are affiliated, but also to their congregants. Nevertheless, the lesson here potentially applies to other types of workplaces. Group interests determine what are legitimate credentials and merit, as much as, if not more than, the skills necessary for a position. This can inform our understanding of persistent job and workplace inequality.

Finally, white hegemony, at least in an environment of purported racial inclusion, is not the result of whites simply working to maintain their dominance. Select African Americans are key contributors to the process. It is appealing to reduce racial issues to a black-versus-white scenario, but such a perspective does not acknowledge the complexity of human relations nor the diversity of preferences, ideas, and experiences within racial groups. I am not implying that most whites do not have an interest in sustaining dominance, nor that most African Americans are satisfied with the status quo. A majority of whites at Crosstown affirmed, to various degrees, a church culture and structure where their preferences were met and white leaders were dominant. And a majority of African Americans favored religious practices, cultural activities, and leadership decisions that would have been more representative of their desires. But white hegemony often depends upon the aid of a contingent of African Americans to sustain its power.

Conclusion: The Elusive Dream

It has been over forty years since Dr. Martin Luther King, Jr., dared us to strive toward amending our past of racial segregation. At the beginning of the twenty-first century, we are seeing positive changes in the religious landscape as it relates to race. Denominations and parachurch organizations are more and more making racial issues important items on their agendas. Churches are working to become places where African Americans and whites worship together. Nevertheless, our racial history and contemporary racial experiences make these endeavors a challenge, and they continue to plague religious organizations' capacity to forge communities that blacks and whites can fully call their own.

I have argued that interracial churches work to the extent that they are, first, comfortable places for whites to attend. This is because whites are accustomed to their cultural practices and ideologies being the norm and to being structurally dominant in nearly every social institution. What this means is that, for interracial churches to stay interracial, racial minorities must be willing to sacrifice their preferences, or they must have already sufficiently acculturated into and accepted the dominant culture and whites' privileged status. Consequently, the chances for a widespread movement of interracial churches are slim. It depends on African Americans' willingness to compromise in the one area of American society where they are able to have power and control: religion. It further depends upon substantial African-American assimilation. Given all of this, is religious racial integration, as it is manifested in so many racially diverse churches in the United States, the best we can hope for? Is the idea of creating cooperative, egalitarian, interracial religious communities where African Americans and whites share life and have equal stakes truly possible?

Dr. Martin Luther King, Jr., inspired a nation afflicted by racial division and injustice to dream of a just and free community of brothers and sisters who openly embrace one another across racial lines. However, Dr. King's message was first and foremost about racial equality. Racial integration is an important component of a racially egalitarian society, but it is not the only one. As churches seek to become interracial, they must not be satisfied with simply having people of different racial groups worship together. They must not even be satisfied with people fellowshipping from time to time outside of church activities. If churches want to realize Dr. King's dream, they must first embrace a dream of racial justice and equality. Interracial churches must be places that all racial groups can call their own, where all racial groups have the power to influence the minor and major decisions of the church, where the culture and experiences of all racial groups are not just tolerated, but appreciated. This demands a radical approach and is certainly a high calling. Whites and racial minorities will have to resist white normativity and structural dominance and fully embrace the cultures, ideas, and perspectives of all racial groups. Otherwise, the dream will remain elusive.

So, I encourage communities, religious or otherwise, that hold the dream of Dr. King as their own, not to accept the convenient counterfeit of mere racial integration but to strive toward becoming communities that celebrate racial justice and equality. For in this, as Dr. King has persuaded us:

> [W]e will be able to speed up that day when all of God's children, black men and white men, Jews and Gentiles, Protestants and Catholics, will be able to join hands and sing in the words of the old spiritual, "Free at last, free at last. Thank God Almighty, we are free at last."

Appendix A: Research Methods

I drew upon both qualitative and quantitative methods for this study. The use of multiple methods, or methodological triangulation, is becoming increasingly common in social scientific research. Employing more than one method can increase the validity of the research, making it more likely that the results truly reflect the phenomenon being examined and are not due to particularities of the methodological approach.[2]

The methods chosen for this study—participant observation, in-depth interviews, and congregational-level surveys—each have their strengths and weaknesses. I hoped to minimize the weaknesses by incorporating the methods together into this research project. The participant observation gave me insight into collective religious practices, interpersonal and intergroup interactions of church affiliates, and other behaviors of the church population.[3] This methodological approach cannot tell us much about people's thoughts, ideas, values, or personal experiences.[4] For those, I relied upon in-depth interviews. Of course, informal conversations are informative. However, the in-depth interviews gave me the opportunity to directly explore informants' views, ideas, and experiences related to interracial congregational life and other race-related issues.[5] The interviews, particularly with the pastors, provided supplemental information about the culture, organizational bureaucracy, and theology of the church.

The participant observation and in-depth interviews were the primary methods used for the case study. A case study offers an understanding of "people in places."[6] The complexities of people's beliefs, ideas, and understandings about themselves and the world around them can be extracted, as can how these perspectives inform their context. The case study facilitated my ability to detail the congregation's religious rituals and practices, such as what happened during worship events, who participated in certain religious practices, and which religious rituals or practices were more sacred than others and why.[7] These practices, attitudes, and interactions were explored over time.[8] I was also able to learn about how interracial churches are structured, that is, who is responsible for what, and what formal and informal norms guide church culture.

The qualitative component of the research design was more central to this study, in the sense that I emphasized the stories of Crosstown Community Church and the narratives of people affiliated with the church over the specific relationships among congregational-level variables. In the mixed-methods scenario, I drew upon the National Congregations Study (NCS) to provide a backdrop to the processes taking place in Crosstown and to demonstrate the extent to which these processes were consistent with what the congregational life of interracial churches in the United States looks like generally.[9] Presupposing that whiteness structures interracial churches, the religious practices and organizational characteristics of interracial churches were compared to those of white churches and of African-American churches to determine whether interracial congregational life emulated that which is more common to white churches more than that which is more common to African-American churches.

Throughout this book, my analysis of the findings from the NCS were based upon a definition of an "interracial" church as one where African Americans and whites each comprised between 10% and 90% of the adult church attendees, and where Latinos and Asians each comprised less than 10% of the adult church attendees. Supplementary analyses based upon an 80:20 cutoff to distinguish interracial and racially homogeneous churches were also conducted. The tables showing these results, as well as the results discussed in chapters 1, 2, and 3, are in appendix C. The quantitative approach provided support for the internal validity of the qualitative results and confirmed that the processes that emerged at Crosstown were trustworthy.[10]

Choosing the Case Study Site

The first step in the qualitative component of the research process was deciding upon a site for the case study. I chose to focus on one religious organization so I could conduct a more thorough and complete examination of interracial congregational life and the complex nature of the processes that govern how interracial churches go about doing the work of being diverse. Churches, of course, participate in auxiliary activities, such as Bible study meetings, small group gatherings, and prayer meetings. However, unlike other organizations, such as workplaces or schools, the main activity of churches, the worship service, occurs only once a week. Consequently, there are relatively limited opportunities, especially in my case as a solo researcher, to observe a church's main organizational activities and to interact with the attendees. Choosing to focus on one congregation allowed me to regularly and frequently observe the case study site over an extended period of time. I was able to go deep, so to speak, with one congregation rather than split my energies conducting ethnographies of multiple congregations, which would have diminished my ability to elucidate the rich detail I was looking to achieve for this book. This facilitated my capacity to better understand the religious culture, congregational life, and people of Crosstown Community Church.

After deciding to focus on one congregation, I proceeded to locate a site willing to be studied for this research. Although interracial churches are uncommon in the United States, I was able to visit several interracial churches in the metropolitan area where the study was conducted before finally choosing the site. These churches varied in racial and class composition. Each of them would have been interesting to study in their own right. However, they posed methodological and theoretical challenges for this study. At least for the case study, I relied upon previous work by Chaves and Higgins[11] and by Christerson and Emerson,[12] who employed an 80:20 ratio to delineate between racially homogeneous and interracial congregations. More specifically, an interracial church is defined as a church where no one racial group comprises more than 80% of the church population. Therefore, I did not consider churches that identified as interracial, but where one racial group in the church comprised more than 80% of the congregation. I also purposively conducted a case study of a church where African Americans and whites were primary groups within the church, each comprising between 20% and 80% of the congregation. Evidence has shown that interracial relations between African Americans and whites in the United States are the least likely to occur compared to relations between whites and other racial minority groups.[13] Churches that did not meet this criterion (this included Latino/white interracial churches, Asian/white interracial churches, and churches that were largely white with a mix of other racial groups) were ultimately not considered. As for other black/white interracial churches I visited, the congregations of these churches were also diverse socioeconomically. Moreover, the socioeconomic differences fell along racial lines. African-American attendees tended to be poorer and lower class, while white attendees tended to be educated and middle class. In a church such as this, it would have been difficult to isolate the effects of race versus those of class on congregational life. If the congregational lives of these churches were more similar to those of white churches, it could reasonably be argued that it was the result of class rather than racial dynamics.

I decided upon Crosstown Community Church because this congregation did not demonstrate these challenges. Admittedly, Crosstown's racial composition does not represent the "average" interracial church in the United States. According to the NCS, interracial churches are on average 33% African American. Crosstown was 65% African American. Yet, this characteristic of the church, as well as other church characteristics, such as the race of the pastor, made the church an ideal case for testing the central thesis of this study. Indeed, if a church like Crosstown, where African Americans comprise a majority of the congregation and the pastor is African American, exhibited a congregational culture that primarily benefits whites, it is probable that this would be evident in churches where African Americans have less of a presence. Furthermore, unlike other black/white interracial churches I considered, Crosstown was largely middle class.[14] Both African Americans and whites held professional jobs; they were managers, engineers, and doctors. This allowed me to control for class. The racial dynamics that could potentially emerge in the church could be more clearly identified.

Research Status

When doing participant observation, it is important to recognize your status in the space you are studying. I was an insider at Crosstown on several dimensions. I had been regularly attending Crosstown for four years and had been a member of the church for two years by the time I began the study. I had seriously deliberated whether to study Crosstown or another interracial church. However, for the reasons discussed above, I decided that Crosstown was well suited as a test case for this study. Additionally, my insider status provided me with considerable access in the church. I observed weekly worship services, choir practices, church dinners, business meetings, special programs and classes, small group meetings, and informal gatherings and activities with church attendees. I shared Sunday church dinners with congregants. I hung out with them at their homes and went out to lunch with them after church. I did not hold a leadership position in the church, but was an active member. I sang in the choir and was a member of the worship team. I also acted as a coordinator for the seminar the church held on race and religion, which is discussed in chapter 2. My primary responsibilities as coordinator included organizing seating in the room where the seminar was held; supplying dry erase markers for the whiteboard; and setting up media equipment, like the VCR and television, before each meeting.

My status as an insider brings my subjectivity into question. To limit this weakness, I asked two members of my dissertation committee to visit Crosstown and to provide me with feedback. Their feedback let me know that my ideas and observations were valid. I also had to regularly negotiate my conflicting identities as a researcher and church member. I prioritized my researcher identity. During informal conversations, I avoided providing my own opinion on topics particularly relevant to the study, such as racially charged controversies in the church, despite my desire to do so. But I cannot say that I was a completely dispassionate participant observer. I happened to be studying the church during a rather volatile period. And if asked my opinion about an issue, I honestly provided it and did engage in conversations.

Additionally, I was less able to relax and enjoy the church services or fully participate in church meetings to the degree I would have liked because I was constantly attuned to what was going on sociologically. I often carried a small pad of paper with me to jot down notes about the content, interactions, and practices at worship services and other church activities. Additionally, as an insider, I had to confront the challenge of observing those not-so-positive attributes about the church and people I was studying. This is particularly challenging because, as an insider, my inclination would be to protect the group from any negative exposure. Revealing less flattering findings about the case study also exposed me, as my own identity and sense of self was tied to the group I was studying.

While there are issues of subjectivity for insider ethnographers, insider status also has its benefits. My insider status afforded me access to church literature and documents that would not have been easily available to me if I did not attend the church. I was also able to gain entrée to less accessible spaces, such as the kitchen, church office, and nursery. My status gave me the kind of invisibility that facilitates the observation of organizational activities and social interactions. For example, I would sometimes walk around the church during worship services to observe other activities that were happening in the church during this time. This may be a very suspicious activity for an outsider that could exclude him or her from gaining further access to the group. I was privy to people's thoughts about various church and social topics during informal conversations to which I would likely not be privy as an outsider. Moreover, I was able to elicit answers to questions that might have been perceived as "being nosey" if asked by someone who was not affiliated with the church. Finally, an important benefit of being an insider is that the researcher is less apt to misinterpret what is being observed, as he or she is fluent with the verbal and cultural language of the study group. For these reasons, I hope that the benefits I gained as an insider balanced the deficits I experienced.

Beginning the Research

At the beginning of the research, I met with Pastor Raymond Barnes to request if I could study the church. I explained that this would include observing church activities and interviewing people who were affiliated with the church. I would provide the church with my findings once the research was completed. I was granted permission to study Crosstown after Pastor Barnes took my request under advisement with the elder board. An announcement was made that I was studying the church for my dissertation during a Sunday worship service. The pastor asked that I stand so that people would recognize me as the attendee who was also conducting a study of the church.

Interactions with attendees on a few occasions made it apparent to me that congregants were cognizant that I was studying the church. However, I did not get the sense that it hindered what they would say or how they would behave in my presence. One incident in particular, early in the research, gave me this impression. The worship service had not yet begun. I was sitting in the pews talking with two attendees about some challenges that the church was facing at the time. I pulled out my pad and jotted down a few notes during our conversation. After a moment or so, one of the attendees said to the other something like "Oh, look at Korie writing down notes for her research" and chuckled. She then continued with what she was saying. I was a little embarrassed and felt rather conspicuous. I decided that I would try to be more discreet in the future. Yet, it was apparent to me that people were aware of my status as researcher and church member. They were comfortable sharing their opinions about church matters in my presence. In other instances, I had the impression that my role as researcher in the church made people more willing to share their views and opinions with me. I felt like informants shared their concerns and frustrations, hoping that I might relay their views to the pastors or others in church leadership. I did not assume the role of informant and relay their thoughts to the church leadership, but these concerns helped to inform future interviews and observations.

Pilot interviews were conducted with ten current attendees and one long-time member. These interviews helped to structure the final interview guides and gave me practice for the final interviews. During the eighteen-month study, forty semistructured interviews, based upon the final interview guides, were conducted with current attendees, pastors, long-time attendees, and previous attendees and pastors. I aimed to represent the racial composition of the church with the interview sample. Sixteen African-American and eleven white current attendees were interviewed. I also interviewed three Asian and Latino attendees. However, I did not focus on the voices of the Asian and Latinos attendees in this book as the limited number of interviews did not provide sufficient data to make any claims about their specific experiences in attending an interracial church. The remaining interviews included the senior pastor, a previous pastor, three long-time members, and five past attendees. All interviews were tape recorded and transcribed.

The interviews lasted one to two and a half hours. All but three of the interviews with attendees were conducted in interviewees' homes. The remaining three interviews were done at the church and at an interviewee's workplace. Pastoral interviews were conducted at the church. All interviews were supplemented with field notes. The field notes provided information about all of my interactions with interviewees about the interview, such as phone conversations requesting interviews, nonverbal communication during the interviews, and the interviews' settings. I was familiar with many of the people who attended the church and was therefore able to directly request most of the interviews. But I did not know most of the interviewees well. In fact, I made a point to not interview people whom I considered to be in my closest social network. The majority of the current and past attendees I interviewed were people to whom I had only spoken in passing before the interview. For past and long-time attendees of the church, I asked the current senior pastor and other church leaders to identify these potential informants. Contact information for previous attendees was provided, and I contacted these interviewees directly.

The research began in January 2002 and ended in June 2003. At the end of the study, 790 pages of interview transcripts and 270 single-spaced field note pages, in addition to community and church literature and documents, were accumulated. Interview data and field notes were analyzed by hand. After reading the interviews and field notes, I coded the data. The data were also analyzed by race to see if particular secondary themes were more or less prevalent among attendees from certain racial groups. The voices heard in this book are exemplars of the themes that emerged in the interviews and observations. The particular quotes represent those that would be most clear to readers.

Throughout this book, pseudonyms are used for all informants, the church, and the surrounding neighborhoods and metropolitan area. I have not revealed any sociodemographic data about the informants beyond their race, gender, and sometimes their family status in order to ensure their anonymity. Too much information provided about informants could expose their identities to fellow congregants. I did not want to take this risk. I have also renamed the communities surrounding Crosstown Community Church to protect the identity of the church and its affiliates. Both Mapleton and Anderson are pseudonyms, and even where they are located in relation to each other has been changed.

Getting Acquainted with Crosstown Community Church

Crosstown was founded in 1921. Historically, the church had been an all-white, predominantly middle-class church. It was originally a member of the American Baptist Association. During the 1950s, Crosstown's regular attendance peaked at 1,100. Long-time attendees proudly described the church as one of the better churches to attend in the metropolitan area during this period. However, Crosstown's attendance slowly dwindled over the next three decades, culminating in a drastic loss of attendees during the late seventies and early eighties that resulted from a split over theological issues.[15] The senior pastor at the time led one of the sides of the divide. He and his supporters adhered to strict beliefs about the kinds of cultural practices in which Christians could participate. Others in the church did not share these views. This divide was very bitter for Crosstown members. After more than twenty years, people still tell the story with intense emotion, both sadness and anger. As an elderly white female member recalled the story, she looked me square in the eyes and, with an expression of firm resolve and stubbornness, told me, "we were not going to let them get away with it." The senior pastor was eventually removed from office. Members who supported the senior pastor also left. This internal division so discouraged other regular attendees and members that many of them also left the church. By the end of the crisis, the attendance had decreased to only about 80 regular attendees at the weekly Sunday worship service.

Not surprisingly, the church was in a weakened state after this crisis. Unable to financially support a full-time senior pastor, the church hired a professor from a local Bible college as a part-time interim pastor. With the direction of this pastor, the church began to orient itself toward the local community, which by this time was racially and economically diverse. From the accounts of church leaders at the time, there were no objections to this new church vision from the predominantly white congregation. The church began to identify as a community church and opened its doors to its African-American neighbors.

Over the years since, attendance at Crosstown increased. About 200 people attended the weekly Sunday morning worship service at the time of this study. And the church also became increasingly racially diverse. The congregation at the time of this study was about 65% African American, 30% white, and 5% Latino and Asian. The church continued to be largely middle class.[17] But it had discontinued its affiliation with the American Baptist Association, because, I was told, the denomination had become too theologically liberal.[18] The church's interracial character became central to its identity. This was exemplified in church symbols and literature. One of the church's logos, for example, was a circle of hands of varying skin tones linked together by each hand holding the wrist of the next. And the church's mission statement claimed that the church was "committed to being an inclusive congregation and being intentional in matters of race and class diversity."

Crosstown's racial diversity was greatly facilitated by its geographic location. The church was located on the southern border of Mapleton, adjacent to the neighborhood of Anderson. It rested on a dividing line between lack and wealth, disadvantage and privilege. Prior to beginning the research, I surveyed Mapleton and Anderson to understand the populations that Crosstown was aiming to serve and to attract to the church. The surveys included collecting historical information on the communities, gathering statistics from the Census Bureau; reading local newspapers; talking with community activists, real estate representatives, and community officials; and noting the type and quality of the housing, public spaces, local businesses, and pedestrian activity.

I learned that both Mapleton and Anderson faced complete racial succession as the twentieth century progressed. During the first half of the twentieth century, Anderson was home for several European immigrant groups, including Germans, Swedes, Italians, and Irish. By 1950, European immigrants made up 14% of the community's population. Racial minorities made up less than 0.5% of the neighborhood's population. However, during the 1960s, things changed. Anderson began to experience a rapid racial turnover. The African-American population increased from less than 1% in 1960 to 32% in 1970. By 1990, Anderson was 86% African American, and by 2000 it was nearly 95% African American. Mapleton similarly faced rapid racial succession. However, its response to an event of racial antagonism worked to create a racially integrated community. The home of the first African American in Mapleton was firebombed twice in 1951. In standing up in defense of this family's rights and offering them support, the community set the tone for things to come. In the 1960s, as other metropolitan neighborhoods changed from nearly all white to nearly all African American, seemingly overnight, Mapleton began to take steps to manage the inevitable change coming its way. The Citizens Committee for Human Rights and the Community Relations Commission were established in 1963. In 1968, one of the nation's first local fair housing ordinances, outlawing discrimination, was passed, and in 1973 the town created a policy statement which claimed that "diversity is [Mapleton's] strength." Through a series of initiatives by the community government and private groups, Mapleton became a model of successful racial integration.

During the early 2000s, Mapleton was a middle- to upper middle-class community. Over 50% of the residents of Mapleton had at least a bachelor's degree, and half of these had graduate degrees.[19] The average annual household income was $82,000. It was also a racially diverse community, with whites and blacks comprising 70% and 22% of Mapleton's population, respectively. Additionally, Mapleton's business district thrived with restaurants, professional services, grocery stores, banks, business offices, coffee shops, boutiques, and a movie theater. The community also hosted festivals, sidewalk sales, and outdoor theater and live music in the parks throughout the year.

In contrast to Mapleton, Anderson was a primarily working-class community in 2000. Two-thirds of Anderson residents graduated from high school. Of these high school graduates, half had at least some college. Although Anderson averaged an annual household income of $43,000, the poverty rate was nearly 20%. Moreover, unlike Mapleton, most of the businesses in Anderson were independent fast food restaurants, such as barbeque and soul food spots, dry cleaners, beauty shops, and liquor stores. As predicted by Massey and Denton,[20] Anderson experienced increased neighborhood deterioration as African Americans were increasingly segregated in this community. Many city lots were vacant and overgrown with weeds or had become resting places for rusting cars and appliances. The neighborhood was also plagued with a pervasive drug culture. According to a community activist in Anderson who attended Crosstown, drugs and gangs were the community's most pressing dilemma. It was not uncommon to see groups of young black men, who appeared to be of high school age or younger, standing on street corners during school hours. During my own observations of the neighborhood, I witnessed, from what I could gather, two separate drug transactions on the streets during broad daylight. These discoveries were purely serendipitous, as I was not searching out this kind of activity. Still, the residents of Anderson demonstrated fortitude and resilience in the face of these challenges. There were more than twenty community organizations in Anderson at the time of the study, each specializing in a particular community support or rebuilding effort. Anderson's community organizations and residents employed multiple strategies, including building rehabilitation, mentoring programs, smoke outs, block clubs, and job placement programs, to combat neighborhood deterioration and social disorganization and to improve the socioeconomic condition of its residents.

National Congregations Study (NCS) Analysis

The NCS was the only data set available with a nationally representative sample of U.S. congregations (at the time of this study), which made it optimal for understanding congregational life in America. The purpose of the NCS analysis was to examine if and how interracial churches differ statistically from racially homogeneous churches along certain congregational characteristics, namely, worship practices, extrareligious activities, and leadership qualities. The NCS was generated using a hypernetwork sampling technique. The sample of congregations in this data set was gathered from nominations provided by a random sample of respondents in the 1998 General Social Survey (GSS), a face-to-face national survey of non-institutionalized English-speaking adults in the United States. Respondents in the 1998 GSS who reported that they attended religious services at least once a year were asked the name and location of their religious congregations. After establishing a sample of congregations generated from these nominations, congregations were approached, and informants, usually priests, ministers, or pastors, were identified for interviews. Data were gathered about these congregations from these key informants. A total of 1,236 cases were generated. As a result of the sampling technique, large congregations were overrepresented in the sample. For this study, the unit of analysis is the congregation. The data used in the analysis were weighted inversely proportional to its size to correct for this overrepresentation.[21]

I also limited the quantitative component of this study to Christian congregations with known religious affiliations. There are only five Christian congregations in the NCS that do not claim a particular denominational or religious affiliation. So, this selection criterion did not greatly reduce the overall sample. An examination that includes non-Christian congregations would be an important contribution to our understanding of interracial relations in religious contexts. However, the non-Christian category in the NCS is quite heterogeneous, including Jews, Muslims, and Hindus among other non-Christian religious groups, making it difficult to draw conclusions about this broadly defined group.

And the number of cases for each specific non-Christian category is quite small.

The analysis was conducted in two stages. Using a Wald test, the differences in means between interracial churches and racially homogeneous churches were first examined. At this stage, the direction of the difference was not tested, only whether or not a difference in the means of the two subpopulations existed. I then employed regression analysis to examine the effect of congregational racial composition (i.e., interracial versus racially homogeneous) on various congregational characteristics. With regression analysis, I could determine whether or not the effect of being an interracial church on congregational characteristics differs from that of racially homogeneous churches. I could further determine the direction of that difference, if indeed one existed. In the case of verbal affirmation, for example, I was able to see whether interracial churches were more or less likely to participate in verbal affirmation than white and African-American churches after taking account of other congregational characteristics.

The operationalizations of the variables used for the quantitative analysis are in appendix B. However, the measures for racial integration and charismatic orientation necessitate further explanation. These variables have either not been quantitatively examined in previous research, or there are other possible measures for these variables that others have employed.

Data are available in the NCS on the percentage of African Americans, whites, Asians, and Latinos in the congregation. Following other research on interracial churches, where racial heterogeneity has been consistently employed as evidence of racial integration, I considered a church racially integrated if there was evidence of racial heterogeneity.[22] I recognize that the 90:10 ratio used to conceptualize an interracial church for the multiple regression analyses is rather inclusive. Other research has used an 80:20 ratio to delineate between interracial and racially homogeneous congregations. However, the number of interracial congregations in the National Congregations Study where African Americans and whites each comprise between 20% and 80% of the adult attendance is less than twenty (after accounting for missing data). This low number of cases is not sufficient for multivariate regression analysis, which I desired for this study. I did conduct supplementary analyses using other operationalizations of an interracial church based upon an 80:20 cutoff, discussed below. The overall results (which I briefly discuss below) were consistent with those from the regression analyses using the 90:10 cutoff, demonstrating that the overall pattern is rather robust.

On average, whites, African Americans, Latinos, and Asians comprised 64%, 33%, 3%, and 1% of interracial churches, respectively. Another approach could have been to examine churches on a continuum of racial heterogeneity. However, churches tended toward homogeneity or integration. This variable would be heavily skewed toward homogeneity if it was a continuous measure, as preliminary analysis of the racial composition of congregations in the NCS and other research has indicated.[23] Furthermore, previous qualitative research suggests that interracial churches possess particular qualities that are unique to them, such as challenges with local racial succession, fluctuation of available resources, and organizational commitments to racial diversity.[24] In this regard, we can think of an interracial church as a distinct type of church. Racial integration could also be construed as evidence of actual cross-racial contact between attendees. The NCS does not provide data on whether or not people of different races are actually interacting in the congregations. However, I suspect that it is likely that people of different races, who voluntarily attend interracial churches, do at some level interact with one another.

I have controlled for charismatic orientation in the survey analysis because interracial congregations are disproportionately charismatic. Variation in outcomes could be potentially attributable to charismatic religion, rather than to racial composition. Charismatic orientation is a proxy for a congregation's adherence to charismatic religious practices. It is not itself a measure of effusive worship style. Charismatic congregations tend to possess a particularly strong emphasis on a personal, experiential religion.[25] Speaking in tongues, healing, and gifts of the Holy Spirit are core characteristics of charismatic religion. Churches that exhibit all of these characteristics are coded as congregations that adhere to charismatic religion. There are charismatic (or Pentecostal) denominations. However, charismatic religion has expanded beyond denominational boundaries into other historically noncharismatic denominations and religious traditions. A majority of Americans who adhere to charismatic religion do not belong to charismatic denominations.[26] Therefore, a measure of whether a congregation adheres to charismatic religion is used instead of Pentecostal denominational affiliation.

As mentioned, I conducted supplementary analyses employing varying operationalizations of interracial and racially homogeneous churches
based upon an 80:20 ratio. Beginning in table C-8, an 80:20 ratio is used
to delineate between interracial churches and white and African-American
churches. The statistical power of these comparisons is particularly low,
with only fifteen black/white interracial churches in the NCS sample.
Therefore, they were not discussed in detail. However, despite the limited
statistical power, significant descriptive comparisons emerged. The bivar-
iate results indicate a similar pattern, which is seen with the more inclusive
analysis employed in chapters 1 through 3. Interracial churches differ from
African-American churches for nine of the twelve indicators examined.
Interracial churches differ from white churches for only four out of the
twelve indicators.

In tables C-9–15, I employ a more inclusive definition of an interracial
church, using the 80:20 cutoff. An interracial church is defined as a
congregation where 20%–80% of adult attendees are white, and 20%–
80% of adult attendees are nonwhite (African American, Latino, and Asian
combined). White churches are congregations where whites comprise
more than 80% of the adult attendees, and nonwhite churches are congregations where African Americans, Latinos, and Asians combined comprise more than 80% of the congregation. For this analysis, multiple
regressions were conducted. The results based upon these conceptualizations of interracial, white, and nonwhite churches affirm the findings
discussed in chapters 1 through 3. This type of interracial church differs
from nonwhite churches along nine of the twelve indicators, but differs from white churches along only three of the twelve indicators.

Sharing the Findings with Crosstown

After completing the research, I gave Pastor Barnes a copy of my dissertation, which was an unpolished, rough draft of this book, as I had committed at the beginning of the research project. Copies were made and
shared with the rest of the pastoral staff and with the elder board. From
what I gathered, they met to discuss the research. I was later asked to
present the findings of the research to the rest of the church leaders,
including deacons and coordinators, suggesting to me that the leaders

generally affirmed the research findings and believed that they might be useful for the church more broadly. The presentation was given on a weekday evening in the fellowship room, where the race and religion seminar was held. A racially diverse group of approximately twenty people was present. Pastor Barnes introduced me, praising the research overall, but also providing a caveat explaining that there may be some findings with which people may not agree. I had the distinct impression that these were findings that either he or members of the pastoral staff and elder board did not affirm.

For the presentation, I highlighted the main hypotheses, explained the key findings of the substantive book chapters, and summarized the conclusions, focusing on the archetypical attendees of interracial churches. People asked questions during and after the presentation and shared their feelings and perspectives on Crosstown's experiences as an interracial church. Several people expressed an appreciation of the research and confirmed my findings. People, both African American and white, nodded their heads in agreement throughout the presentation. As I summarized the six archetypical categories of interracial church attendees, a few people said, "that one is me." After the presentation, one African-American woman told me that I told it "like it was" without holding anything back. Later, a white man shared similar sentiments with me. He expressed that I really exposed the white leadership, of which he is a member, but justly so, in his opinion. While it was not my intention to "call people out" or "tell it like it is," people's responses to the presentation led me to believe that the findings of this book resonated, in no small way, with their experiences.

Appendix B: National Congregations Study Variables and Operationalizations

Variables	Operationalizations
Dependent Variables	
Verbal affirmation	Dummy variable: Congregation coded 1 if a person in the congregation said amen or other words of approval during the most recent worship service. Otherwise 0.
Hand raising	Dummy variable: Congregation coded 1 if a person in the congregation raised his/her hand during the most recent worship service. Otherwise 0.
Spontaneous worship	Dummy variable: Congregation coded 1 if a person in the congregation jumped, shouted, or danced spontaneously during the most recent worship service. Otherwise 0.
Worship service length	Number of minutes most recent worship service lasted.
Choir participation	Dummy variable: Congregation coded 1 if, during the most recent worship service, a choir sang in the service. Otherwise 0.
Time of greeting	Dummy variable: Congregation coded 1 if, during the most recent worship service, the congregation participated in a time where people greeted each other by shaking hands or some other way. Otherwise 0.

(continued)

Variables	Operationalizations
Community involvement	Scale 0–9 (overall Cronbach's alpha = 0.60). Items in the scale are based upon dichotomous measures of whether or not the congregation: participated in giving cash to the needy; helping the needy in any way; donating cash to individuals or organizations; feeding the hungry; building or repairing homes; helping the homeless; programs ministering to prison inmates; programs relating to community service in any way; and/or programs focusing on health needs.
Political involvement	Scale 0–8 (overall Cronbach's alpha = 0.67). Items in the scale are based upon dichotomous measures of whether or not the congregation participated in political discussions; shared political opportunities with other congregants; registered voters; lobbied political officials; marched for a political issue; provided voter guides; invited political candidates to speak; and/or invited government officials to speak at the church.
Racial/ethnic heritage preservation	Dummy variable: Congregation coded 1 for having a group that met within past 12 months to discuss the racial/ethnic heritage of a specific group. Otherwise 0.
Race-related discussions	Dummy variable: Congregation coded 1 for having a group that met within past 12 months to discuss race-related topics. Otherwise 0.
African-American pastor	Dummy variable: Congregation coded 1 if head pastor is African American. Otherwise 0.
Nonwhite pastor	Dummy variable: Congregation coded 1 if head pastor is nonwhite. Otherwise 0.
White pastor	Dummy variable: Congregation coded 1 if head pastor is white. Otherwise 0.
Independent Variables	
African-American church	Dummy variable: Congregation coded 1 if more than 90% of adult attendees are African American. Otherwise 0.
African-American (80:20) church	Dummy variable: Congregation coded 1 if more than 80% of adult attendees are African American. Otherwise 0.
White church	Dummy variable: Congregation coded 1 if more than 90% of adult attendees are white. Otherwise 0.
White (80:20) church	Dummy variable: Congregation coded 1 if more than 80% of adult attendees are white. Otherwise 0.
Nonwhite (80:20) church	Dummy variable: Congregation coded 1 if more than 80% of adult attendees are African American, Asian, and/or Latino. Otherwise 0.

(continued)

Variables	Operationalizations
Interracial church	Dummy variable: Congregation coded 1 if between 10% and 90% of adult attendees are white *and* between 10% and 90% of adult attendees are African American *and* Asians and Latinos each comprise less than 10% of the adult attendees. Otherwise 0.
Interracial (80:20) church	Dummy variable: Congregation coded 1 if between 20% and 80% of adult attendees are white *and* between 20% and 80% of adult attendees are African American *and* Asians and Latinos each comprise less than 20% of the adult attendees. Otherwise 0.
Nonwhite/white interracial (80:20) church	Dummy variable: Congregation coded 1 if between 20% and 80% of adult attendees are white *and* between 20% and 80% of adult attendees are African American, Asian, and/or Latino. Otherwise 0.
Percentage with bachelor's degree	Percentage of adult participants with a four-year degree
Percentage with no high school diploma	Percentage of adult participants who have less than a high school diploma
Charismatic orientation	Dummy variable: Congregation coded 1 if attendees practice speaking in tongues, healing, and gifts of the Holy Spirit. Otherwise 0.
Percentage under 35	Percentage of adult participants who are younger than 35 years old
Percentage over 60	Percentage of adult participants who are older than 60 years old
Conservative Protestant	Dummy variable: Congregation coded 1 if conservative Protestant. Otherwise 0.
Liberal Protestant	Dummy variable: Congregation coded 1 if liberal Protestant. Otherwise 0.
Catholic	Dummy variable: Congregation coded 1 if Catholic. Otherwise 0.
South	Dummy variable: Congregation coded 1 if located in the South. Otherwise 0.
Church size	Number of people who participate in congregation's religious activities

Appendix C: Tables

TABLE C-I. Means of Worship Styles and Practices by Interracial, White, and African-American Churches[a]

	Interracial Churches	White Churches	African-American Churches
Spontaneous worship	32%	4%**	61%**
	(.074)	(.008)	(.047)
Verbal affirmation	63%	48%+	93%**
	(.076)	(.021)	(.026)
Hand raising	51%	34%*	90%**
	(.079)	(.020)	(.030)
Worship service length	90 minutes	70 minutes**	128 minutes**
	(5.27)	(.890)	(4.05)
Choir participation	61%	72%	89%**
	(.077)	(.019)	(.031)
Time of greeting	20%	20%	8%+
	(.063)	(.017)	(.026)
N	41	553	107

Significance of difference between interracial (black/white) and white churches or interracial (black/white) and African-American churches: +p < .10 *p < .05 **p < .01, two-tailed.
Standard errors in parentheses.
Data are weighted inversely proportional to congregation size to correct for an overrepresentation of larger congregations in the sample.
a. The definitions for the racial compositions for this table are as follows: Interracial (black/white) churches include congregations where African Americans and whites each comprise between 10% and 90% of adult attendees, and Asians and Latinos each comprise less than 10% of adult attendees. White churches include congregations where whites comprise more than 90% of adult attendees. African-American churches include congregations where African Americans comprise more than 90% of adult attendees.

TABLE C-2. Odds Ratios of Select Worship Practices Predicted by Interracial, White, and African-American Churches (net of other factors)[a]

Independent Variables	Spontaneous Worship	Verbal Affirmation	Hand raising
African-American church[b]	3.17*	4.71**	8.60**
	(1.58)	(2.67)	(4.25)
White church[b]	.156**	.854	.800
	(.076)	(.355)	(.301)
Percentage under 35 years old	1.02**	1.02*	1.01[+]
	(.009)	(.007)	(.006)
Percentage over 60 years old	.986	0.996	.981**
	(.009)	(.006)	(.005)
Percentage with no high school diploma	1.00	1.02*	1.00
	(.009)	(.009)	(.007)
Percentage with bachelor's degree	.984*	.990**	1.00
	(.007)	(.004)	(.004)
Size of congregation	1.00	1.00	1.00
	(.000)	(.000)	(.000)
South	1.69[+]	1.37	1.00
	(.509)	(.281)	(.197)
Catholic[c]	.112**	.231**	.867
	(.088)	(.067)	(.239)
Liberal Protestant[c]	.193**	.166**	.421**
	(.093)	(.036)	(.092)
Charismatic	3.46*	6.31*	13.75**
	(1.73)	(4.91)	(10.48)
N	701	701	701

Significance of difference between interracial (black/white) and white churches or interracial (black/white) and African-American churches: $^+p < .10$ $^*p < .05$ $^{**}p < .01$, two-tailed.

Standard errors in parentheses.

Data are weighted inversely proportional to congregation size to correct for an overrepresentation of larger congregations in the sample.

a. The definitions for the racial compositions for this table are as follows: Interracial (black/white) churches include congregations where African Americans and whites each comprise between 10% and 90% of adult attendees, and Asians and Latinos each comprise less than 10% of adult attendees. White churches include congregations where whites comprise more than 90% of adult attendees. African-American churches include congregations where African Americans comprise more than 90% of adult attendees.

b. Reference category is interracial church.

c. Reference category is conservative Protestant.

TABLE C-3. Coefficients/Odds Ratios of Select Worship Practices Predicted by Interracial, White, and African-American Churches (net of other factors)[a]

Independent Variables	Worship Service Length Coefficients[d]	Choir Participation Odds Ratios[e]	Time of Greeting Odds Ratios[e]
African-American church[b]	33.59**	6.99**	.288*
	(4.56)	(3.27)	(.164)
White church[b]	−14.83**	1.72	.852
	(4.01)	(.612)	(.366)
Percentage under 35 years old	.187**	.999	.973**
	(.064)	(.006)	(.008)
Percentage over 60 years old	−.080	1.00	.994
	(.054)	(.005)	(.006)
Percentage with no high school diploma	−.013	.999	1.00
	(.065)	(.006)	(.008)
Percentage with bachelor's degree	−.055	1.00	1.00
	(.037)	(.004)	(.004)
Size of congregation	.000	1.00*[f]	1.00
	(.000)	(.000)	(.000)
South	3.40[+]	2.05**	.976
	(1.97)	(.423)	(.210)
Catholic[c]	−21.25**	1.13	.192**
	(2.95)	(.340)	(.097)
Liberal Protestant[c]	−9.43**	1.98**	.976
	(2.24)	(.437)	(.226)
Charismatic	15.79**	.875	.162[+]
	(4.41)	(.401)	(.171)
Constant	90.75**	—	—
	(5.08)		
N	701	701	701

Significance of difference between interracial (black/white) and white churches or interracial (black/white) and African-American churches: [+]p < .10 *p < .05 **p < .01, two-tailed.

Standard errors in parentheses.

Data are weighted inversely proportional to congregation size to correct for an overrepresentation of larger congregations in the sample.

a. The definitions for the racial compositions for this table are as follows: Interracial (black/white) churches include congregations where African Americans and whites each comprise between 10% and 90% of adult attendees, and Asians and Latinos each comprise less than 10% of adult attendees. White churches include congregations where whites comprise more than 90% of adult attendees. African-American churches include congregations where African Americans comprise more than 90% of adult attendees.

b. Reference category is interracial church.

c. Reference category is conservative Protestant.

d. OLS regression

e. Logistic regression

f. Odds ratio is 1.0007. While statistically significant, this odds ratio demonstrates a minimally substantive difference.

TABLE C-4. Means of Social and Civic Activities by Interracial, White, and African-American Churches[a]

	Interracial Churches	White Churches	African-American Churches
Community involvement	1.80	1.66	1.07**
	(.266)	(.068)	(.129)
Political involvement	1.6	1.10*	2.14
	(.316)	(.056)	(.188)
Race-related discussions	24%	20%	29%
	(.068)	(.016)	(.044)
Racial/ethnic heritage preservation	15%	4%**	35%*
	(.056)	(.009)	(.046)
N	41	558	107

Significance of difference between interracial (black/white) and white churches or interracial (black/white) and African-American churches: $p < .10$ *$p < .05$ **$p < .01$, two-tailed.

Standard errors in parentheses.

Data are weighted inversely proportional to congregation size to correct for an overrepresentation of larger congregations in the sample.

a. The definitions for the racial compositions for this table are as follows: Interracial churches include congregations where African Americans and whites each comprise between 10% and 90% of adult attendees, and Asians and Latinos each comprise less than 10% of adult attendees. White churches include congregations where whites comprise more than 90% of adult attendees. African-American churches include congregations where African Americans comprise more than 90% of adult attendees.

TABLE C-5. Coefficients of Select Social and Civic Activities Predicted by Interracial, White, and African-American Churches (net of other factors)[a]

Independent Variables	Community Involvement	Political Involvement
African-American church[b]	−2.46	.893**
	(.280)	(.266)
White church[b]	−1.88	−.190
	(.246)	(.234)
Percentage under 35 years old	−.004	.002
	(.004)	(.004)
Percentage over 60 years old	.000	−.004
	(.003)	(.003)
Percentage with no high school diploma	−.007[+]	.003**
	(.004)	(.004)
Percentage with bachelor's degree	.010**	.006**
	(.002)	(.002)
Size of congregation	.000**[d]	.000**[d]
	(.000)	(.000)
South	−.241*	−.220[+]
	(.121)	(.115)
Catholic[c]	.176	.247
	(.180)	(.172)
Liberal Protestant[c]	.629**	.198
	(.137)	(.131)
Charismatic	.071	1.21**
	(.264)	(.251)
Constant	1.35**	.907**
	(.312)	(.300)
N	706	706

Significance of difference between interracial (black/white) and white churches or interracial (black/white) and African-American churches: [+]p < .10 *p < .05 **p < .01, two-tailed.

Standard errors in parentheses.

Data are weighted inversely proportional to congregation size to correct for an overrepresentation of larger congregations in the sample.

a. The definitions for the racial compositions for this table are as follows: Interracial (black/white) churches include congregations where African Americans and whites each comprise between 10% and 90% of adult attendees, and Asians and Latinos each comprise less than 10% of adult attendees. White churches include congregations where whites comprise more than 90% of adult attendees. African-American churches include congregations where African Americans comprise more than 90% of adult attendees.

b. Reference category is interracial church.

c. Reference category is conservative Protestant.

d. The coefficient is .0002. While statistically significant, this odds ratio demonstrates a minimally substantive difference.

TABLE c-6. Odds Ratios of Select Social and Civic Activities Predicted by Interracial, White, and African-American Churches (net of other factors)[a]

Independent Variables	Race-Related Discussions	Racial/Ethnic Heritage Preservation
African-American church[b]	2.59*	6.78**
	(1.23)	(3.84)
White church[b]	.977	.335*
	(.419)	(.185)
Percentage under 35 years old	1.00	1.01
	(.007)	(.009)
Percentage over 60 years old	.996	1.01
	(.006)	(.009)
Percentage with no high school diploma	.998	.988
	(.008)	(.010)
Percentage with bachelor's degree	1.02**	1.02*
	(.004)	(.006)
Size of congregation	1.00**[d]	1.00+[e]
	(.000)	(.000)
South	.946	.854
	(.198)	(.267)
Catholic[c]	.497+	1.62
	(.187)	(.705)
Liberal Protestant[c]	1.86**	.835
	(.441)	(.337)
Charismatic	2.31*	3.20*
	(.916)	(1.50)
Constant	—	—
N	706	706

Significance of difference between interracial (black/white) and white churches or interracial (black/white) and African-American churches: [+]p < .10 *p < .05 **p < .01, two-tailed.

Standard errors in parentheses.

Data are weighted inversely proportional to congregation size to correct for an overrepresentation of larger congregations in the sample.

a. The definitions for the racial compositions for this table are as follows: Interracial (black/white) churches include congregations where African Americans and whites each comprise between 10% and 90% of adult attendees, and Asians and Latinos each comprise less than 10% of adult attendees. White churches include congregations where whites comprise more than 90% of adult attendees. African-American churches include congregations where African Americans comprise more than 90% of adult attendees.

b. Reference category is interracial church.

c. Reference category is conservative Protestant.

d. The coefficient is 1.0004. While statistically significant, this odds ratio demonstrates a minimally substantive difference.

e. The coefficient is 1.0002. While statistically significant, this odds ratio demonstrates a minimally substantive difference.

TABLE C-7. Means of Race for Head Pastors by Interracial, White, and African-American Churches[a]

	Interracial Churches	White Churches	African-American Churches
African-American head pastor	28%	0.2%**	93%**
	(.066)	(.002)	(.024)
White head pastor	68%	98%**	7%**
	(.069)	(.006)	(.024)
N	47	586	116

Significance of difference between interracial (black/white) and white churches or interracial (black/white) and African-American churches: [+]p < .10 *p < .05 **p < .01, two-tailed.

Standard errors in parentheses.

Data are weighted inversely proportional to congregation size to correct for an overrepresentation of larger congregations in the sample.

a. The definitions for the racial compositions for this table are as follows: Interracial (black/white) churches include congregations where African Americans and whites each comprise between 10% and 90% of adult attendees, and Asians and Latinos each comprise less than 10% of adult attendees. White churches include congregations where whites comprise more than 90% of adult attendees. African-American churches include congregations where African Americans comprise more than 90% of adult attendees.

TABLE C-8. Means of Congregational Practices and Characteristics by
Interracial (80:20), White (80:20), and African-American (80:20) Churches[a]

Independent Variables	Interracial Churches (80:20)	White Churches (80:20)	African-American Churches (80:20)
Spontaneous worship	27%	6%**	58%*
	(.118)	(.009)	(.043)
Verbal affirmation	47%	49%	92%**
	(.133)	(.019)	(.023)
Hand raising	47%	36%	90%**
	(.133)	(.018)	(.026)
Worship service length	96 minutes	71 minutes**	127 minutes**
	(8.78)	(.858)	(3.45)
Choir participation	73%	71%	86%
	(.118)	(.017)	(.030)
Time of greeting	13%	19%	8%
	(.091)	(.015)	(.024)
Race-related discussions	27%	22%	32%
	(.118)	(.016)	(.042)
Racial/ethnic heritage preservation	0%	7%	35%**
	(.000)	(.010)	(.042)
Community involvement	1.87	1.65	1.05*
	(.456)	(.060)	(.110)
Political involvement	0.8	1.19	2.2*
	(.261)	(.052)	(.182)
African-American clergy	20%	.1%**	93%**
	(.107)	(.001)	(.022)
White clergy	67%	98%**	6%**
	(.126)	(.006)	(.021)
N	15	688	130

Significance of difference between interracial (black/white) and white churches or interracial (black/white) and African-American churches: $^{+}p < .10$ $^{*}p < .05$ $^{**}p < .01$, two-tailed.

Standard errors in parentheses.

Data are weighted inversely proportional to congregation size to correct for an overrepresentation of larger congregations in the sample.

a. The definitions for the racial compositions for this table are as follows: Interracial (80:20) churches include congregations where African Americans and whites each comprise between 20% and 80% of adult attendees, and Asians and Latinos each comprise less than 20% of adult attendees. White (80:20) churches include congregations where whites comprise more than 80% of adult attendees. African-American (80:20) churches include congregations where African Americans comprise more than 80% of adult attendees.

TABLE C-9. Means of Worship Styles and Practices by Nonwhite/White
Interracial (80:20), White (80:20), and Nonwhite (80:20) Churches[a]

	Nonwhite/White Interracial Churches	White Churches	Nonwhite Churches
Spontaneous worship	13%	5%**	53%**
	(.032)	(.009)	(.041)
Verbal affirmation	54%	48%	87%**
	(.047)	(.020)	(.027)
Hand raising	63%	36%**	84%**
	(.045)	(.019)	(.027)
Worship service length	76 minutes	70 minutes*	121 minutes**
	(2.61)	(.830)	(3.51)
Choir participation	66%	72%	84%**
	(.044)	(.018)	(.030)
Time of greeting	12%	20%*	6%+
	(.031)	(.016)	(.020)
N	115	619	149

Significance of difference between interracial (nonwhite/white) and white churches or interracial (non-white/white) and African-American churches: $^+p < .10$ $^*p < .05$ $^{**}p < .01$, two-tailed.

Standard errors in parentheses.

Data are weighted inversely proportional to congregation size to correct for an overrepresentation of larger congregations in the sample.

a. The definitions for the racial compositions for this table are as follows: Nonwhite/white interracial (80:20) churches include congregations where nonwhites (African Americans, Asians, and Latinos combined) and whites each comprise between 20% and 80% of adult attendees. White (80:20) churches include congregations where whites comprise more than 80% of adult attendees. Nonwhite (80:20) churches include congregations where nonwhites (African Americans, Asians, and Latinos combined) comprise more than 80% of adult attendees.

TABLE C-10. Odds Ratios of Select Worship Practices Predicted by Nonwhite/ White Interracial (80:20), White (80:20), and Nonwhite (80:20) Churches (net of other factors)[a]

Independent Variables	Spontaneous Worship	Verbal Affirmation	Hand Raising
Nonwhite (80:20) church[b]	4.02**	3.21**	2.71**
	(1.54)	(1.11)	(.865)
White (80:20) church[b]	.288**	.889	.491**
	(.111)	(.222)	(.116)
Percentage under 35 years old	1.02*	1.02**	1.02**
	(.007)	(.006)	(.005)
Percentage over 60 years old	.983*	.997	.988**
	(.008)	(.005)	(.005)
Percentage with no high school diploma	1.07	1.01*	1.01
	(.007)	(.007)	(.006)
Percentage with bachelor's degree	.986*	.990**	.993[+]
	(.006)	(.003)	(.003)
Size of congregation	1.00	1.00*[d]	1.00
	(.000)	(.000)	(.000)
South	1.39	1.34	1.01
	(.361)	(.109)	(.174)
Catholic[c]	.004**	.165**	.772
	(.027)	(.040)	(.174)
Liberal Protestant[c]	.284**	.186**	.462**
	(.115)	(.037)	(.092)
Charismatic	3.36**	1.34	2.82**
	(1.29)	(.450)	(.977)
N	883	883	883

Significance of difference between nonwhite/white interracial and white churches or nonwhite/white interracial and nonwhite churches: [+]$p < .10$ *$p < .05$ **$p < .01$, two-tailed.

Standard errors in parentheses.

Data are weighted inversely proportional to congregation size to correct for an overrepresentation of larger congregations in the sample.

a. The definitions for the racial compositions for this table are as follows: Nonwhite/white interracial (80:20) churches include congregations where nonwhites (African Americans, Asians, and Latinos combined) and whites each comprise between 20% and 80% of adult attendees. White (80:20) churches include congregations where whites comprise more than 80% of adult attendees. Nonwhite (80:20) churches include congregations where nonwhites (African Americans, Asians, and Latinos combined) comprise more than 80% of adult attendees.

b. Reference category is nonwhite/white interracial church.

c. Reference category is conservative Protestant.

d. The coefficient is 1.0002. While statistically significant, this odds ratio demonstrates a minimally substantive difference.

TABLE C-11. Coefficients/Odds Ratios of Select Worship Practices Predicted by Nonwhite/White Interracial (80:20), White (80:20), and Nonwhite (80:20) Churches (net of other factors)[a]

Independent Variables	Worship Service Length Coefficients[d]	Choir Participation Odds Ratios[e]	Time of Greeting Odds Ratios[e]
Nonwhite (80:20) church[b]	32.70**	3.64**	.251**
	(3.13)	(1.18)	(.120)
White (80:20) church[b]	−11.06**	1.33	.777
	(2.61)	(.327)	(.264)
Percentage under 35 years old	.137*	1.00	.972**
	(.055)	(.005)	(.008)
Percentage over 60 years old	−.118*	1.00	.966
	(.047)	(.005)	(.006)
Percentage with no high school diploma	−.048	1.00	.997
	(.056)	(.005)	(.008)
Percentage with bachelor's degree	−.046	1.00	1.00
	(.034)	(.003)	(.004)
Size of congregation	−.002*	1.00**[f]	.999
	(.000)	(.000)	(.000)
South	4.30*	2.05**	.854
	(1.80)	(.384)	(.176)
Catholic[c]	−25.83**	1.42	.099**
	(2.38)	(.352)	(.050)
Liberal Protestant[c]	−10.40**	2.12**	1.11
	(2.10)	(.441)	(.244)
Charismatic	11.42**	.590[+]	.488
	(3.15)	(.179)	(.268)
Constant	91.16**	—	—
	(3.69)		
N	883	883	883

Significance of difference between nonwhite/white interracial and white churches or nonwhite/white interracial and nonwhite churches: [+]p < .10 *p < .05 **p < .01, two-tailed.

Standard errors in parentheses.

Data are weighted inversely proportional to congregation size to correct for an overrepresentation of larger congregations in the sample.

a. The definitions for the racial compositions for this table are as follows: Nonwhite/white interracial (80:20) churches include congregations where nonwhites (African Americans, Asians, and Latinos combined) and whites each comprise between 20% and 80% of adult attendees. White (80:20) churches include congregations where whites comprise more than 80% of adult attendees. Nonwhite (80:20) churches include congregations where nonwhites (African Americans, Asians, and Latinos combined) comprise more than 80% of adult attendees.

b. Reference category is nonwhite/white interracial church.

c. Reference category is conservative Protestant.

d. OLS regression

e. Logistic regression

f. The coefficient is 1.0005. While statistically significant, this odds ratio demonstrates a minimally substantive difference.

TABLE C-12. Means of Social and Civic Activities by Nonwhite/White Interracial (80:20), White (80:20), and Nonwhite (80:20) Churches[a]

	Nonwhite/White Interracial (80:20) Churches	White (80:20) Churches	Nonwhite (80:20) Churches
Community involvement	1.6	1.7	1.1**
	(.134)	(.064)	(.110)
Political involvement	1.6	1.2**	2.2*
	(.169)	(.054)	(.173)
Race-related discussions	23%	21%	30%
	(.039)	(.016)	(.038)
Racial/ethnic heritage	15%	6%**	34%**
preservation activities	(.033)	(.009)	(.039)
N	116	624	150

Significance of difference between interracial (nonwhite/white) and white churches or interracial (nonwhite/white) and African-American churches: $^+p < .10$ $^*p < .05$ $^{**}p < .01$, two-tailed.

Standard errors in parentheses.

Data are weighted inversely proportional to congregation size to correct for an overrepresentation of larger congregations in the sample.

a. The definitions for the racial compositions for this table are as follows: Nonwhite/white interracial (80:20) churches include congregations where nonwhites (African Americans, Asians, and Latinos combined) and whites each comprise between 20% and 80% of adult attendees. White (80:20) churches include congregations where whites comprise more than 80% of adult attendees. Nonwhite (80:20) churches include congregations where nonwhites (African Americans, Asians, and Latinos combined) comprise more than 80% of adult attendees.

TABLE C-13. Coefficients of Social and Civic Activities Predicted by Nonwhite/ White Interracial (80:20), White (80:20), and Nonwhite (80:20) Churches (net of other factors)[a]

Independent Variables	Community Involvement	Political Involvement
Nonwhite (80:20) church[b]	−.080	.849**
	(.187)	(.192)
White (80:20) church[b]	−.050	−.133
	(.157)	(.160)
Percentage under 35 years old	−.004	.001
	(.003)	(.003)
Percentage over 60 years old	.000	−.003
	(.002)	(.003)
Percentage with no high school diploma	−.009**	.004
	(.003)	(.004)
Percentage with bachelor's degree	.009**	.006**
	(.002)	(.002)
Size of congregation	.000**[d]	.000**[d]
	(.000)	(.000)
South	−.205[+]	−.143
	(.109)	(.111)
Catholic[c]	.282	.338*
	(.143)	(.146)
Liberal Protestant[c]	.636**	.238[+]
	(.127)	(.129)
Charismatic	.094	1.015**
	(.187)	(.190)
Constant	1.14**	.800**
	(.222)	(.226)
N	890	890

Significance of difference between nonwhite/white interracial and white churches or nonwhite/white interracial and nonwhite churches: [+]$p < .10$ *$p < .05$ **$p < .01$, two-tailed.

Standard errors in parentheses.

Data are weighted inversely proportional to congregation size to correct for an overrepresentation of larger congregations in the sample.

a. The definitions for the racial compositions for this table are as follows: Nonwhite/white interracial (80:20) churches include congregations where nonwhites (African Americans, Asians, and Latinos combined) and whites each comprise between 20% and 80% of adult attendees. White (80:20) churches include congregations where whites comprise more than 80% of adult attendees. Nonwhite (80:20) churches include congregations where nonwhites (African Americans, Asians, and Latinos combined) comprise more than 80% of adult attendees.

b. Reference category is nonwhite/white interracial church.

c. Reference category is conservative Protestant.

d. The coefficient is .0002. While statistically significant, this odds ratio demonstrates a minimally substantive difference.

TABLE C-14. Odds Ratios of Social and Civic Activities Predicted by Nonwhite/White Interracial (80:20), White (80:20), and Nonwhite (80:20) Churches (net of other factors)[a]

Independent Variables	Race-Related Discussions	Racial/Ethnic Heritage Activities
Nonwhite (80:20) church[b]	1.72[+]	4.40**
	(.536)	(1.56)
White (80:20) church[b]	.746	.467*
	(.201)	(.161)
Percentage under 35 years old	1.00	1.01
	(.006)	(.007)
Percentage over 60 years old	.999	1.00
	(.005)	(.004)
Percentage with no high school diploma	1.00	1.01
	(.006)	(.007)
Percentage with bachelor's degree	1.01**	.997
	(.003)	(.007)
Size of congregation	1.00**[d]	1.00
	(.000)	(.000)
South	.884	.7955
	(.167)	(.210)
Catholic[c]	.876	1.71[+]
	(.231)	(.538)
Liberal Protestant[c]	2.15**	1.27
	(.465)	(.419)
Charismatic	1.87*	2.04*
	(.541)	(.673)
Constant	—	—
N	890	890

Significance of difference between nonwhite/white interracial and white churches or nonwhite/white interracial and nonwhite churches: [+]$p < .10$ *$p < .05$ **$p < .01$, two-tailed.

Standard errors in parentheses.

Data are weighted inversely proportional to congregation size to correct for an overrepresentation of larger congregations in the sample.

a. The definitions for the racial compositions for this table are as follows: Nonwhite/white interracial (80:20) churches include congregations where nonwhites (African Americans, Asians, and Latinos combined) and whites each comprise between 20% and 80% of adult attendees. White (80:20) churches include congregations where whites comprise more than 80% of adult attendees. Nonwhite (80:20) churches include congregations where nonwhites (African Americans, Asians, and Latinos combined) comprise more than 80% of adult attendees.

b. Reference category is nonwhite/white interracial church.

c. Reference category is conservative Protestant.

d. The coefficient is 1.0002. While statistically significant, this odds ratio demonstrates a minimally substantive difference.

TABLE C-15. Means of Race of Head Pastor of Nonwhite/White Interracial (80:20), White (80:20), and Nonwhite (80:20) Churches[a]

	Interracial Churches	White Churches	Nonwhite Churches
Nonwhite head pastor	11%	2%**	81%**
	(.029)	(.006)	(.032)
White head pastor	82%	94%**	15%**
	(.036)	(.009)	(.029)
N	116	626	151

Significance of difference between interracial (nonwhite/white) and white churches or interracial (non-white/white) and nonwhite churches: $^+$p < .10 *p < .05 **p < .01, two-tailed.

Standard errors in parentheses.

Data are weighted inversely proportional to congregation size to correct for an overrepresentation of larger congregations in the sample.

a. The definitions for the racial compositions for this table are as follows: Nonwhite/white interracial (80:20) churches include congregations where nonwhites (African Americans, Asians, and Latinos combined) and whites each comprise between 20% and 80% of adult attendees. White (80:20) churches include congregations where whites comprise more than 80% of adult attendees. Nonwhite (80:20) churches include congregations where nonwhites (African Americans, Asians, and Latinos combined) comprise more than 80% of adult attendees.

Appendix D: Interview Guides

Current Crosstown Community Church Attendee

1. What is your race?
2. What is your ethnicity?
3. What is the highest level of education you have achieved?
4. Do you work outside of the home? If yes, is your job full or part time? What do you do?
5. Did you ever serve in the military? In which branch did you serve? How long were you in the service?

6. During high school, was the neighborhood where you lived racially diverse? Which racial groups (e.g., blacks, whites, Asians, Latinos) were represented? What was the approximate proportion of each group?
7. How about your high school, was it racially diverse? Which racial groups were represented? What was the approximate proportion of each group?
8. Who were your closest friends during high school? Please just give me initials or first names only.

9. For each friend during high school, ask:
    a. Where did you meet _____ (e.g., church, neighborhood, school, etc.)?
    b. What was _____ gender?
    c. What was _____ race?
10. Did you grow up in a Christian home?
11. If so, how would you describe (*childhood church*)?
    a. What was the denomination of this church?
    b. What was the racial composition of this church?
    c. Approximately how many people attended this church?
12. How regularly did your family attend the Sunday services there?
13. How would you describe the Sunday services at this church?
    a. How would you describe the worship music?
    b. What were the sermons like?
    c. What did you enjoy about the Sunday services?

PREVIOUS CHURCH

14. Were you attending a church before coming to Crosstown?
15. If so, how long were you going to (*previous church*)?
16. What first attracted you to (*previous church*)?
17. How would you describe (*previous church*)?
    a. What was the denomination of this church?
    b. What was the racial composition of this church?
    c. Approximately how many people attended this church?
18. How regularly did you attend the Sunday services there?
19. How would you describe the Sunday services?
    a. How would you describe the worship music at this church?
    b. What were the sermons like?
    c. What did you enjoy about the Sunday services?

CROSSTOWN

20. How long have you been going to Crosstown?
21. What first attracted you to Crosstown?
22. How regularly would you say you attend the Sunday services?
23. Besides the Sunday services, what ministries or groups are you involved in?

24. Do you have children? Do your children participate in youth group or the Sunday children's service? How about other children's activities at Crosstown?

25. What do you enjoy about being at Crosstown?

26. Do you have any frustrations about Crosstown?

27. What do you think about the Sunday services? What do you enjoy about them? What would you like to see change?

28. What do you think about the way the (*ministry(ies) they are involved in*) are organized? What would you like to see changed?

29. Have you ever thought about leaving Crosstown? If so, what were the main factors in considering leaving? What made you decide to stay?

30. What do you think about the racial/ethnic diversity at Crosstown? What does this add to the church? Does it make anything more difficult, in your opinion?

31. Do you feel like you have a group of close friends at the church? Would you say that they are your closest friends, or do you have closer friends outside of church?

32. Who would you say are your top three closest friends that go to Crosstown, in order of closeness? Please just give me initials or first names only.

33. Who would you say are your top three closest friends that don't go to Crosstown, in order of closeness? Please just give me initials or first names only.

34. Would you say you are closer to (*Crosstown friend #1*) or (*outside friend #1*)? Would you say you are closer to (*Crosstown friend #2*) or (*outside friend #2*)? Would you say you are closer to (*Crosstown friend #3*) or (*outside friend #3*)?

35. What is the race or ethnicity of each of these six friends?

36. What is the highest level of education of each of these six friends?

37. Do any of these friends work outside the home? If so, what do each of them do?

IDENTITY

38. How would you describe yourself (e.g., race, faith, job, marital status, etc.)? *or* When you think about who you are, what comes to mind?

39. Please look through this stack of cards and pull out all that apply. If there is something that is not on the cards, there are blank cards you can fill out to add to the list.

40. (After interviewee pulls out the cards): From top to bottom, order the cards in level of closeness to you or from the one you most identify with to the one you least identify with.

    a. What does it mean to you to be (black, white, etc.)?

RACIAL ATTITUDES

41. On average, blacks have worse jobs, income, and housing than white people. Why do you think this is? Do you think this should be solved? If so, how?

42. Does racism still exist in the United States? Why do you think it still/no longer exists?

43. What, if anything, should the church do about racial inequality?

Former Crosstown Community Church Attendee

BACKGROUND

1. What is your race?
2. What is your ethnicity?
3. What is the highest level of education you have achieved?
4. Do you work outside of the home? If yes, is your job full or part time? What do you do?
5. Did you ever serve in the military? In which branch did you serve? How long were you in the service?

CROSSTOWN EXPERIENCE

1. When and how long did you attend Crosstown?
2. What first attracted you to Crosstown?
3. How regularly would you say you attended the Sunday services?
4. What do you think about the Sunday services at Crosstown? What did you enjoy about them? What would you have liked to see change?
5. Besides the Sunday services, were you involved in other ministries or groups?

6. What do you think about the way the (*other ministry(ies) mentioned*) was organized? Was there anything that you would have liked to see changed?

7. Do you have children? Did your children participate in the youth group or the Sunday children's service? How about other children's activities at Crosstown?

8. Did you enjoy being at Crosstown? If so, what did you enjoy about being at Crosstown?

9. Did you have any frustrations with Crosstown? If so, what were they?

10. What were the main factors that led you to leave Crosstown?

11. What did you think about the racial/ethnic diversity at Crosstown? Do you think racial/ethnic diversity added anything to the church? Do you think it made anything more difficult, in your opinion?

12. Do you feel like you had a group of close friends at Crosstown? Would you say that they were your closest friends at the time, or did you have closer friends outside of church?

13. Who would you say your top three closest friends were at Crosstown, in order of closeness, when you attended the church? Please just give me first names or initials.

14. What is the race or ethnicity of each of these three friends?

15. What is the highest level of education of each of these friends?

16. Do any of these friends work outside the home? If so, what do each of them do?

17. Are you still friends with these people?

CURRENT CHURCH EXPERIENCE

18. Do you currently attend a church?

19. If so, how long have you been going to (*current church*)?

20. What first attracted you to (*current church*)?

21. How would you describe (*current church*)?

    a. What is the denomination of this church?

    b. What is the racial composition of this church?

    c. Approximately how many people attend this church?

22. How regularly would you say you attend the Sunday services there?

23. How would you describe the Sunday services?
    a. How would you describe the worship music at this church?
    b. What are the sermons like?
    c. What do you enjoy about the Sunday services?
    d. Is there anything you would like to see changed?
24. Besides the Sunday services, are you involved in other ministries or groups?
25. What do you think about the way the (small groups or ministries they are involved in) are organized? What, if anything, would you like to see changed?
26. Do you feel like you have a group of close friends at this church? Would you say that they are your closest friends, or do you have closer friends outside of church?
27. Who would you say are your top three closest friends that go to (current church), in order of closeness? Please just give me initials or first names only.
28. Who would you say are your top three closest friends that don't go to (current church), in order of closeness? Please just give me initials or first names only.
29. Would you say you are closer to (current church friend #1) or (outside friend #1)? Would you say you are closer to (current church friend #2) or (outside friend #2)? Would you say you are closer to (current church friend #3) or (outside friend #3)?
30. What is the race or ethnicity of each of these six friends?
31. What is the highest level of education of each of these six friends?
32. Do any of these friends work outside the home? If so, what do each of them do?
33. What do you enjoy about being at (current church)?
34. Do you have any frustrations about (current church)?
35. Have you ever thought about leaving (current church)? If so, what were the main factors in considering leaving? What made you decide to stay?

IDENTITY

36. How would you describe yourself (e.g., race, faith, job, marital status, etc.)? or When you think about who you are, what comes to mind?

37. Please look through this stack of cards and pull out all that apply. If there is something that is not on the cards, there are blank cards you can fill out to add to the list.

38. (After interviewee pulls out the cards): From top to bottom, order the cards in level of closeness to you or from the one you most identify with to the one you least identify with.

    a. What does it mean to you to be (*black, white, etc.*)?

RACIAL ATTITUDES

44. On average, blacks have worse jobs, income, and housing than white people. Why do you think this is? Do you think this should be solved? If so, how?

45. Does racism still exist in the United States? Why do you think it still/no longer exists?

46. What, if anything, should the church do about racial inequality?

Current Pastor

1. How long have you been pastor at Crosstown?

2. Have you been a pastor at other churches? (If yes, go to the next questions. Otherwise, skip to question 7.)

3. How many other churches have you pastored?

4. At the last church you pastored before this one, how long were you the pastor?

5. What was your pastoral rank (i.e., senior pastor, assistant pastor, youth pastor, etc.)?

6. How would you describe the last church you pastored?

    a. What was the denomination of this church?

    b. How would you describe the worship music at this church?

    c. What was the racial composition of this church?

    d. What was the mission statement or central ministry focus of this church? (If there was a third church, repeat questions 6a–6d.)

7. Do you have formal religious educational training (i.e., seminary, Bible college, etc.)? If yes, what kind of training have you had?

8. Did you attend church growing up?

9. If so, how would you describe this church?
   a. What was the denomination of this church?
   b. How would you describe the worship music at this church?
   c. What was the racial composition of the church?
   d. What were the sermons like?
10. You mentioned earlier that you have been at Crosstown for (*length of time*). What were the deciding factors that led you to come to pastor Crosstown?
11. What was Crosstown like when you first came?
    a. What was the racial composition at that time?
    b. In what ways was the worship style at the time similar or different from what it is now?
    c. What about the leadership structure, was it similar to how it is now (i.e., was there an elder and deacon board)?
    d. I realize you are the first black pastor of the church. Did you feel welcomed and supported by the congregation?
12. Does the church have any programs or strategies that are for the specific purpose of fostering or creating racial diversity? If so, what are they?
13. Do you think there are specific challenges that come with Crosstown being an interracial church? If so, can you give me some examples of what those challenges are?
14. Are there rewards to Crosstown being an interracial church? If so, can you give me some examples of these rewards?
15. Do you think it is important for churches, in general, to be interracial? Explain further.
16. Are there rewards that you feel you gain as a pastor of an interracial church?
17. Are there challenges that you have encountered as a pastor of an interracial church? If so, what are some of those challenges? Have you been able to overcome these challenges? If so, how did you or the church do this?
18. Are you involved in any pastors' groups? Can you tell me about them?
    a. What is the purpose(s) of this group(s)?
    b. Where do you meet and how often?
    c. What churches are represented by the pastors who attend this group(s)?
    d. What is the racial composition of the group?

19. Over the past year, has the church participated in any activities with other churches? Can you tell me about the events and the churches that partnered with the church?

Former Pastor

1. How long were you a pastor at Crosstown? When did you become a pastor at Crosstown?
2. Have you been a pastor at other churches? (If yes, go to the next questions. Otherwise, skip to question 7.)
3. How many other churches have you pastored?
4. At the last church you pastored, before coming to Crosstown, how long were you the pastor?
5. What was your pastoral rank (i.e., senior pastor, assistant pastor, youth pastor, etc.)?
6. How would you describe this church?
   a. What was the denomination of this church?
   b. How would you describe the worship music at this church?
   c. What was the racial composition of this church?
   d. What was the mission statement or central ministry focus of this last church you pastored? (If there was a third church, repeat questions 6a–6d.)
7. Do you have formal religious educational training (i.e., seminary, Bible college, etc.)? If yes, what kind of training have you had?
8. Did you attend church growing up?
9. If so, how would you describe this church?
   a. What was the denomination of this church?
   b. How would you describe the worship music at this church?
   c. What was the racial composition of the church?
   d. What were the sermons like?
10. You mentioned earlier that you were at Crosstown for (*length of time*). What were the deciding factors that led you to come to pastor Crosstown?
11. What was Crosstown like when you first came?
    a. What was the racial composition at that time?
    b. In what ways was the worship style at this time similar or different from when you left?

    c. What about the way the church leadership was organized, did it change during your tenure at the church (i.e., was there an elder and deacon board)?

    d. (If at the church during Pastor Raymond Barnes' appointment ask): Pastor Raymond Barnes is the first black pastor of Crosstown. Did you feel he was welcomed and supported by the congregation? Were there any conflicts or concerns about his appointment?

12. Did the church have any programs or strategies that were for the specific purpose of fostering or creating racial diversity? If so, what were they?

13. Do you think there were specific challenges that came with Crosstown being an interracial church? If so, can you give me some examples of what those challenges were?

14. Were there rewards to Crosstown being an interracial church? If so, can you give me some examples of what those rewards were?

15. Do you think it is important for churches in general to be interracial? Explain further.

16. Were there rewards that you feel you specifically gained as a pastor of an interracial church?

17. Were there challenges that you specifically encountered as a pastor of an interracial church? If so, what were some of those challenges? Were you able to overcome those challenges? If so, how did you or the church do this?

Long-Time Crosstown Attendee

1. How long have you been attending Crosstown?
2. What was the church like when you first came?

    a. How many people attended the Sunday services?

    b. What were some of the other programs or activities that went on at the church?

    c. Were most of the people from the local community or were people from throughout the metropolitan area?

    d. Who was the pastor at the time? What was he like?

    e. What was the racial/ethnic makeup of the church at the time?

3. How has the church changed since you've been here?

4. What do you think new members of Crosstown should know about the history of the church?

5. What are the most important or significant events in Crosstown's history?

6. When did African Americans begin attending the church?

7. Was there any concern among the members with African Americans coming to the church?

8. Pastor Barnes is the first African-American pastor of this church. Were there any members who did not approve of Pastor Barnes' appointment as senior pastor? If so, what were some of the reasons?

Notes

INTRODUCTION

1. King 2000.

2. See Skinner 1968 and Perkins 1976 for more on Thomas Skinner's and John Perkins's experiences with and thoughts on racial reconciliation. Also take a look at Emerson and Smith 2000: 54–55 for a definition of racial reconciliation.

3. Some examples include Anderson 2004; Cenkner 1996; Foster 1997; Law 1996; Perkins and Rice 1993; and Ortiz 1996, among others.

4. Emerson and Smith 2000.

5. For schools, see James 1989; Anderson 1988; Franklin 2000; Montejano 1987; Takaki 1989; Walters 2001; Reardon and Yun 2002. For workplaces, see Collins 1995; Tomaskovic-Devey 1993; Fosu 1993; Wilson 1995; Anderson and Shapiro 1996; Semyonov et al. 1984. For neighborhoods, see Massey and Denton 1987, 1993; Meyer 2000; Jackson 1985; Frey and Farley 1996; Harris 2001.

6. Lesick 1980.

7. Emerson and Smith 2000: 47–48.

8. Blau 1977, 1984.

9. Throughout the book, I use "African American" and "black" interchangeably to refer to people of African descent who live in the United States.

10. Wilkes and Iceland 2004.

11. Tomaskovic-Devey 1993; Fosu 1993; Beck et al. 1980; Kulis and Shaw 1996; Collins 1997; Wilson 1995; Anderson and Shapiro 1996; Semyonov et al. 1984.

12. Emerson and Woo 2006 propose that churches that begin as racially diverse are more likely to develop and sustain racially egalitarian religious organizations. They point to Bridgeway Community Church, which was started by an interracial team of leaders, as an exemplar of such a church. However, Priest and Priest 2007 tell the story of a church that originated out of a merger between an African-American church and a white church as a response to a call to racial integration. Unlike Bridgeway, this church rather swiftly reproduced white structural and cultural dominance, suggesting that other factors, in addition to historical origins, matters for interracial churches' ability to develop and sustain racially egalitarian organizations.

13. See Cornell and Hartman 1988.

14. Whites have been shown to be more averse to interracial interactions with African Americans than are Latinos and Asians (Warren and Twine 1997). This is evident in interracial marriage rates where black/white interracial marriage is the least common interracial marriage combination (Qian 1997, 1999). Furthermore, black/white residential segregation remains considerably higher than Latino/white and Asian/white residential segregation (Frey and Farley 1996; Massey et al. 1994).

15. The seven major historic black denominations that comprise the black church are the African Methodist Episcopal (AME); the African Methodist Episcopal Zion (AMEZ); the Christian Methodist Episcopal (CME); the National Baptist Convention, USA, Incorporated (NBC); the National Baptist Convention of America, Unincorporated (NBCA); the Progressive National Baptist Convention (PNBC); and the Church of God in Christ (COGIC) (Lincoln and Mamiya 1990: 1).

16. Mays and Nicholson 1933; Frazier 1964; Morris 1984.

17. Borkholder 1999.

18. Omi and Winant 1994; Bonilla-Silva 2001.

19. Cornell and Hartman 1988.

20. Guglielmo 2003.

21. See Lopez (1996) for more on the United States' naturalization laws.

22. Doane 2003.

23. Whiteness is most often referred to in the literature as a racial identity (Doane 2003; Lipsitz 1998; Flagg 1993; Lopez 1996; Frankenberg 1993; Lewis 2004; Roediger 1991). But it is also referred to as (and at times in conjunction with) "the state of being white" (Lopez 1996), an "ideological order" (Hartigan 1999, 2003), a social category (Doane 2003; Lopez 1996), and a social position or location within a racial hierarchical structure (Doane 2003; Andersen 2003; Lewis 2004; Mills 2003; Almaguer 1994).

24. Montagu 1974; Gould 1981; Davis 1991.

25. Jacobson 1999; Lopez 1996; Davis 1991.

26. Davis 1991.

27. Davis 1991.

28. For whites' better opportunities at securing home financing, see Yinger 1995, Munnell et al. 1996, Oliver and Shapiro 1995; living in better neighborhoods, see Jargowsky 1997, Jackson 1985, Massey and Denton 1993; attending higher-quality schools, see Nettles and Perna 1997, Allen et al. 2002; obtaining more stable employment, see Harris and Farley 2000; obtaining more prestigious, higher-waged jobs, see Semyonov et al. 1984, Tomaskovic-Devey 1993, Fosu 1993, Kulis and Shaw 1996, Collins 1997; and evading prison sentences, see LaFree 1985, Myers 1979, Kennedy 1997.

29. All three of these do not have to be present to ensure racial dominance. South Africa is one example of this as whites were structurally advantaged despite being a numerical minority in the country.

30. Doane 2003: 7.

31. Peggy McIntosh, in her essay on white privilege, enumerated these ways in which she, as a white woman, experiences everyday white privilege. See McIntosh 1988.

32. For more on the ability to define racial boundaries, see Lopez 1996 and Davis 1991. For studies that show local communities' and the federal government's role in instituting policies and programs that blatantly discriminate against African Americans and Latinos, see Massey and Denton 1993; and Jackson 1985. For more on whites' influence on educational systems, see Scheurich and Young 1998; Asante 1991; Wills 1996; and Epstein 1998.

33. Doane 2003; Andersen 2003; Flagg 1993.

34. Lewis 2004; Hartigan 1999.

35. Lipsitz 1998: vii.

36. Bobo and Zubrinsky 1996; Kluegel and Smith 1982; Schuman, Steeh, and Bobo 1985; Kinder and Sears 1981; Sears 1988; Bonilla-Silva 1997, 2001, 2003.

37. Lipsitz 1998.

38. Lewis 2004.

39. Flagg 1993: 983.

40. Williams 1997; Flagg 1993.

41. Waters 1990.

42. Terry 1981; Feagin and Vera 1995; Tatum 1997; Martin et al. 1996; Flagg 1993.

43. Loescher 1948.

44. Reimers 1965. Also see Boles 1988 for more on race and religion during the antebellum era in the United States.

45. Frazier 1964.

46. Reimers 1965.

47. Frazier 1964; Reimers 1965; McPherson 1975.

48. Frazier 1964.

49. Lincoln and Mamiya 1990.

50. Reimers 1965: 31.

51. Mays and Nicholson 1933; Morris 1984.

52. Mays and Nicholson 1933; Frazier 1964; Morris 1984.

53. Mays and Nicholson 1933; Frazier 1964; Morris 1984.

54. Mays and Nicholson 1933; Lincoln 1974.

55. Morris 1984: 5.

56. There is evidence that some northerners, particularly northern aboli-tionists, did not adhere to white supremacy (Dumond 1972). Nevertheless, the general view was that blacks were of a subordinate race, even if they should not be enslaved (Reimers 1965).

57. Litwack 1961: 199–201, originally from the *Journal of the Proceedings of the Annual Convention of the Protestant Episcopalian Church in the State of New York* (1846), 72.

58. Reimers 1965, originally from *Religious Herald* 9 (January 8, 1874): 2. Also see Harvey 2003 for more on the role of religion in racial ideologies.

59. Even leaders in the abolitionist movement were hesitant to challenge be-liefs about racial difference and segregation, as revealed by the Lane Rebels movement in Cincinnati, Ohio (Lesick 1980).

60. Cole 1966; Emerson and Smith 2000.

61. Reimers 1965.

62. Matthews 1997.

63. Luker 1991: 72.

64. Kramer 1954.

65. Reimers 1965; Oldham 1935.

66. Reimers 1965.

67. Reimers 1965.

68. Reimers 1965.

69. Parker 1968.

70. Manis 1987.

71. Catchings 1952.

72. The Episcopalian denomination, for example, developed committees and policies specifically aimed at increasing racial diversity. However, the extent to which these policies have been actualized is limited (Shattuck 2000).

73. Dougherty 2003.

74. Emerson and Smith 2000.

75. See Chaves et al. 1999 for more on the methodology used to generate the National Congregations Study.

76. I use pseudonyms to protect the identities of the case study church and its attendees from those who read the book but also from people affiliated with the church. On very few occasions, I also changed other characteristics of inter-viewees, such as gender, to further ensure that their identities are concealed from other Crosstown affiliates. I explained to Pastor Barnes and other pastors inter-viewed that, given their position in the church, I would not be able to hide their identities to this degree, particularly from people who attend the church.

77. Orum, Feagin, and Sjoberg 1991: 2.

CHAPTER 1

1. Ammerman 1997: 55.

2. Chaves 1998.

3. According to Emerson and Smith 2000, in 90% of American congregations, 90% of the people are of one race (135–136).

4. Mitchell 1970: 162–177. Also see Hamilton 1972; Pipes 1970; Spencer 1987; Stewart 1997.

5. See Emerson and Smith 2000: 76–80 for more.

6. Eldredge 2001.

7. Cymbala and Merrill 1997.

8. *Christianity Today* is an evangelical magazine issued monthly.

9. Interviewees were not prompted to consider Crosstown's worship or music style specifically.

10. Barrett 1974; Frazier 1964; Herskovits 1970; Lincoln and Mamiya 1990; Mitchell 1970; Pinn 2002; Pitts 1989, 1991; Raboteau 1978, 1995.

11. DuBois 2003: 136.

12. Pitts 1989: 282.

13. Music is also integral to this process. The music style of African-American worship, rooted in African music traditions, serves to develop "spiritual transport" (Lincoln and Mamiya 1990).

14. This is not to say that white congregations and African-American congregations do not vary when it comes to participation in effusive worship. White, younger, and charismatic congregations are known to participate in such practices (Shibley 1998). There are, of course, African-American congregations that do not participate in shouting or other forms of effusive worship. Nevertheless, there is consistent evidence that African-American churches are inclined to participate in shouting and other forms of effusive worship practices (Raboteau 1978, 1995; Lincoln and Mamiya 1990; Nelson 1996).

15. *Culture* is understood to include norms, behaviors, values, beliefs, and symbols. See Peterson (1979) for a review of how culture is conceptualized more broadly in the United States. Also see Murdock 1945.

CHAPTER 2

1. Drake and Cayton 1970; Lincoln and Mamiya 1990; Morris 1984.

2. Chaves and Higgins 1992.

3. Chappell 2004 argues that the structure of religion in the United States, which has simultaneously acted as a unifying force in the black community and as a moment for fissure among whites in the United States (southern whites in particular) has facilitated sociopolitical movements, like the Civil Rights movement. The imbalance in the centrality of religion among whites and African Americans is what Chappell argues to be one of the key reasons for the Civil

Rights movement's success. Other research comparing the social and political participation of white and African-American Christians in the United States includes Barnes 2004; Beyerlein and Chaves 2003; Cavendish 2000; Chaves 1999; Chaves and Higgins 1992; Chaves and Tsitsos 2001; Cnaan et al. 2004; Cnaan and Boddie 2001; Owens and Smith 2005; Tsitsos 2003; Wood 1994. It is suggested that nonwhite Christian traditions' greater participation levels in extra-religious social and civic activities is because nonwhite Christians possess a more collectivistic and communal world view than do white Christians (Bellah et al. 1996; Emerson and Smith 2000; Stevens-Arroyo 1998; Lincoln and Mamiya 1990).

4. Morris 1984; Pattillo-McCoy 1998; Alex-Assensoh 2004.

5. Beyerlein and Chaves 2003 find that African-American churches are particularly inclined to participate in political activities. However, they also note that churches "specialize" in different kinds of political activities based upon their racial composition and religious tradition.

6. Chaves 2004 similarly reports that American churches are not inclined to participate in community or social activities.

7. Warner 1988; Roozen et al. 1984; Mock 1992.

8. The communities where participating churches were located did not have a large proportion of African-American churches. In my survey of Mapleton specifically, I was able to find only one predominantly African-American church.

9. Emerson and Smith 2000.

10. Emerson and Smith 2000.

11. Lincoln and Mamiya 1990; Warner 1988; Roozen et al. 1984.

12. See Emerson and Smith 2000: 76 for more on the cultural toolkit of white evangelicals.

CHAPTER 3

1. The NCS only has data on the race of head clergy. Of course, more measures in the NCS of leadership characteristics, particularly as they relate to race, would better inform our understanding of the role of race in the structure of leadership in interracial churches, as well as how interracial churches compare to other churches along these sorts of characteristics.

2. Finke and Dougherty 2002 find that seminary training affects the religious beliefs, ideologies, and social networks of church pastors so much that it is not uncommon for church pastors to differ from their congregations on religious beliefs and doctrine. Moreover, seminary-trained pastors are tied to a broader social network that extends beyond the congregation. The ties to this social network provide pastors with valuable social capital. Consequently, seminary-trained pastors' main reference groups include those which are part of their broader seminary-based social network.

3. "Brother" or "sister" in this context is slang used to refer to people who identify as black or African American.

4. Christerson, Edwards, and Emerson 2005 find that white families with children perceive that attending an interracial church is a potential detriment to their children. In these instances, while attending an interracial church may have been very important to them initially, once they have to consider the impact of attending an interracial church on their children, multiracial interaction is no longer a priority in selecting a church.

5. This is according to the youth pastor, who had collected attendance information on the youth who attended church youth programs.

6. Church members are regular attendees who have completed an "Introduction to Crosstown" Sunday school class. During the class, people learn about the church's history and its specific religious beliefs and tenets. They also participate in an interview with a member of the elder board to establish the congruity of their religious beliefs with those of the church. After having completed the class and interview, the elder board decides whom they will recommend to the church as candidates for church membership. During a quarterly church business meeting, existing church members vote on the cohort of church member candidates. Members, unlike regular attendees, are able to vote on church business and can be considered for lay leadership positions. During my time at Crosstown, I never witnessed the congregation deny membership to a church member candidate.

7. Warner 1993.

8. Christerson, Edwards, and Emerson 2005 talk more about why whites are more likely to leave interracial churches in *Against All Odds: The Struggle for Racial Integration in Religious Organizations*.

9. Emerson et al. 2001; Crowder 2000; Lewis et al. 2004; Logan et al. 1996; Quillian 1999; South and Crowder 1997; Bobo and Zubrinsky 1996.

10. Lipsitz 1998 introduces the idea of "investing" in whiteness. He argues that white Americans invest in whiteness as a means of maintaining their structural advantage.

11. Lareau 1987; Lamont and Lareau 1988; Lareau and Horvat 1999; Bourdieu 1977, 1986; Bourdieu and Passeron 1977; DiMaggio 1982; DiMaggio and Mohr 1985.

12. Guglielmo 2003; Ignatiev 1995; Brodkin 1998; Roediger 1991. For European immigrants, in particular, this has often meant holding racist beliefs about and engaging in discriminatory acts against African Americans.

13. Lamont and Lareau 1988; Kingston 2001.

14. Lareau and Horvat 1999; Brubaker 1993; Robbins 1991.

15. Lamont and Lareau 1988.

CHAPTER 4

1. Blau 1977.

2. Thoits 1996.

3. McCall and Simmons 1978; Stryker 1968.

4. Thoits 1996; Hoggs et al. 1996.

5. Hoggs et al. 1996; McCall and Simmons 1978.

6. Tajfel 1981: 255.

7. Waters 1990.

8. Waters 1990 argues that these ethnic ties are also symbolic because they are not necessarily reflective of whites' true ancestry. Whites choose European ethnic identities that they perceive to have the most distinctive cultural traits.

9. Bobo et al. 1997; Lopez 1996; Jacobson 1999.

10. Frankenberg 1993.

11. Williams 1997; Doane 1997, 2003.

12. Broman et al. 1988; Allen et al. 1989.

13. Demo and Hughes 1990; Rosenberg and Simmons 1972; Rosenberg 1979.

14. Demo and Hughes 1990; Harris 1995.

15. Harris 1995.

16. Sigelman and Welch 1993; Sigelman et al. 1996; Emerson and Smith 2000.

17. See Gurin, Miller, and Gurin 1980, Broman et al. 1988, Demo and Hughes 1990, Thompson 1992, Tajfel 1978 for more. The third dimension, a perspective on the social structural location of the racial group, has been primarily used in past research to conceptualize racial and ethnic identity for blacks in particular (Toomer 1975; Tajfel 1978).

18. I would like to thank Elise Martel and Maria Krysan for helping me to develop this methodological approach.

19. The identities listed on the cards were mother, father, single mom, single dad, daughter, son, grandfather, grandmother, upper class, middle class, working class, lower class, blue collar, tradesman, student, professional, educated, homemaker, retired, unemployed, employed, wealthy, poor, Christian, saved, evangelical, Bible believing, agnostic, atheist, urban, suburban, rural, female, male, immigrant, foreigner, African American, black, white, Caucasian, Native American, Asian, Latino, American, disabled, Democrat, Republican, married, wife, husband, divorced, widow, widower, single, adult, young adult, middle aged, senior citizen.

20. In the identity literature, identity is often conceptualized as a "feeling of closeness" to a particular group (Broman et al. 1988; Demo and Hughes 1990; Harris 1995).

21. Other research has found that African-American and Native American ministers discuss their racial experiences within a framework of suffering and loss. These ministers further contribute their spiritual growth and development to these experiences (Davidson et al. 2003; D'Antonio et al. 2001).

22. Terry 1981; Feagin and Vera 1995; Tatum 1997; Martin et al. 1996.

23. It is important to note the potential effect of the interviewer's race on interviewees' responses for this section of the interview particularly. The race of the interviewer has been shown to bias interviewees' responses (Hatchett and

Schuman 1975; Krysan 1998; Schuman and Converse 1971). Respondents are prone to provide responses which are suspected to not offend an "other" race interviewer or that are considered socially desirable. Asked by an African-American interviewer to share their thoughts and perspectives on black/white social inequality, white respondents may be less inclined to employ individually oriented explanations, such as lack of motivation or biological inferiority. However, the open-ended structure of the interview questions allowed me to deconstruct interviewees' responses more thoroughly and to more accurately assess their understanding of and capacity to apply particular explanations to racial inequality. Nonetheless, this method afforded interviewees the least amount of "privacy," and they may have favored a particular explanation over another because of supposed interviewer expectations.

24. I followed Emerson and Smith's (2000: 86–87, 99–106, 123–127) question format here.

25. Emerson and Smith 2000.

26. Emerson and Smith 2000.

27. Emerson and Smith 2000.

28. I cannot definitively say that African Americans' inclination to draw upon a meritocratic ideology to explain racial inequality is due to selection bias or other factors. However, other research has also found that African Americans consistently draw upon meritocracy as an explanation for racial inequality (Bonilla-Silva and Embrick 2001). They argue that this is because African Americans, as a minority group, are influenced by the dominant views and ideologies.

29. Waters 1990; Frankenberg 1993; Terry 1981; Feagin and Vera 1995; Tatum 1997; Martin et al. 1996.

30. Emerson and Smith 2000.

31. Peggy McIntosh observed a similar paradox among whites. She shared in her personal reflections on whiteness, "as a white person, I realized I had been taught about racism as something which puts others at a disadvantage, but had been taught not to see one of its corollary aspects, white privilege, which puts me at an advantage" (McIntosh 1988: 220–229).

32. Becker 1998; Marti 2005.

33. Marti 2005.

34. Marti 2005: 181.

35. Emerson and Smith 2000.

36. Teachman et al. 2000.

37. For more on jobs see Collins 1995; neighborhood experiences, see Pattillo-McCoy 1999; and access to wealth, see Oliver and Shapiro 1995.

CHAPTER 5

1. Sigelman et al. 1996; Ellison and Powers 1994; Emerson et al. 2002; Fong and Isajiw 2000.

2. Samuelson and Zeckhauser 1988.

3. One interviewee, while she hadn't regularly interacted with African Americans as a teenager, had lived in an interracial neighborhood and attended an interracial high school with Asians.

4. Iannaccone 1990.

5. There was only one white interviewee who attended a church as a youth where nonwhites also attended. However, the worship practices and style of this church were similar to what other white interviewees said about their childhood churches.

6. I followed the social network question format of Christerson and Emerson 2003.

CHAPTER 6

1. Blau 1977.

2. McPherson et al. 1992; Popielarz and McPherson 1995; McPherson and Smith-Lovin 1987.

3. Popielarz and McPherson 1995.

4. McPherson et al. 1992; Popielarz and McPherson 1995.

5. Popielarz and McPherson 1995.

6. Wuthnow 1988; Gay and Ellison 1993.

7. Emerson and Smith 2000.

8. Emerson and Smith 2000: 155.

9. Christerson and Emerson 2003.

10. Bates 1975; Lears 1985.

11. Femia 1975.

12. Gramsci 1971.

13. Bates 1975; Golding 1992.

14. Bates 1975; Adamson 1980.

15. Simms 1999; Bates 1975.

16. Sernett 1975.

17. See Simms 1999 for more on the role of religion in counterhegemonic movements during slavery.

18. Jackson 1985; Omi and Winant 1994; Bates 1975; Golding 1992.

19. Bates 1975: 363.

20. The American dream, often symbolized by owning a home, has been more easily attained by whites, ostensibly providing evidence of its validity for all groups. Yet, structural conditions, such as race-based federal housing policies, have made it more difficult for subordinate racial groups to gain a good education or build wealth. Housing policies implemented by the Federal Housing Authority initially restricted FHA loans to all-white neighborhoods. The ability to take out government-insured thirty-year mortgages, the first of their kind, opened up the possibility of the American dream to thousands of white families. Whites

with very little money could begin the path toward home ownership. Since good public education and wealth are tied to home ownership, these racist policies were also ensuring the dominant status of whites for future generations. See Kenneth Jackson's *Crabgrass Frontier* (1985) for more.

21. Bonilla-Silva 2001; Omi and Winant 1994; Lewis 2004.

22. See 137–166 in Bonilla-Silva 2001 for more on the different frames of color-blind ideology.

23. Bonilla-Silva and Embrick 2001.

24. Bonilla-Silva and Embrick 2001: 60

25. Bonilla-Silva and Embrick 2001; Lears 1985. See Poulantzas 1982 for more on the impact of dominant ideologies on subordinate classes.

26. Omi and Winant 1994.

27. Morris 1984.

28. Omi and Winant 1994.

29. Omi and Winant 1994: 68.

30. Stevens-Arroyo 1995. Also see Billings and Scott 1994 for a review of the literature on the role of religion in oppositional movements.

31. Quoted from J. S. Mills (1848) in Gaertner, Pattanaik, and Suzumera 1991: 162.

32. Becker 1998 has similarly shown that interracial churches downplay the sociopolitical content of race and rather focus on personal experiences in an effort to minimize potential discord and to create ties among church members. A potential outcome of emphasizing personal experiences and identities is that religious, social, or political activities that could potentially threaten unity, even if these activities are congruent with their religious tradition and culture in general, are avoided.

33. Morris 1984: 7.

34. Doane 2003; Lopez 1996; Lewis 2004; Takaki 1993; Lipsitz 1998; Williams 1997.

35. Emerson and Woo 2006. Also see Marti 2005; and Christerson, Edwards, and Emerson 2005 for more examples.

36. Bonilla-Silva 2003; Lewis 2005.

APPENDIX A

1. Jick 1979; Tashakkori and Teddlie 1998; Denzin 1978; Patton 1990.

2. Campbell and Fiske 1959; Greene et al. 1989; Jick 1979.

3. Lofland and Lofland 1995.

4. Bernard 1995; Tashakkori and Teddlie 1998.

5. Bernard 1995; Tashakkori and Teddlie 1998; Babbie 1989; Lofland and Lofland 1995.

6. Zussman 2004.

7. I drew upon *Studying Congregations: A New Handbook*, edited by Nancy Ammerman, Jackson W. Carroll, Carl S. Dudley, and William McKinney, as well as other methodological texts, for guidance on conducting participant observation of Crosstown.

8. For more on case studies, see Feagin, Orum, and Sjoberg 1991.

9. Tashakkori and Teddlie 1998.

10. Tashakkori and Teddlie 1998.

11. Chaves and Higgins 1992.

12. Christerson and Emerson 2003.

13. Warren and Twine 1997; Qian 1997, 1999; Frey and Farley 1996; Massey et al. 1994.

14. This estimate was provided by a member of the pastoral staff. Data from informal conversations and the in-depth interviews confirm this assessment.

15. This account of the theological positions of the church during the split is solely based upon interviews with current long-time members. Hence, the depiction may be biased against those who left the church. However, whatever the specifics of the reasons for this division, this split was theologically, not racially, based.

16. According to Emerson and Woo's typology of interracial churches, Crosstown would be considered a "survival embracing" church. These churches, after experiencing a precipitous drop in attendance for a variety of reasons, re-evaluate their missions to minister to people from diverse backgrounds. Emerson and Woo 2006: 57.

17. This is an estimate from a member of the pastoral staff.

18. The church no longer strongly identifies with its Baptist roots.

19. Demographic data provided on Mapleton and Anderson are from the 2000 census.

20. Massey and Denton 1993.

21. See Chaves 1998 and Chaves et al. 1999 for more on the weighting procedures for the National Congregations Study.

22. Christerson and Emerson 2003; Smith 1993; Emerson and Kim 2003; and Wedam 1999 are examples of previous research that has operationalized interracial churches as evidence of racial heterogeneity in the organization. Nevertheless, what constitutes racial integration is debatable and has been for some time in academic circles, ranging from racial heterogeneity to complete pluralism, including the integration of values, ideas, and norms (Bogardus 1958).

23. Dougherty 2003 found that the modal church is completely racially homogeneous in the United States.

24. See Emerson and Kim 2003; and Christerson et al. 2005 for more.

25. Cerillo 1999; Shibley 1998; Spittler 1999; Synan 1971.

26. Smidt et al. 1999.

Bibliography

Adamson, W. L. 1980. *Hegemony and Revolution: A Study of Antonio Gramsci's Political and Cultural Theory.* Berkeley: University of California Press.

Alba, Richard D., John R. Logan, and Brian Stults. 2000. "How Segregated Are Middle Class African-Americans?" *Social Problems* 47:543–558.

Alex-Assensoh, Yvette M. 2004. "Taking the Sanctuary to the Streets: Religion, Race, and Community Development in Columbus, OH." *Annals of the American Academy of Political and Social Sciences* 594:79–91.

Allen, Richard L., Michael C. Dawson, and Ronald E. Brown. 1989. "A Schema-Based Approach to Modeling an African-American Racial Belief System." *American Political Science Review* 83: 421–441.

Allen, Walter, Marguerite Bonous-Hammarth, and Robert Ternishi. 2002. *Stony the Road We Trod . . . The Black Struggle for Higher Education in California.* San Francisco, CA: James Irvine Foundation.

Almaguer, Tomas. 1994. *Racial Fault Lines: The Historical Origins of White Supremacy in California.* Berkeley: University of California Press.

Ammerman, Nancy Tatom. 1997. *Congregation and Community.* New Brunswick, NJ: Rutgers University Press.

Ammerman, Nancy T., Jackson W. Carroll, Carl S. Dudley, and William McKinney (eds.). 1992. *Studying Congregations: A New Handbook.* Nashville, TN: Abingdon.

Andersen, Margaret L. 2003. "Whitewashing Race: A Critical Perspective on Whiteness," in *White Out: The Continuing Significance of Racism,* edited by Ashley W. Doane and Eduardo Bonilla-Silva, 21–34. New York: Routledge.

Anderson, David. 2004. *Multicultural Ministry: Finding Your Church's Unique Rhythm.* Grand Rapids, MI: Zondervan.

Anderson, Deborah, and David Shapiro. 1996. "Racial Differences in Access to High-Paying Jobs and the Wage Gap between Black and White Women." *Industrial and Labor Relations Review* 49:273–286.

Anderson, James. D. 1988. *The Education of Blacks in the South, 1860–1935.* Chapel Hill: University of North Carolina Press.

Asante, Molefi Kete. 1991. "The Afrocentric Idea in Education." *Journal of Negro Education* 60:170–180.

Babbie, Earl. 1989. *The Practice of Social Research.* Belmont, CA: Wadsworth.

Barnes, Sandra L. 2004. "Priestly and Prophetic Influences on Black Church Social Services." *Social Problems* 51:202–221.

Barrett, Leonard E. 1974. *Soul-Force: African Heritage in Afro-American Religion.* Garden City, NY: Anchor Press/Doubleday.

Bates, Thomas R. 1975. "Gramsci and the Theory of Hegemony." *Journal of the History of Ideas* 36:351–366.

Beck, E. M., Patrick M. Horan, and Charles M. Tolbert. 1980. "Industrial Segmentation and Labor Market Discrimination." *Social Problems* 28: 113–130.

Becker, Penny Edgell. 1998. "Making Inclusive Communities: Congregations and the 'Problem' of Race." *Social Problems* 45:451–471.

Bellah, Robert N., Richard Madsen, William M. Sullivan, Ann Swidler, and Steven M. Tipton. 1996. *Habits of the Heart: Individualism and Commitment in American Life.* Berkeley: University of California Press.

Bernard, H. Russell. 1995. *Research Methods in Anthropology: Qualitative and Quantitative Approaches.* Thousand Oaks, CA: Sage.

Beyerlein, Kraig, and Mark Chaves. 2003. "The Political Activities of Religious Congregations in the United States." *Journal for the Scientific Study of Religion* 42:229–246.

Billings, Dwight, and Shanna L. Scott. 1994. "Religion and Political Legitimation." *Annual Review of Sociology* 20:173–202.

Blau, Peter M. 1977. *Inequality and Heterogeneity: A Primitive Theory of Social Structure.* New York: Free Press.

———. 1984. *Crosscutting Social Circles.* Orlando, FL: Academic.

Bobo, Lawrence, James Kluegel, and Ryan Smith. 1997. "Laissez-Faire Racism: The Crystallization of a Kinder, Gentler, Anti-Black Ideology," in *Racial Attitudes in the 1990s: Continuity and Change,* edited by S. Tuch and J. Martin, 15–42. Westport, CT: Praeger.

Bobo, Lawrence, and Camille Zubrinsky. 1996. "Attitudes on Residential Integration: Perceived Status Differences, Mere In-Group Preference, or Racial Prejudice?" *Social Forces* 74:883–909.

Bogardus, Emory. 1958. "Integration as a Current Concept." *Sociology and Social Research* 42:207–212.

Boles, John B. (ed.). 1988. *Masters and Slaves in the House of the Lord: Race and Religion in the American South 1740–1870.* Lexington: University of Kentucky Press.

Bonilla-Silva, Eduardo. 1997. "Rethinking Racism: Toward a Structural Interpretation." *American Sociological Review* 62:465–480.

———. 2001. *White Supremacy and Racism in the Post–Civil Rights Era.* Boulder, CO: Lynne Rienner.

———. 2003. *Racism without Racists: Color-Blind Racism and the Persistence of Racial Inequality in the United States.* New York: Rowman and Littlefield.

Bonilla-Silva, Eduardo, and David G. Embrick. 2001. "Are Blacks Color Blind Too? An Interview-Based Analysis of Black Detroiters' Racial Views." *Race and Society* 4:47–67.

Borkholder, Joy. 1999. "For Richer, for Poorer." *Generation Quarterly* 7:5.

Bourdieu, Pierre. 1977. "Cultural Reproduction and Social Reproduction," in *Power and Ideology in Education*, edited by Jerome Karabel and A. H. Halsey, 487–511. New York: Oxford University Press.

———. 1986. "The Forms of Capital," in *Handbook of Theory and Research for the Sociology of Culture*, edited by John Richardson, 241–258. New York: Greenwood.

Bourdieu, Pierre, and Jean-Claude Passeron. 1977. *Reproduction in Education, Society and Culture.* Beverly Hills, CA: Sage.

Brewer, Marilynn B. 1991. "The Social Self: On Being the Same and Different at the Same Time." *Personality and Social Psychology Review* 17:475–482.

———. 1999. "The Psychology of Prejudice: Ingroup Love or Outgroup Hate?" *Journal of Social Issues* 55:429–444.

Brodkin, Karen. 1998. *How Jews Became White Folks and What That Says about Race in America.* New Brunswick, NJ: Rutgers University Press.

Broman, Clifford L., Harold W. Neighbors, and James S. Jackson. 1988. "Racial Group Identification among Black Adults." *Social Forces* 67: 146–159.

Brubaker, Rogers. 1993. "Social Theory as Habitus," in *Bourdieu: Critical Perspectives*, edited by Craig C. Calhoun, Edward LiPuma, and Moishe Postone, 212–235. Chicago: University of Chicago Press.

Campbell, Donald T., and D. W. Fiske. 1959. "Convergent and Discriminant Validation by the Multitrait-Multimethod Matrix." *Psychological Bulletin* 54:297–312.

Carmines, Edward G., and James A. Stimson. 1989. *Issue Evolution*. Princeton, NJ: Princeton University Press.

Catchings, L. Maynard. 1952. "Interracial Activities in Southern Churches." *Phylon* 13:54–56.

Cavendish, James C. 2000. "Church-Based Community Activism: A Comparison of Black and White Catholic Congregations." *Journal for the Scientific Study of Religion* 39:64–77.

Cenkner, William (ed.). 1996. *The Multicultural Church: A New Landscape in U.S. Theologies*. New York: Paulist Press.

Cerillo, Augustus. 1999. "The Beginnings of American Pentecostalism: A Historiographical Overview," in *Pentecostal Currents in American Protestantism*, edited by Edith L. Blumhofer, Russell P. Spittler, and Grant A. Wacker, 229–259. Urbana: University of Illinois Press.

Chappell, David. 2004. *A Stone of Hope: Prophetic Religion and the Death of Jim Crow*. Chapel Hill: University of North Carolina Press.

Chaves, Mark. 1998. *National Congregations Study*. Data file and codebook. Tucson: University of Arizona, Department of Sociology.

———. 1999. "Religious Congregations and Welfare Reform: Who Will Take Advantage of 'Charitable Choice'?" *American Sociological Review* 64: 836–846.

———. 2004. *Congregations in America*. Cambridge, MA: Harvard University Press.

Chaves, Mark, and Lynn M. Higgins. 1992. "Comparing the Community Involvement of Black and White Congregations." *Journal for the Scientific Study of Religion* 31:425–440.

Chaves, Mark, Mary Ellen Koneiczky, Kraig Beyerlein, and Emily Barman. 1999. "The National Congregations Study: Background, Methods and Selected Results." *Journal for the Scientific Study of Religion* 38:458–476.

Chaves, Mark, and William Tsitsos. 2001. "Congregations and Social Services: What They Do, How They Do It, and with Whom." *Nonprofit and Voluntary Sector Quarterly* 30:660–683.

Christerson, Brad, and Michael O. Emerson. 2003. "The Costs of Diversity in Religious Organizations: An In-Depth Case Study." *Sociology of Religion* 64:163–182.

Christerson, Brad, Korie L. Edwards, and Michael O. Emerson. 2005. *Against All Odds: The Struggle for Racial Integration in Religious Organizations*. New York: New York University Press.

Cole, Charles C. 1966. *The Social Ideas of the Northern Evangelists 1826–1860*. New York: Octagon.

Collins, Sharon M. 1995. *Black Corporate Executives: The Making and Breaking of a Black Middle Class*. Philadelphia, PA: Temple University Press.

———. 1997. "Black Mobility in White Corporations: Up the Corporate Ladder but Out on a Limb." *Social Problems* 44:55–67.

Cornell, Stephen, and Douglas Hartman. 1988. "Mapping the Terrain:
    Definitions," in *Ethnicity and Race: Making Identities in a Changing World*,
    edited by Stephen Cornell and Douglas Hartman, 15–37. Thousand
    Oaks, CA: Pine Forge.

Cnaan, Ram, and Stephanie C. Boddie. 2001. " Philadelphia Census of
    Congregations and Their Involvement in Social Service Delivery." *Social
    Service Review* 75:559–580.

Cnaan, Ram, Jill W. Sinha, and Charlene C. McGrew. 2004. "Congregations
    as Social Service Providers: Services, Capacity, Culture, and Organiza-
    tional Behavior." *Administration in Social Work* 28:47–68.

Crowder, Kyle. 2000. "The Racial Context of White Mobility: An Individual
    Level Assessment of the White Flight Hypothesis." *Social Science
    Research* 29:223–257.

Cymbala, Jim and Dean Merrill. 1997. *Fresh Wind, Fresh Fire: What Happens
    When Gods Spirit Invades the Hearts of His People*. Grand Rapids, MI:
    Zondervan.

D'Antonio, William, James Davidson, Dean Hoge, and Katherine Meyer.
    2001. *American Catholics: Gender, Generation and Commitment*. Walnut
    Creek, CA: Rowman and Littlefield.

Davidson, James, Thomas Walters, Bede Cisco, Katherine Meyer, and Charles
    Zech. 2003. *Lay Ministers and Their Spiritual Practices*. Indianapolis, IN:
    OSV Press.

Davis, F. James. 1991. *Who Is Black? One Nation's Definition*. University Park:
    Pennsylvania State University Press.

Delaney, David. 1998. *Race, Place and Law 1836–1948*. Austin: University of
    Texas Press.

Demo, David H., and Michael Hughes. 1990. "Socialization and Racial
    Identity among Black Americans." *Social Psychology Quarterly* 53:
    364–374.

Denzin, Norman K. 1978. *Sociological Methods: A Sourcebook*. New York:
    McGraw-Hill.

DiMaggio, Paul. 1982. "Cultural Capital and School Success: The Impact of
    Status Culture Participation on the Grades of U.S. High School
    Students." *American Sociological Review* 47:189–201.

DiMaggio, Paul, and John Mohr. 1985. "Cultural Capital, Educational At-
    tainment, and Marital Selection." *American Journal of Sociology* 90:
    1231–1261.

Doane, Ashley W. 1997. "White Identity and Race Relations in the 1990s," in
    Perspectives on Current Social Problems, edited by Gregg Lee Carter, 151–
    159. Boston: Allyn and Bacon.

———. 2003. "Rethinking Whiteness Studies," in *White Out: The Continuing
    Significance of Racism*, edited by Ashley W. Doane and Eduardo Bonilla-
    Silva, 1–18. New York: Routledge.

Dougherty, Kevin. 2003. "How Monochromatic Is Church Membership? Racial-Ethnic Diversity in Religious Community." *Sociology of Religion* 64:65–85.

Drake, St. Clair, and Horace R. Cayton. 1970. *Black Metropolis: A Study of Negro Life in a Northern City.* New York: Harcourt, Brace.

DuBois, W. E. B. 2003. *The Negro Church.* New York: Altamira.

Dumond, Dwight L. 1972. "The Abolition Indictment of Slavery," in *The Abolitionists: Means, Ends, and Motivations,* edited by Hugh Hawkins, 22–48. Lexington, MA: Heath.

Eldredge, John. 2001. *Wild at Heart: Discovering the Secret's of a Man's Soul.* Nashville, TN: Thomas Nelson, Inc.

Ellison, Christopher G., and Daniel A. Powers. 1994. "The Contact Hypothesis and Racial Attitudes among Black Americans." *Social Science Quarterly* 75:385–400.

Emerson, Michael O. and Rodney Woo. 2006. *People of the Dream: Multiracial Congregations in the United States.* Princeton, NJ: Princeton University Press.

Emerson, Michael O., and Karen Chai Kim. 2003. "Interracial Congregations: An Analysis of Their Development and a Typology." *Journal for the Scientific Study of Religion* 42:217–227.

Emerson, Michael O., Rachel T. Kimbro, and George Yancey. 2002. "Contact Theory Extended: The Effects of Prior Racial Contact on Current Social Ties." *Social Science Quarterly* 83 (3):745–761.

Emerson, Michael O., and Christian Smith. 2000. *Divided by Faith: Evangelical Religion and the Problem of Race in America.* New York: Oxford University Press.

Emerson, Michael O., George Yancey, and Karen Chai. 2001. "Does Race Matter in Residential Segregation? Exploring the Preferences of White Americans." *American Sociological Review* 66:922–935.

Epstein, Terrie. 1998. "Deconstructing Differences in African-American and European-American Adolescents' Perspectives on U.S. History." *Curriculum Inquiry* 28:397–423.

Farley, Reynolds, and William H. Frey. 1994. "Changes in the Segregation of Whites from Blacks during the 1980s: Small Steps toward a More Integrated Society." *American Sociological Review* 59:23–45.

Feagin, Joe R., Anthony M. Orum, and Gideon Sjoberg (eds.). 1991. *A Case for the Case Study.* Chapel Hill: University of North Carolina Press.

Feagin, Joe R., and Hernan Vera. 1995. *White Racism: The Basics.* New York: Routledge.

Femia, J. 1975. "Hegemony and Consciousness in the Thought of Antonio Gramsci." *Political Studies* 23:28–48.

Finke, Roger, and Kevin D. Dougherty. 2002. "The Effects of Professional Training: The Social and Religious Capital Acquired in Seminaries." *Journal for the Scientific Study of Religion* 41:103–120.

Fireside, Harvey. 2004. *Separate and Unequal: Homer Plessy and the Supreme Court Decision That Legalized Racism*. New York: Carroll and Graf.

Flagg, Barbara. 1993. "'Was Blind, but Now I See': White Race Consciousness and the Requirement of Discriminatory Intent." *Michigan Law Review* 91:953.

Fong, Eric, and Wsevolod W. Isajiw. 2000. "Determinants of Friendship Choices in Multiethnic Society." *Sociological Forum* 15 (2):249–271.

Foster, Charles R. 1997. *Embracing Diversity: Leadership in Interracial Churches*. Herndon, VA: Alban Institute.

Fosu, Augustin Kwasi. 1993. "Do Black and White Women Hold Different Jobs in the Same Occupation? A Critical Analysis of the Clerical and Service Sectors." *Review of the Black Political Economy* (Spring):67–81.

Frankenberg, Ruth. 1993. *White Women, Race Matters: The Social Construction of Whiteness*. Minneapolis: University of Minnesota Press.

Franklin, John Hope. 2000. *From Slavery to Freedom: A History of African Americans*, 8th ed. New York: McGraw-Hill.

Frazier, E. Franklin. 1964. *The Negro Church in America*. New York: Schocken.

Frey, William H., and Reynolds Farley. 1996. "Latino, Asian, and Black Segregation in U.S. Metropolitan Areas: Are Multi-Ethnic Metros Different?" *Demography* 33:35–50.

Gaertner, Samuel L., John F. Dovidio, Jason A. Nier, Christine M. Ward, and Brenda S. Banker. 1999. "Across Cultural Divides: The Values of a Superordinate Identity," in *Cultural Divides: Understanding and Overcoming Group Conflict*, edited by Deborah A. Prentice and Dale T. Miller, 173–212. New York: Russell Sage Foundation.

Gaertner, Samuel L., Jeffrey Mann, Audrey Murrell, and John F. Dovidio. 1989. "Reducing Intergroup Bias: The Benefits of Recategorization." *Journal of Personality and Social Psychology* 57:239–249.

Gaertner, Wulf, Prasanta Pattanaik, and Kotara Suzumera. 1991. "Individual Rights Revisited." *Economica* 59:161–177.

Gay, David A. and Christopher G. Ellison. 1993. "Religious Subcultures and Political Tolerance: Do Denominations Still Matter?" *Review of Religious Research* 34: 311–333.

Gilkes, Cheryl Townsend. 1998. "Plenty Good Room: Adaptation in a Changing Black Church," in *The Annals of the American Academy of Political and Social Science: American Religions in the Twenty-First Century*, edited by Wade Clark Roof, 101–121. Thousand Oaks, CA: Sage.

Golding, S. 1992. *Gramsci's Democratic Theory: Contributions to a Post-Liberal Democracy*. Toronto: University of Toronto Press.

Goodwin, Carole. 1979. *The Oak Park Strategy: Community Control of Racial Change*. Chicago, IL: University of Chicago Press.

Gould, Stephen Jay. 1981. *The Mismeasure of Man*. New York: Norton.

Gramsci, A. 1971. *Selections from the Prison Notebooks*, edited by Q. Hoare and G. N. Smith. New York: International Publishers.

Greene, Jennifer C., Valerie J. Caracelli, and Wendy F. Graham. 1989. "Toward a Conceptual Framework for Mixed-Method Evaluation Designs." *Educational Evaluation and Policy Analysis* 11:255–274.

Guglielmo, Thomas. 2003. *White on Arrival: Italians, Race, Color, and Power in Chicago 1890–1945*. New York: Oxford University Press.

Gurin, Patricia, Arthur H. Miller, and Gerald Gurin. 1980. "Stratum Identification and Consciousness." *Social Psychology Quarterly* 43:30–47.

Hamilton, Charles V. 1972. *The Black Preacher in America*. New York: Morrow.

Harris, David. 1995. "Exploring the Determinants of Adult Black Identity: Context and Process." *Social Forces* 74:227–241.

Harris, David R. 2001. "Why Are Whites and Blacks Averse to Black Neighbors?" *Social Science Research* 30:100–116.

Harris, David R., and Reynolds Farley. 2000. "Demographic, Economic, and Social Trends," in *New Directions: African Americans in a Diversifying Nation*, edited by James S. Jackson. Washington, DC: National Policy Association.

Hartigan, John, Jr. 1999. *Racial Situations: Class Predicaments of Whiteness in Detroit*. Princeton, NJ: Princeton University Press.

———. 2003. "Who Are These White People? 'Rednecks,' 'Hillbillies,' and 'White Trash' as Marked Racial Subjects," in *White Out: The Continuing Significance of Racism*, edited by Ashley W. Doane and Eduardo Bonilla-Silva, 95–112. New York: Routledge.

Harvey, Paul. 2003. " 'A Servant of Servants Shall He Be': The Construction of Race in American Religious Mythologies," in *Religion and the Creation of Race and Ethnicity*, edited by Craig R. Prentiss, 13–27. New York: New York University Press.

Hatchett, Shirley, and Howard Schuman. 1975. "White Respondents and Race-of-Interviewer Effects." *Public Opinion Quarterly* 39:523–528.

Herskovits, Melville J. 1970. *The Myth of the Negro Past*. Gloucester, MA: Smith.

Hoggs, Michael A., Deborah J. Terry, and Katherine M. White. 1996. "A Tale of Two Theories: A Critical Comparison of Identity Theory with Social Identity Theory." *Social Psychology Quarterly* 55:255–269.

Iannaccone, Laurence. 1990. "Religious Practice: A Human Capital Approach." *Journal for the Scientific Study of Religion* 29:297–314.

Ignatiev, Noel. 1995. *How the Irish Became White*. New York: Routledge.

Jackson, Kenneth T. 1985. *Crabgrass Frontier: The Suburbanization of the United States*. New York: Oxford University Press.

Jacobson, Matthew Frye. 1999. *Whiteness of a Different Color: European Immigrants and the Alchemy of Race*. Cambridge, MA: Harvard University Press.

James, David. 1989. "City Limits on Racial Inequality: The Effects of City-Suburb Boundaries on Public School Desegregation, 1968–1976." *American Sociological Review* 54:963–985.

Jargowsky, Paul A. 1997. *Poverty and Place: Ghettos, Barrios, and the American City.* New York: Russell Sage Foundation.

Jeung, Russell. 2002. "Asian American Pan-Ethnic Formation and Congregational Cultures," in *Religions in Asian America: Building Faith Communities,* edited by Pyong Gap Min and Jung Ha Kim, 215–243. Walnut Creek, CA: Altamira.

Jick, Todd D. 1979. "Mixing Qualitative and Quantitative Methods: Triangulation in Action." *Administrative Science Quarterly* 24:602–611.

Kennedy, Randall. 1997. *Race, Crime, and the Law.* New York: Pantheon.

Kinder, Donald R., and David O. Sears. 1981. "Prejudice and Politics: Symbolic Racism versus Racial Threats to the Good Life." *Journal of Personality and Social Psychology* 40:414–431.

King, Martin Luther, Jr. 2000. *Why We Can't Wait.* New York: Signet Classics.

Kingston, Paul W. 2001. "The Unfulfilled Promise of Cultural Capital Theory." *Sociology of Education* (Extra issue):88–99.

Kluegel, James R., and Eliot R. Smith. 1982. "Whites' Beliefs about Blacks' Opportunity." *American Sociological Review* 47:518–532.

Kramer, Alfred. 1954. "Racial Integration in Three Protestant Denominations." *Journal of Educational Sociology* 28:59–68.

Krivo, Lauren J., Ruth D. Peterson, Helen Rizzo, and John R. Reynolds. 1998. "Race, Segregation, and the Concentration of Disadvantage: 1980–1990." *Social Problems* 45:61–80.

Krysan, Maria. 1998. "Privacy and the Expression of White Racial Attitudes: A Comparison across Three Contexts." *Public Opinion Quarterly* 62:506–544.

Kulis, Stephen S., and Heather E. Shaw. 1996. "Racial Segregation among Postsecondary Workers." *Social Forces* 75:575–591.

LaFree, Gary D. 1985. "Official Reactions to Hispanic Defendants in the Southwest." *Journal of Research in Crime and Delinquency* 22:213–237.

Lamont, Michele, and Annette Lareau. 1988. "Cultural Capital: Allusions, Gaps, and Glissandos in Recent Theoretical Developments." *Sociological Theory* 6:153–168.

Lareau, Annette. 1987. "Social Class Differences in Family-School Relationships: The Importance of Cultural Capital." *Sociology of Education* 60:73–85.

Lareau, Annette, and Erin McNamara Horvat. 1999. "Moments of Social Inclusion and Exclusion: Race, Class, and Cultural Capital in Family-School Relationships." *Sociology of Education* 72:37–53.

Law, Eric H. F. 1996. *The Bush Was Blazing, but Not Consumed.* St. Louis, MO: Chalice.

Lears, T. J. Jackson. 1985. "The Concept of Cultural Hegemony: Problems and Possibilities." *American Historical Review* 90:567–593.

Lesick, Lawrence Thomas. 1980. *The Lane Rebels: Evangelicalism and Antislavery in Antebellum America*. Metuchen, NJ: Scarecrow.

Lewis, Amanda E. 2004. "'What Group?' Studying Whites and Whiteness in the Era of 'Color-Blindness.'" *Sociological Theory* 22:623–646.

———. 2005. *Race in the Schoolyard: Negotiating the Color Line in Classrooms and Communities*. New Brunswick, NJ: Rutgers University Press.

Lewis, Amanda E., Maria Krysan, Sharon M. Collins, Korie Edwards, and Geoff Ward. 2004. "Institutional Patterns and Transformations: Race and Ethnicity in Housing, Education, Labor Markets, Religion, and Criminal Justice," in *The Changing Terrain of Race and Ethnicity*, edited by Maria Krysan and Amanda E. Lewis, 67–119. New York: Russell Sage.

Lincoln, C. Eric. 1974. *The Black Church since Frazier*. New York: Schocken.

Lincoln, C. Eric, and Lawrence H. Mamiya. 1990. *The Black Church in the African American Experience*. Durham, NC: Duke University Press.

Lipsitz, George. 1998. *The Possessive Investment in Whiteness: How White People Profit from Identity Politics*. Philadelphia: Temple University Press.

Litwack, Leon. 1961. *North of Slavery*. Chicago: University of Chicago Press.

Loescher, Frank S. 1948. *The Protestant Church and the Negro: A Pattern of Segregation*. Westport, CT: Negro Universities Press.

Lofland, John, and Lyn H. Lofland. 1995. *Analyzing Social Settings: A Guide to Qualitative Observation and Analysis*. Belmont, CA: Wadsworth.

Logan, John R., Richard D. Alba, and Shu-Yin Leung. 1996. "Minority Access to White Suburbs: A Multiregional Comparison." *Social Forces* 74:851–881.

Logan, John R., Brian J. Stults, and Reynolds Farley. 2004. "Segregation of Minorities in the Metropolis: Two Decades of Change." *Demography* 41:1–22.

Lopez, Ian F. Haney. 1996. *White by Law: The Legal Construction of Race*. New York: New York University Press.

Luker, Ralph E. 1991. *The Social Gospel in Black and White: American Racial Reform 1885–1912*. Chapel Hill: University of North Carolina Press.

Manis, Andrew Michael. 1987. *Southern Civil Religions in Conflict: Black and White Baptists and Civil Rights, 1947–1957*. Athens: University of Georgia Press.

Marti, Gerardo. 2005. *A Mosaic of Believers: Diversity and Innovation in a Multiethnic Church*. Bloomington: Indiana University Press.

Martin, Judith N., Robert L. Krizek, Thomas K. Nakayama, and Lisa Bradford. 1996. "Exploring Whiteness: A Study of Self-Labels for White Americans." *Communication Quarterly* 44:125–144.

Martin, Waldo E. 1998. *Brown vs. Board of Education: A Brief History with Documents*. Boston: Bedford/St. Martin's.

Massey, Douglas S., and Nancy Denton. 1987. "Trends in the Residential Segregation of Blacks, Hispanics and Asians: 1970–1980." *American Sociological Review* 52:802–825.

———. 1993. *American Apartheid: Segregation and the Making of the Underclass.* Cambridge, MA: Harvard University Press.

Massey, Douglas S., Andrew B. Gross, and Kumiko Shibuya. 1994. "Migration, Segregation and the Geographic Concentration of Poverty." *American Sociological Review* 59:425–445.

Matthews, Donald G. 1997. "Religion and the South: Authenticity and Purity—Pulling Us Together, Tearing Us Apart," in *Religious Diversity and American Religious History*, edited by Walter H. Conser, Jr., and Sumner B. Twiss, 72–101. Athens: University of Georgia Press.

Mays, Benjamin E., and Joseph W. Nicholson. 1933. *The Negro's Church.* New York: Russell and Russell.

McCall, George, and J. L. Simmons. 1978. *Identities and Interactions: An Examination of Human Associations in Everyday Life.* New York: Free Press.

McIntosh, Peggy. 1988. "White Privilege and Male Privilege: A Personal Account of Coming to See Correspondences through Work in Women's Studies," in *Race, Class and Gender: An Anthology*, edited by Margaret L. Andersen and Patricia Hill Collins, 220–229. Belmont, CA: Wadsworth.

McPherson, James M. 1975. *The Abolitionist Legacy: From Reconstruction to NAACP.* Princeton, NJ: Princeton University Press.

McPherson, J. Miller, Pamela A. Popielarz, and Sonja Drobnic. 1992. "Social Networks and Organizational Dynamics." *American Sociological Review* 57:153–170.

McPherson, J. Miller, and Lynn Smith-Lovin. 1987. "Homophily in Voluntary Organizations: Status Distance and the Composition of Face-to-Face Groups." *American Sociological Review* 52:370–379.

Meyer, Stephen Grant. 2000. *As Long as They Don't Move Next Door: Segregation and Racial Conflict in American Neighborhoods.* Lanham, MD: Rowman and Littlefield.

Mills, Charles. 2003. "White Supremacy as Sociopolitical System: A Philosophical Perspective," in *White Out: The Continuing Significance of Racism*, edited by Ashley W. Doane and Eduardo Bonilla-Silva, 35–48. New York: Routledge.

Mitchell, Henry H. 1970. *Black Preaching.* Philadelphia: Lippincott.

Mock, Alan K. 1992. "Congregational Religious Styles and Orientations to Society: Exploring Our Linear Assumptions." *Review of Religious Research* 34:20–33.

Montagu, Ashley. 1974. *Man's Most Dangerous Myth: The Fallacy of Race*, 5th ed. New York: Oxford University Press.

Montejano, David. 1987. *Anglos and Mexicans in the Making of Texas, 1836–1986.* Austin: University of Texas Press.

Morris, Aldon. 1984. *The Origins of the Civil Rights Movement: Black Communities Organizing for Change.* New York: Free Press.

Munnell, Alicia H., Geoffrey M. B. Tootell, Lynn E. Browne, and James McEneaney. 1996. "Mortgage Lending in Boston: Interpreting HMDA Data." *American Economic Review* 86:25–53.

Murdock, George. 1945. "The Common Denominator of Cultures," in *The Sciences of Man in the World Crisis*, edited by Ralph Linton, 123–142. New York: Columbia University Press.

Myers, Martha A. 1979. "Offender Parties and Official Reactions: Victims and the Sentencing of Criminal Defendants." *Sociological Quarterly* 20: 529–540.

Nelson, Timothy J. 1996. "Sacrifice of Praise: Emotion and Collective Participation in an African-American Worship Service." *Sociology of Religion* 57:379–396.

Nettles, Michael T., and L. W. Perna. 1997. *The African American Education Data Book.* Fairfax, VA: Frederick D. Patterson Research Institute of the College Fund.

Newhall, Amy Marcus, Norman Miller, Rolf Holtz, and Marilynn Brewer. 1993. "Cross-Cutting Category Membership with Role Assignment: A Means of Reducing Intergroup Bias." *British Journal of Social Psychology* 32:125–146.

Nyden, Philip, Michael Maly, and John Lukehart. 1997. "The Emergence of Stable Racially and Ethnically Diverse Urban Communities: A Case Study of Nine U.S. Cities." *Housing Policy Debate* 8:491–534.

Oldham, Joseph H. 1935. *Christianity and the Race Problem.* New York: Doran.

Oliver, Melvin L., and Thomas M. Shapiro. 1995. *Black Wealth/White Wealth: A New Perspective on Racial Inequality.* New York: Routledge.

Omi, Michael, and Howard Winant. 1994. *Racial Formation in the United States: From the 1960s to 1990s.* New York: Routledge.

Ondrich, Jan, Alex Stricker, and John Yinger. 1999. "Do Landlords Discriminate? The Incidence and Causes of Racial Discrimination in Rental Housing Markets." *Journal of Housing Economics* 8:185–204.

Ortiz, Manuel. 1996. *One New People: Models for Developing a Multiethnic Church.* Downers Grove, IL: InterVarsity.

Orum, Anthony M., Joe R. Feagin, and Gideon Sjoberg. 1991. "The Nature of the Case Study," in *A Case for the Case Study*, edited by Joe R. Feagin, Anthony M. Orum, and Gideon Sjoberg, 1–26. Chapel Hill: University of North Carolina Press.

Owens, Michael Leo, and R. Drew Smith. 2005. "Congregations in Low-Income Neighborhoods and the Implications for Social Welfare Policy Research." *Nonprofit and Voluntary Sector Quarterly* 34:316–339.

Park, Robert E. 1944. *Black Gods of the Metropolis*. Philadelphia: University of Pennsylvania Press.

Parker, James. 1968. "The Interaction of Negroes and Whites in an Integrated Church Setting." *Social Forces* 46:359–366.

Pattillo-McCoy, Mary. 1998. "Church Culture as a Strategy of Action in the Black Community." *American Sociological Review* 63:767–784.

———. 1999. *Black Picket Fences: Privilege and Peril among the Black Middle Class*. Chicago, IL: University of Chicago Press.

Patton, Michael Quinn. 1990. *Qualitative Evaluation and Research Methods*. Newbury, CA: Sage.

Perkins, John H. 1976. *Let Justice Roll Down: John Perkins Tells His Own Story*. Glendale, CA: Regal Books.

Perkins, Spencer, and Chris Rice. 1993. *More than Equals: Racial Healing for the Sake of the Gospel*. Downers Grove, IL: InterVarsity.

Peterson, Richard A. 1979. "Revitalizing the Culture Concept." *Annual Review of Sociology* 5:137–166.

Pinn, Anthony B. 2002. *Black Church in the Post–Civil Rights Era*. Maryknoll, NY: Orbis.

Pipes, William H. 1970. *Say Amen, Brother! Old-Time Negro Preaching: A Study in American Frustration*. Westport, CT: Negro Universities Press.

Pitts, Walter. 1989. "'If You Caint Get the Boat, Take a Log': Cultural Reinterpretation in the Afro-Baptist Ritual." *American Ethnologist* 16:279–293.

———. 1991. "Like a Tree Planted by the Water: The Musical Cycle in the African-American Baptist Ritual." *Journal of American Folklore* 104: 318–339.

Popielarz, Pamela A., and J. Miller McPherson. 1995. "On the Edge or In Between: Niche Position, Niche Overlap, and the Duration of Voluntary Association Memberships." *American Journal of Sociology* 101:698–720.

Poulantzas, N. 1982. *Political Power and Social Classes*. London: Verso.

Priest, Kersten Bayt, and Robert J. Priest. 2007. "Divergent Worship Practices in the Sunday Morning Hour: Analysis of an 'Interracial' Church Merger Attempt," in *This Side of Heaven: Race, Ethnicity, and Christian Faith*, edited by Robert J. Priest and Alvaro L. Nieves, 275–293. New York: Oxford University Press.

Qian, Zhenchao. 1997. "Breaking the Racial Barriers: Variations in Interracial Marriage between 1980 and 1990." *Demography* 34:263–276.

———. 1999. "Who Intermarries? Education, Nativity, Region, and Interracial Marriage, 1980 and 1990." *Journal of Comparative Family Studies* 30 (4):579–597.

Quillian, Lincoln. 1999. "Migration Patterns and the Growth of High Poverty Neighborhoods." *American Journal of Sociology* 105:1–37.

Raboteau, Alfred J. 1978. *Slave Religion: The "Invisible Institution" in the Antebellum South*. New York: Oxford University Press.

———. 1995. A *Fire in the Bones: Reflections on African-American Religious History*. Boston: Beacon.

Rankin, Bruce H., and James M. Quane. 2000. "Neighborhood Poverty and the Social Isolation of Inner-City African American Families." *Social Forces* 79:139–164.

Reardon, Sean F., and John T. Yun. 2002. *Private School Racial Enrollments and Segregation*. Cambridge, MA: Harvard University, Civil Rights Project.

Reimers, David M. 1965. *White Protestantism and the Negro*. New York: Oxford University Press.

Robbins, Derek. 1991. *The Work of Pierre Bourdieu*. Boulder, CO: Westview.

Roediger, David R. 1991. *The Wages of Whiteness: Race and the Making of the American Working Class*. New York: Verso.

Roozen, David A., William McKinney, and Jackson W. Carroll. 1984. *Varieties of Religious Presence*. New York: Pilgrim.

Rosenberg, Morris. 1979. *Conceiving the Self*. New York: Basic.

Rosenberg, Morris, and Roberta G. Simmons. 1972. *Black and White Self Esteem: The Urban School Child*. Washington, DC: American Sociological Association.

Saltman, Juliet. 1990. *A Fragile Movement: The Struggle for Neighborhood Stabilization*. New York: Greenwood.

Samuelson, William, and Richard Zeckhauser. 1988. "Status Quo Bias in Decision Making." *Journal of Risk and Uncertainty* 1:7–59.

Sassoon, A. S. 1980. *Gramsci's Politics*. London: Croom Helm.

Scheurich, James Joseph, and Michele D. Young. 1998. "Rejoinder: In the United States of America, in Both Our Souls and Sciences, We Are Avoiding Racism." *Educational Researcher* 27:27–32.

Schuman, Howard, and Jean M. Converse. 1971. "The Effects of Black and White Interviewers on Black Responses in 1968." *Public Opinion Quarterly* 35:44–68.

Schuman, Howard, Charlotte Steeh, and Lawrence Bobo. 1985. *Racial Attitudes in America: Trends and Interpretations*. Cambridge, MA: Harvard University Press.

Sears, David O. 1988. "Symbolic Racism," in *Eliminating Racism: Means and Controversies*, edited by Phyllis A. Katz and Dalmas A. Taylor, 53–84. New York: Plenum.

Semyonov, Moshe, Danny R. Hoyt, and Richard I. Scott. 1984. "Place, Race and Differential Occupational Opportunities." *Demography* 21:259–270.

Sernett, Milton C. 1975. *Black Religion and American Evangelicalism: White Protestants, Plantation Missions, and the Flowering of Negro Christianity, 1787–1865*. Metuchen, NJ: Scarecrow Press.

Shattuck, Gardiner H., Jr. 2000. *Episcopalians and Race: Civil War to Civil Rights*. Lexington: University of Kentucky Press.

Shibley, Mark A. 1998. "Contemporary Evangelicals: Born-Again and World Affirming." *Annals of the American Academy of Political and Social Science* 558:67–87.

Sigelman, Lee, Timothy Bledsoe, and Susan Welch. 1996. "Making Contact? Black-White Social Interaction in an Urban Setting." *American Journal of Sociology.* 101:1306–1332.

Sigelman, Lee, and Susan Welch. 1993. "The Contact Hypothesis Revisited: Black-White Interaction and Positive Racial Attitudes." *Social Forces* 71:781–795.

Simms, R. 1999. "The Politics of Religion in Plantation Society: A Gramsian Analysis," in *Research in the Social Scientific Study of Religion*, edited by J. M. Greer and D. O. Moberg, 91–177. Leiden: Brill.

Skinner, Tom. 1968. *Black and Free*. Grand Rapids, MI: Zondervan Publishing House.

Smidt, Corwin E., Lyman A. Kellstedt, John C. Green, and James L. Guth. 1999. "The Spirit-Filled Movements in Contemporary America: A Survey Perspective," in *Pentecostal Currents in American Protestantism*, edited by Edith L. Blumhofer, Russell P. Spittler, and Grant A. Wacker, 111–130. Urbana: University of Illinois Press.

Smith, Richard A. 1993. "Creating Stable Racially Integrated Communities: A Review." *Journal of Urban Affairs* 15:115–140.

South, Scott J., and Kyle Crowder. 1997. "Escaping Distressed Neighborhoods: Individual, Community, and Metropolitan Influences." *American Journal of Sociology* 102:1040–1084.

Spencer, Jon Michael. 1987. *Sacred Symphony: The Chanted Sermon of the Black Preacher*. New York: Greenwood.

Spittler, Russell P. 1999. "Corinthian Spirituality: How a Flawed Anthropology Imperils Authentic Christian Existence," in *Pentecostal Currents in American Protestantism*, edited by Edith L. Blumhofer, Russell P. Spittler, and Grant A. Wacker, 3–22. Urbana: University of Illinois Press.

Stevens-Arroyo, Anthony M. 1995. "Latino Catholicism and the Eye of the Beholder: Notes Towards a New Sociological Paradigm." *Latino Studies Journal* 6:22–55.

———. 1998. "The Latino Religious Resurgence." *Annals of the American Academy of Political and Social Science: Americans and Religions in the Twenty-First Century* (July):163–177.

Stewart, Carlyle F. 1997. *Soul Survivors: An African American Spirituality*. Louisville, KY: Westminster/John Knox.

Stryker, Sheldon. 1968. "Identity Salience and Role Performance: The Relevance of Symbolic Interaction Theory for Family Research." *Journal of Marriage and the Family* 30:558–564.

Synan, Vinson. 1971. *The Holiness-Pentecostal Movement in the United States.* Grand Rapids, MI: Eerdmans.

Tajfel, Henri. 1978. *Differentiation between Social Groups.* London: Academic.

———. 1981. *Human Groups and Social Categories: Studies in Social Psychology.* Cambridge: Cambridge University Press.

Takaki, Ronald T. 1989. *Strangers from a Different Shore: A History of Asian Americans.* Boston: Little, Brown.

———. 1993. *A Different Mirror: A History of Multicultural America.* Boston: Little, Brown.

Tashakkori, Abbas, and Charles Teddlie. 1998. *Mixed Methodology: Combining Qualitative and Quantitative Approaches.* Thousand Oaks, CA: Sage.

———. 2003. *Handbook of Mixed Methods in Social & Behavioral Sciences.* Thousand Oaks, CA: Sage.

Tatum, Beverly Daniel. 1997. *Why Are All the Black Kids Sitting Together in the Cafeteria? and Other Conversations about Race.* New York: Basic.

Teachman, Jay D. Lucky M. Tedrow, and Kyle D. Crowder. 2000. "The Changing Demography of America's Families." *Journal of Marriage and Family* 62: 1234–1246.

Terry, Robert W. 1981. "The Negative Impact on White Values," in *Impacts of Racism on White Americans,* edited by Benjamin P. Bowser and Raymond G. Hunt, 119–151. Beverly Hills, CA: Sage.

Thoits, Peggy A. 1996. " 'Me's and We's': Forms and Functions of Social Identities," in *Self and Identity: Fundamental Issues,* edited by Richard D. Ashmore and Lee Jussim, 106–136. Oxford: Oxford University Press.

Thomas, Brook. 1997. *Plessy v. Ferguson: A Brief History with Documents.* Boston: Bedford.

Thompson, Vetta L. Sanders. 1992. "A Multifaceted Approach to the Conceptualization of African-American Identification." *Journal of Black Studies* 23:75–85.

Tomaskovic-Devey, Donald. 1993. *Gender and Racial Inequality at Work: The Sources and Consequences of Job Segregation.* Ithaca, NY: ILR Press.

Toomer, Jethro W. 1975. "Beyond Being Black: Identification Alone Is Not Enough." *Journal of Negro Education* 44:184–199.

Tsitsos, William. 2003. "Race Differences in Congregational Social Service Activity." *Journal for the Scientific Study of Religion* 42:205–215.

Walters, Pamela Barnhouse. 2001. "Educational Access and the State: Historical Continuities and Discontinuities in Racial Inequality in American Education." *Sociology of Education* (Extra issue):35–49.

Warner, R. Stephen. 1988. *New Wine in Old Wineskins: Evangelicals and Liberals in a Small-Town Church.* Berkeley: University of California Press.

———. 1993. "Work in Progress toward a New Paradigm for the Sociological Study of Religion in the United States." *American Journal of Sociology* 98:1044–1093.

Warren, Jonathan W., and Frances Winddance Twine. 1997. "White Americans, the New Minority? Non-Blacks and the Ever-Expanding Boundaries of Whiteness." *Journal of Black Studies* 28:200–218.

Waters, Mary. 1990. *Ethnic Options: Choosing Identities in America*. Berkeley: University of California Press.

Wedam, Elfriede. 1999. "Ethno-Racial Diversity within Indianapolis Congregations." *Research Notes* 2 (4).

Wellman, David T. 1993. *Portraits of White Racism*. New York: Cambridge University Press.

Wilkes, Rima and John Iceland. 2004. "Hypersegregation in the Twenty-First Century." *Demography* 41: 23–36.

Williams, Patricia J. 1997. *Seeing a Color-Blind Future: The Paradox of Race*. New York: Noonday.

Wills, John J. 1996. "Who Needs Multicultural Education? White Students, U.S. History, and the Construction of a Usable Past." *Anthropology and Education Quarterly* 27:365–389.

Wilson, Frank Harold. 1995. "Rising Tide or Ebb Tide? Recent Changes in the Black Middle Class in the U.S., 1980–1990." *Research in Race and Ethnic Relations* 8:21–55.

Wilson, William Julius. 1987. *The Truly Disadvantaged: The Inner City, the Underclass, and Public Policy*. Chicago: University of Chicago Press.

———. 1997. *When Work Disappears: The World of the New Urban Poor*. New York: Random House.

Wood, Richard L. 1994. "Faith in Action: Religious Resources for Political Success in Three Congregations." *Sociology of Religion* 55:397–417.

Wright, Eric Olin. 1997. *Class Counts: Comparative Studies in Class Analysis*. New York: Cambridge University Press.

Wuthnow, Robert. 1988. *The Restructuring of American Religion: Society and Faith Since World War II*. Princeton, NJ: Princeton University Press.

Yinger, John. 1995. *Closed Doors, Opportunities Lost*. New York: Russell Sage Foundation.

Zubrinsky, Camille L., and Lawrence Bobo. 1996. "Prismatic Metropolis: Race and Residential Segregation in the City of Angels." *Social Science Research* 25:335–374.

Zussman, Robert. 2004. "People in Places." *Qualitative Sociology* 27:351–363.

Index